CONFLICT, WAR & REVOLUTION: *MY LIFE*

Alessandra Kozlowska

CONFLICT, WAR & REVOLUTION: *MY LIFE*

Edited by

Andrew George-Perutz

SEREN

Seren is the book imprint of
Poetry Wales Press Ltd
57 Nolton Street, Bridgend, Wales, CF31 3AE
www.serenbooks.com
Facebook: facebook.com/SerenBooks
Twitter: @SerenBooks

ISBNs
Hardback – 978-1-78172-449-1
Ebook – 978-1-78172-450-7
Kindle – 978-1-78172-451-4

A CIP record for this title is available from the British Library.

The publisher acknowledges the financial assistance
of the Welsh Books Council.

Printed by TJ International, Cornwall.

Contents

Introduction

It is my greatest regret that I only met my grandmother a handful of times, but even on those few occasions she proved herself to be a natural storyteller. Her reminisces of life were to me the stuff of dreams and legend, tales from storybooks with names that I could only imagine ever existing. Princes and paupers, men with the stature of bears and gentle pianists, exotic hotels in even more exotic locations, oil barons, wars and revolutions, riches and rags. Everything was in this melting pot of a life that she had led.

Not that my own life had been uneventful, or so I thought! I am married with two daughters and six grandchildren. My wife, Penelope, was a dancer with the Royal Ballet and we spent many years living and working abroad for a multinational corporation. I was posted to Sri Lanka during the civil war with the Tamil Tigers. Curfews, bombs and killings were commonplace and came close to home when one of our staff was kidnapped and murdered on the east coast of Sri Lanka in Batticaloa. We lived for two and a half years in Cambodia, where we were inadvertently involved in the spat between Prince Ranariddh and Hun Sen. Caught up in the eventual coup by the Cambodian People's Party we had finally to be evacuated by military aircraft to Bangkok. I spent time in Nigeria and witnessed first-hand the problems there, and visited China when the road from the airport to Beijing was lined with soldiers and Shanghai was essentially just on one side of the Yangtze River!

My mother had always spoken of grandmother's memoirs, although they appeared to have been lost in various moves and relocations. Meantime I relied upon faded photographs, photocopied documents and newspaper cuttings to keep my memories alive. My curiosity was further piqued by an article I found written by Carroll W. Parcher of the *Glendale News* (now part of the *Los Angeles Times*) in 1945. Parcher wrote a regular column whilst he was in Italy during the Second World War. He would frequently include a thumbnail sketch of 'interesting characters' he had met – and one of these characters was my grandmother, Alessandra. However, it was some years after my mother died that I came across an old tin box full of documents, papers and pictures. Amongst these was a faded green folder, and hand-written on the front were the words: Alessandra Perutz, with a sticky label stating 'Mother's Book'.

Inside the almost bleached folder were 283 pages of flimsy carbon paper, each filled with a faded typescript that, on closer examination, was written in Italian! I sat down and began to translate, and with each passing page I realised that my life paled into insignificance in comparison. I was taken on a roller-coaster ride through perhaps the most turbulent times of our history. Revolutions, uprisings, wars, assassinations, times of affluence and times of hardship, and times when money had no value! I was captivated, and once again entranced, by Grandmother.

The fact that these pages and her story are now experiencing a wider audience is thanks to a variety of people. My travels abroad helped to confirm places, streets and sometimes even houses. I thank Carol Matthews and Colin Playle for their work in correcting spelling and tense, highlighting inconsistencies and fanning the flames of my sometimes flagging will-power having received yet another rejection from an agent. Finally I received a huge fillip from a publisher – an email from Mick Felton of Seren that said he thought it was an interesting story and wished to see the manuscript. Then, for me, the reward of all my grandmother's hard work, the acceptance to publish.

It leaves me only to say this is Grandmother's story, in her own words.

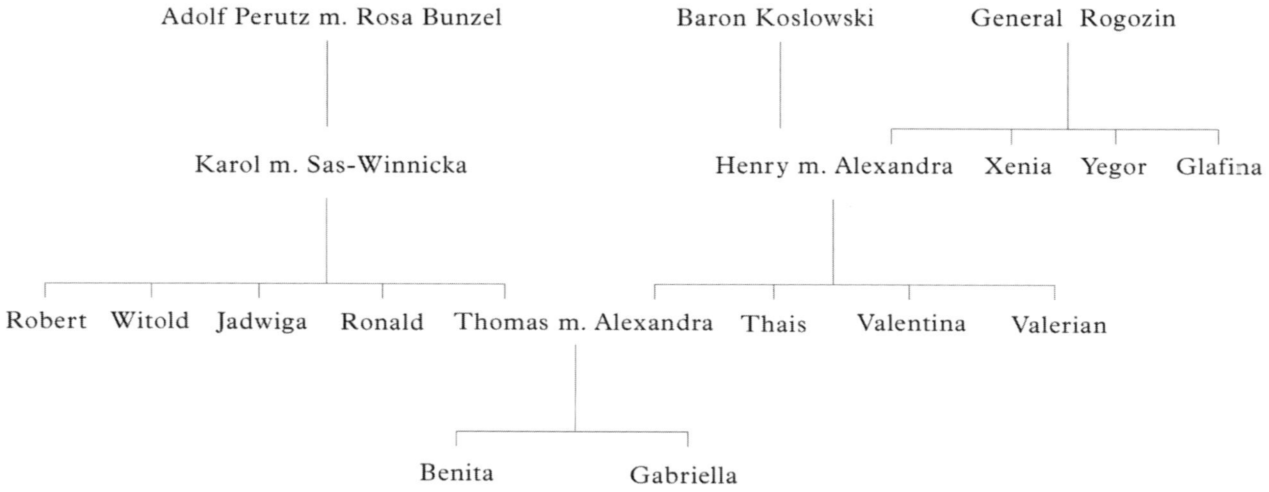
Adolf Perutz m. Rosa Bunzel
Baron Koslowski
General Rogozin
Karol m. Sas-Winnicka
Henry m. Alexandra
Xenia
Yegor
Glafina
Robert
Witold
Jadwiga
Ronald
Thomas m. Alexandra
Thais
Valentina
Valerian
Benita
Gabriella

A Glimpse into the Future

I can still remember my last day at school in Marinsk. It was a clear spring morning and the holidays were about to begin. At the Institute Marinsk for Girls the last lesson of the term would be geography with Professor Zaleski.

The professor's preferred way of treating any lesson was with the use of a magic lantern and on the last day, and last lesson of term, it would be no different. Africa was his chosen subject. The blinds had been drawn and the lamp in the lantern threw a warm orange window of light onto the wall at the front of the classroom. There was a sharp click as the professor inserted his first slide into the holder; a moment of shadow as he pushed the slide across and into the lens of the lantern and, suddenly, a bright landscape sprang to life. An immense sea of yellow sand stretched from one side of the picture to the other. It was topped by the azure blue of a burning sky, and jutting from the yellow sand into that azure sky were the enormous monuments of the Pharaohs, the pyramids, flanked by the massive sphinxes. Completing the tableau in the foreground were two camels with their Bedouin guides.

Sitting at the rear of the schoolroom my imagination had run riot. The Professor's deep baritone voice described Egypt and painted pictures of the Pharaohs and of the lives of those ancient Egyptians. But the oppressive nature of the Egyptian desert, the melancholy look of the camels and the sophisticated arrogance of the Bedouins, coupled with the warmth of the classroom and the smell of the burning oil from the lantern, had begun to make me feel nauseous. As the Professor continued to click softly through the slides, I had crept quietly out of the classroom and into the grounds of the Institute.

Sitting on a bench beneath the boughs of an old oak tree I gazed around me. I noticed the differing shades of green. That of the grass was soft, the trees darker and the bushes multi-hued. Set amongst all this was the contrast of the flowers with their bright splashes of colour. I could pick out the scent of lime trees, which were in flower, and I heard the sounds of the birds with their spring song and, at that moment, I decided I would never – could never – trade the beauty of my country for the wealth of the Pharaohs.

My thoughts were interrupted as, in the distance, the Institute's janitor, Nikita, appeared. He wore a long blue livery coat adorned with gold braid, and was vigorously ringing a large bronze hand bell which sounded not only the end of the lesson, but also the end of term.

A swarm of students crowded through the large double front doors of the Institute onto the broad avenue that cut through the gardens. They were dressed uniformly in maroon pilgrim dresses with white over-aprons, both of which reached down to their ankles and, with their black shoes and white ankle socks, they resembled the large dahlia flowers which grew around the grounds. Their chattering voices grew louder as they crossed the grounds, and spread through the air like the warbling of birds. I made my way, with the others, out through the large wrought iron gates at the entrance to the grounds and towards home. I passed the dacha of the General and I slowed to greet his widow, who was tending her beloved geraniums on the flower-filled terrace. Two sheepdogs, inseparable companions of the widow, lay prostrate on the terrace. Their half-closed eyes followed the majestic peacocks that strutted regally across the lawns towards the fountains that flowed below the terrace into a large pond filled with flowers and fish. I had been so fascinated by this scene that, without realising, I found myself at the gates of our own dacha in Marinsk and, interestingly, at the gates of a new chapter in my life.

My mother, Alessandra (Sania), was the daughter of General Ilya Fedorovitch Rogozny and my father, Enrico (Henry) Kozlowski was the son of Baron Kozlowski. The Baron had been a general of the Tsar's army during the second war with Turkey and, as a reward for his heroism, had received from the Tsar a gift of lands in the Caucasus. In 1900 my parents had purchased a further large tract of land in Ekaterinodar on the banks of the Kuban River. Ekaterinodar had been founded on January 12, 1794 as Yekaterinodar, and this original name meant 'Catherine's Gift', recognizing both Catherine the Great's grant of land in the Kuban region to the Black Sea Cossacks (created from the former Zaporozhian Cossacks) and Saint Catherine of Alexandria, who was considered to be the patron saint of the city.

My father then set about building a luxurious palace. With forty-eight rooms across two storeys and large crystal windows that overlooked the gardens beneath, it was his triumph. Large conservatory doors opened onto the vast terraces that surrounded the house. From those terraces stone steps guided you down to the lawns and gardens below. A long gravel avenue, bordered by fragrant lilac trees, led away from the house down to the tall iron gates through which, if you were on the outside, you could glimpse a view of the entire façade of the house. When the flowerbeds and the lilac trees were in full bloom the soft breeze across the grounds would scent the whole of the palace with spring.

It was from the dacha Marinsk to this new palace that we would move to during the holidays. Despite the comfort and luxury lavished on the new property in Ekaterinodar, and even with the knowledge that the dacha in Marinsk would be kept as a summerhouse, we children had not been happy. Myself, my sisters Thais and Valentina, and my brothers Vladimir and Valerian had begun to wage a small war on my parents. Once it had been announced that we would be moving to the city we had realised how much we had taken for granted our surroundings in Marinsk. It was in Marinsk that we had taken our first steps, gone to our first schools and made our first friends. We recalled the games we had played in the gardens, the woods and the forests surrounding the dacha, how we had learned to get close to nature and the wild animals, learned to ride, and shoot, and hunt. We were becoming Cossacks. The announcement of the move to Ekaterinodar had aroused alarm and we all, continually, told our parents that we would never, ever, be happy again, that we could not be happier elsewhere. We had insisted that if we were to move to the new house we would have to take our pets, our horses – the list was endless.

So it was that our arrival in Ekaterinodar had been more of a circus than that of a family. Accompanied by a variety of dogs, cats, ponies, horses and even our donkey, a carriage had taken us from the station at Ekaterinodar to our new home. We passed through those impressively tall gates with studied indifference and the only thing that aroused an iota of curiosity or interest, particularly amongst the boys, was the family crest of an eagle bearing a horseshoe engraved into the glass of the large doors at the front of the house. However, children's memories are short-lived and new experiences soon replaced those we missed in Marinsk, though each summer we would go back to our dacha in Marinsk, which had indeed become our summer residence.

Ekaterinodar was changing and developing. Over the years the lighting oil was replaced by electricity and, in the main street, the first tram arrived. It was a small wagon equipped with a large bell that rang almost continuously and which, together with the prolonged whistling of the tram drivers, brought along with it all those things that represent big cities. Colour and noise surrounded you whilst frightened horses galloped wildly pulling carriages upon which imposing coachmen sat impassively guiding their steeds whilst those inside prayed for salvation!

In June 1905 our quiet world had been shaken and, unknowingly, we were given a glimpse of the future. A silken cloth was briefly lifted from a gypsy's crystal ball and revealed, in its cloudy interior, a taste of what was to come.

In the garden our cat lay in the shadows of the vine that ran along the trellis, quietly watching for any birds that should dare step on his territory. My father and mother had been having breakfast on the terrace and reading the newspapers when Timote, their old retainer, appeared at the foot of the steps of the terrace. He announced breathlessly that he had just returned from the city and had seen a massive event on the main street. It was unfortunate that as loyal as Timote was he was also quite illiterate and had been unable to decipher the inscriptions on the placards that were being carried around by the crowds. Although he did describe, rather too vividly, the appearance of the revolutionary red flag with the skull of death that was being waved by the marchers and protestors. His ignorance was such that all hopes of further illumination or filling in any gaps were pointless. Timote reasoned and philosophised only to the extent of his knowledge, which was limited. He would put on his scales of justice solely two arguments: the good and the bad. He was now experiencing unfamiliar emotions and took it upon himself to explain that he was unable to offer any further information. Timote was the darling of the family and although he held the post of head butler it was very much a sinecure. Timote did not realize the gravity of the events that were unfolding in the city and, having dispensed what he did know, left any further judgement to the family. As he would do at these times he sat down on the steps of the terrace engrossed in thought and trying to understand what was happening.

My parents had been more than a little troubled by what Timote had reported. Scant as the information had been, it was obvious that disquieting events were taking place in the city, and they were discussing among themselves the seriousness of the situation and the consequences that could ensue. All the children were at their academies in the city and my parents assumed they would be safe and, as yet, nothing further had been heard to arouse additional suspicions. Around noon my father had decided to go to the city centre to see if he could obtain more precise information of what was happening. However, just as he was leaving the house, they heard a sudden salvo of gunfire from the direction of the city.

My mother grew pale and terrified, her voice shook with fear as she said "They're shooting!" Timote, true to type, phlegmatically repeated what, to him, was purely an observation. "They're shooting."

My mother's thoughts went immediately to the children who, hopefully, were still at their academies in the city centre. My father tried to calm everyone. He told them that the children would be safe in school, and would almost certainly be under the protection of the masters. Nonetheless this insight did little to calm nerves, nerves that were further severely rattled by the sound of horses galloping past their gates.

"Cossacks!" my parents exclaimed together, and they both ran to the gates from which they could observe the road leading to the governor's palace. From their vantage point they could see a great swarm of protestors moving through the city centre and, behind them the Cossack cavalry with their raised whips trying to disperse the crowds.

One witness had escaped from the multitude and paused by the gates. He told my father that the demonstrators had put in the front row of the mob all the boys taken from schools and were using them as a shield! Without exchanging a word my parents ran to where the crowds had gathered, expecting to find their children but at the same time hoping they were still safe in school.

The central square was in chaos; there was a sea of bodies surrounding the governor's palace and, behind this multitude, the Cossacks, pushing, shouting, and trying to clear a path through the protestors. There seemed to be no way through the mob.

The Cossacks continued to try to restore order. "Away!" they shouted, "Move away!" and their horses pushed further and further into the crowd. My parents were trapped. Moving neither forward nor back, they were caught between the chaos of the crowd and the mounted Cossacks. They tried to twist their way through the throng of bodies to reach a clearing where stood the monument to Catherine the Great.

"Move!" shouted a voice above them and my mother looked up. "Move!" threatened a Cossack and my mother, with her large gazelle eyes, pleaded with him to help them through to find their children.

"Here – go find your children!" The Cossack shouted and helped my parents through to the relative safety of the square. Behind the monument, seemingly blissfully unaware of what was happening around them, sat Valentina, Vladimir and Valerian reading the comics that filled the pockets of their uniforms. My parents seized them thankfully and, still trembling, pulled them down a side alley to lead them home without further incident. Thais and myself, who were found by the housekeeper, were already in front of the house, waiting, worrying but then relieved that everyone was once again safe. We saw my parents coming towards us and ran to greet them, to tell them how we managed to escape the mob and not be dragged into the crowd, how the gatekeeper of the school kept us hidden in his home in order that the protestors would not find us, and how our housekeeper found us and brought us back home safely.

The ferment of the revolution was spreading now throughout Russia. Every day the newspapers carried more sensational news; the assassinations of ministers and military rulers, strikes that alternated with mass arrests, summary trials and executions. In Ekaterinodar the anarchist party terrified the men of local government. The anarchists imposed draconian conditions: threatening them, telling them to leave their office within twenty-four hours under pain of death. The threats were ignored at their peril and more than one official suffered the consequence of their bravery.

The battle lines between the Bolsheviks (the workers) and the Cossacks (the nobility) had been drawn but the Bolshevik anarchists still held huge sway and power, primarily through threats and fear. Blackmail of landowners and the aristocracy became stock in trade and, with access to government records and papers, they easily identified their targets and would request specified sums of money to be handed over at a certain place. Alongside this demand was the warning that should the victim involve the police, or default on payment, the outcome was effectively: death to you and everyone in your family!

It would have been impossible to list the names of all the victims but, unsurprisingly, in any list the revolutionaries held they could not miss the name of my father – Henry Kozlowski. As we sat at home having breakfast one morning we heard a single gunshot that seemed to come from the wrought iron gates at the front of the house. Timote crept down through the bushes to see what was happening and found, tied to the gate's railing, an envelope. Not being able to read he merely took the envelope from the gate and, returning to the house, gave it to my mother. The note was addressed to Baron Kozlowski and, suspecting she knew exactly what it would contain, my mother passed it immediately to my father. As anticipated it was a ransom demand. Set out in unequivocal terms was a demand for 50,000 roubles together with clear directions that dictated where in the city my father should be, and at what time he should be there. As with all other blackmail demands received by the wealthy this was under the threat of death not only to my mother and father but also to the family as a whole, including Timote, the housekeeper and all the staff.

There was much discussion between my mother and father as to whether the ransom demand should be met, whether it should be ignored or indeed whether we should report it to the police. My father told everyone he would make the decision the next morning but that evening, with a sum of fifty thousand roubles in a small bag, my father left the house without telling any member of his family. He arrived early at the proposed meeting place and waited for the blackmailers. Seven o'clock came and passed with no sign of a blackmailer wanting to meet my father. A further half an hour passed and still there was no sign. Fearing that perhaps he had the wrong meeting place my father began to walk up and down the main street, looking down all the small side streets and into dark hallways and alleyways, but there was still no indication of anyone wanting or waiting to meet him. My father came back to the original meeting place and waited a further fifteen minutes. With still no contact having been made my father once again began to pace up and down the main street, now getting worried that perhaps his family was in danger. He again began to check the alleys and side streets this time more thoroughly, looking into shadowed doorways and passageways. It was this unusual and suspicious behaviour that brought him to the attention of two policemen. The policemen were familiar with my father and his habits, of which wandering up and down the main street in the city centre was not one. They did not approach him straightaway but instead went directly to inform the police chief, Colonel Gernisk, of this unusual pattern of behaviour. The Colonel knew immediately what was happening but was also aware of the consequences that could occur. He set off in his coach and came alongside my father and asked, politely, "Tell me Mr Kozlowski, are you practising to walk from Ekaterinodar to Karlsbad?" My father had explained he was just taking some fresh air after a heavy dinner, at which point Colonel Gernisk offered to give my father a ride home in his carriage, an offer that could hardly be refused. Later that evening, after explaining everything to the family, it came as no surprise to anyone that another gunshot was heard coming from the direction of the main gates. A further letter had been attached to the railings containing an identical death threat and similar demands for money. This time, however, my father was offered police protection and the house was surrounded and guarded by soldiers. No one could leave the house without an escort of armed Cossacks.

The terror of the revolutionary government continued unabated. The young, full of enthusiasm, fought for new ideas and to obtain adequate laws. Students and children of the intelligentsia put themselves in danger seeking to improve the lives of farmers and workers across Russia. Thousands of these young men, strong and courageous, suffered from summary military judgment and the resulting verdict. They were proud to bear the scars of the beatings, and torture they received, and were stoic in their acceptance of making the endless journey towards Siberia. They were energised by the hope that their sacrifice would lead to new land reforms and democratic elections for parliament. The revolutionary movement and the attitude of the government could be compared to a game of chess.

Manifestos were written and discarded but eventually, in October 1905 under pressure from his advisers who feared he would lose his throne, Nicholas II reluctantly agreed to sign the 'October Manifesto'. This promised the granting of civil liberties, a cabinet government, and a legislative Duma elected on a wide franchise. The Manifesto's proclamation was met with jubilation in the streets on 17 October 1905; there were spontaneous demonstrations of support in all the major cities. The strikes officially ended or quickly collapsed and a political amnesty was offered. There was euphoria, a sense that Russia was now entering a new era of Western constitutionalism and freedom.

Infatuation – with Boys and Oil!

After a long period of both political and economic stagnation, Russia began to wake up and recognise the benefits of private initiatives and enterprise. My father had been transfixed for some time by the discovery of oil, both in Maikop in 1866 and Grozny in 1897, and had decided that he should spearhead the exploration of the subterranean layers of the Caucus. The decision taken, he began to work out a plan and devise a strategy of where and when. If you needed to know where my father was he would invariably be found hunched over piles of maps, which were spread out across the library table, intent on making calculations and taking notes. Or he would be with his geologist Professor Karl Bogdanovich establishing priorities and preferred exploration sites. Finally, after many months of dedicated research and measurement, Timote was ordered to start the necessary preparations for the departure of his master for the sites identified and proposed by the geologist. They were isolated places, with limited means of communication apart from horse-drawn carriages. The roads to reach these points required travellers to go through dense forests infested with bandits that endangered the life of an unwary traveller. Early one morning, with all preparations complete, my father prepared to depart accompanied by an escort armed with rifles and revolvers.

The driver slapped the reins, and with a cry of 'Avanti' the grazing horses snapped to attention and soon disappeared from sight as the family gathered on the terrace to wave goodbye. Nobody was sure when my father would return: I think we all knew it would be a good few months; indeed my mother was concerned that perhaps he wouldn't return at all, and would be targeted by the bandits and revolutionaries that still ran riot in the dense forests of the Caucasus!

Shortly after my father left to go prospecting for oil, my mother received the welcome announcement of the imminent arrival of her sister Xenia Culbertson and her husband from America. Xenia was three years older than my mother and, at the age of 23, had been widowed when she lost her first husband in the Turkish War in 1877. A year later she had lost her first-born son to a malignant fever. Oil had been the reason that her second husband Almon Culbertson, drawn to the Caucasus by the reports of the discovery of large oil fields, had first met Xenia at her father's estate. They married in 1881 and moved to a new life in America. Xenia now had three sons with Almon; Eugene the eldest at 24, Ely at 19 and finally, the baby of the group Sascha who was 17.

Ely, the brightest of the three children, had just been expelled from the Rostov Gymnasium! The school had been in a state of high anticipation with the expected visit from the Chief Inspectorate of all Russian schools. He had been scheduled to arrive with all the pomp and ceremony that was to be expected of such an event; a highly decorated coach drawn by four prized horses, and a broad red carpet flanked by the teachers and senior students of the gymnasium. As the clock struck noon a coach and four white horses, immaculately groomed and presented, drew into the school grounds and stopped by the red carpet. The rather overweight principal waddled over, anxious to anticipate the footman who was about to open the door of the carriage for the distinguished guest.

However instead of the resplendent inspector out had jumped Ely, with his books under his arm and a swagger in his step. There was a moment of complete and utter silence followed by sniggers and then roars of laughter from the students. The principal stood and stared at Ely with apoplectic rage, ordered him back into the coach and sent him home. Although the real coach and party did arrive moments later the damage had been done. A letter suggesting that Ely may be better suited to another gymnasium had been swiftly dispatched to his father.

Ely Culbertson would eventually make his reputation and cement his fame as the American contract bridge entrepreneur and personality dominant during the 1930s. He would play a major role in the popularisation of the new game and was widely regarded as 'the man who made Contract Bridge'. Always seen as a great showman he became rich, was highly extravagant, and lost and gained fortunes several times over.

The youngest son Sascha, conversely, was considered something of a musical prodigy and his father had decided he would take him to Prague to study under the famous Professor Ševčík. Sascha, as with Ely, would also achieve the heights of his talents and would achieve fame, if not fortune, as a brilliant concert violinist, although his influences would remain Gypsy, Russian and Cossack music.

Eugene was perhaps the least cerebral but the most physical of the three. He enjoyed the outdoor life, was an accomplished horseman and found most sports came to him with utmost ease. Xenia's husband had already departed for Austria taking Sascha with him, leaving Xenia, Ely and Eugene alone for the first time.

So these were the circumstances in which our family waited for the arrival of my mother's sister and our cousins. Timote had been dispatched to the gates to keep a watchful eye for the carriage, and to provide ample warning to we girls of the arrival of our guests.

A while later Timote rushed up to the house to announce their imminent arrival and then, still breathless, ran back down to open the gates and let in their carriage. We all gathered in the hall. Thais with her brown complexion, bright eyes, beautiful mouth and ready smile that revealed a treasure of enviable teeth was gay, talented and full of confidence and she dominated me, the younger sister. By contrast, I was of milder character, blonde with fair skin and blue-green eyes. That day I wore a blue dress adorned with two freshly-picked white roses, but was in awe and admiration of Thais, wearing a white muslin dress, striped in blue and offset with a belt of red lacquered leather.

The carriage drew up to the portico at the front of the house and we could see the shadows of the occupants inside. We were all gathered in the hall, my mother at the front, tall, slim and elegant with her fine classic features and delicate complexion. She was wearing a pleated pink tea-gown and at her neck was a pinwheel brooch of amethysts and pearls.

Timote, who had been hanging on to the back of the carriage, leapt off and ran round to open the doors and release the occupants. Kisses and hugs, charged with emotion and smiles, were exchanged. Compliments were intermingled with exclamations of joy and coupled with the timid glances of the cousins as each became aware of the other. The housekeeper showed the visitors to their rooms, and Timote began the laborious task of sorting the cabin trunks and ensuring that the correct luggage arrived in the right rooms.

My mother, Thais and myself waited for our guests in the dining room. For a while only the gentle bubbling song of the boiling samovar accompanied the whispered conversation between Thais and myself. This rapidly turned to an evaluation of the boys, Eugene the athlete, versus Ely the studious. After our visitors arrived in the dining room it was Eugene who monopolised the conversation. He was tall and had the traits of his father; a charming raconteur, his conversation was witty and lively as he recounted episodes of his student life in Monaco. Ely, younger, blonde with blue eyes, sat looking bored. There was a gap in the conversation and Ely quite suddenly asked: "How long do you really think the calm will last in this country of yours?"

There was silence and general consternation in the room. Ely had touched upon a subject that was taboo for the whole family. Following the uprising and riots in the town, the danger the children had been placed in from the anarchists, the ransom demands and the ongoing threat to our family, this was not an area they particularly wished to visit or discuss. Xenia scolded Ely and said she didn't want to hear any more of this absurd talk.

The mood in the room changed and, in an attempt to regain some composure, it was suggested that perhaps the boys would like to accompany the girls to the stables and go for a ride around the grounds. The two sisters, my mother Sania and Xenia, meanwhile sat on the terrace. A slight breeze ruffled the cherry trees and the soft petals of the blossom were scattered like confetti. The fragrant scent of the lime trees and the flowers filled the air and delighted the two sisters and they watched as Eugene, Ely, Thais and myself cantered around the grounds and up the avenue leading to and from the house.

Xenia spoke about Sascha and his exceptional talent on the violin, and his acceptance by Professor Ševčík in Prague for further tuition. They laughed as Xenia recounted the story of Ely and the inspectorate at the Rostov Academy. Xenia had been praying that Ely would pass his exams in order to progress to baccalaureate, and she had been waiting at the Academy when everything had unfolded, the arrival of the coach, the appearance of Ely and the reaction of the overweight, and indeed overwrought, principal.

Xenia had dragged Ely, almost by the ear, into her carriage and galloped home. The joke had cost Ely his certificate of baccalaureate, and given her constant concern about his future. Sania proposed that she would contact Professor Gerasimov from the Lyceum in Ekaterinodar who might be able to offer assistance by way of private tuition. This idea was accepted and a few weeks later, on the advice of Professor Gerasimov, Ely left with him for a small secluded dacha on the banks of the Black Sea, free from worldly amusements and distractions, and far more appropriate to study.

Ely's departure coincided with the return of my father from the prospecting trip for oil in the forests of the Caucasus. The strength of the geological findings of Professor Bogdanovich had cemented Henry's conviction that there was oil beneath the ground, and in significant enough quantities to make it a viable proposition. My father had decided that he was willing, on the basis of the research, to take the financial risk. The land he had surveyed with Professor Bogdanovich was Maikop, owned by the Cossacks, and therefore the purchase and leasing formalities demanded special governmental negotiations. The inevitable delays of bureaucratic procedure prevented my father from going to our summer dacha back in Marinsk. Therefore it was Xenia and Eugene together with my mother, my sisters Thais and Valentina and my brothers Vladimir and Valerian who set off for the long trip to the country and to what was now our summer house.

After long hours of travel by train we arrived at the small station in Marinsk, and continued our journey by carriage on a hot dusty road that ran through endless plantations of sunflower and tobacco, before finally turning onto the long shady avenue that led us to the private entrance of the villa.

Almost before the carriages had come to a halt, the boys were out and had rushed across the gardens and through to the orchard behind, where the trees were laden with apples, pears, peaches and limes. Having filled their pockets with a variety of fruit, they immediately headed off to the gamekeeper's lodge to introduce Eugene to Vasili. Vasili was a giant of a man, an archetypal Cossack. He must have stood at least two metres tall, with a huge barrel of a chest and the biggest, blackest, bushiest beard that covered the whole of the lower part of his face. His eyes were the colour of coal and glittered beneath his large hat and huge, overgrown eyebrows that were almost as long as his beard! He had, for many a year, been the favoured gamekeeper at the dacha and had built up a fearsome reputation as a fabled huntsman. He lived in the small lodge, a little way from the main dacha, in the middle of a shady grove of ancient olive trees. Vasili did not disappoint. He may not have had a quite so fabulous a story but, nevertheless, his latest trophy that was something to behold. A young black bear, on a leash, that was walking alongside him, perfectly at home and quite unperturbed by the excitement of the youngsters that now surrounded him. The boys spent hours enjoying Vasili's hospitality and relishing and reliving his stories. When they finally began to make their way back to the dacha, the farm workers were finishing in the fields, darkness was beginning to fall and, on the wind, they could hear the voices of the farmers as they sang to celebrate the end of the day.

The walk down the road back to the dacha was completed in silence. By the time they reached the house with their heads full of the wonderful stories from Vasili, and their minds numb from the long train and carriage journey, the need for rest and sleep was overwhelming. The day of our arrival drew to a close and we never slept more soundly. We did not hear the hunter's shots in the night, the chorus of the frogs from the ponds and river, the sound of the clocks striking the hour, or the whispering of the wind through the trees.

Every morning we awoke to the sounds of the birds singing. The younger members of the family would discuss over breakfast what they thought the programme for the day should be, and always it would include Vasili. They rode through the forests, they fished the lakes and practised shooting with Vasili, but the greatest pleasure was the picnic. Horse drawn carts were laden with all the provisions and utensils necessary to feed the adults, the children and the servants. Another cart, this time with a little more comfort, was detailed to transport us along the little used road, to cross the rivers at the shallow fords and to wind their way through the narrow tracks that led through the forests. We would arrive at emerald green meadows and there would unpack the carts and lay out a sumptuous buffet of cold meats, cheeses, fruit, bread and cakes. The children would play in the forest, listening to the birds, keeping watch for the bears, while the adults would enjoy the splendid views, veiled in a slight opalescent tinge, like a filmy curtain, that seemed to unite the fields with the sky. Across the horizon the soft breeze of the afternoon would ruffle swathes of golden corn rolling like waves of the sea in the light wind.

The two sisters, Sania and Xenia, would lie on a large plaid blanket of soft wool, contemplating the panorama around them and, for a while, they would forget the disquiet that they had experienced. The only cloud on the horizon was the persistent malaise of Sania, who would denounce the symptoms with a casual wave of her hand.

For everybody the picnic on the last day of our holiday was unforgettable. We had set about collecting wood to light a fire. Buckets of water were brought from the nearby spring and the cook and housekeeper began to prepare a feast to end all feasts! In the large pots and pans that hung over the fire were prepared dishes to make our mouths water. Chicken and Greek rice were cooked with fragrant herbs whose aromatic sweet scent filled the air. This just served to increase the appetite of the hungry company. Pizzas and ravioli prepared Russian-style were accompanied by excellent tea made in the samovar with the water collected from the spring-fed stream. Salads that came from around the world, Russian, French and Italian; and those that came from around the garden, pepper, tomato, and potato, would all appear on the large tablecloth spread across the grass... finally lunch was ready!

The holidays came to an end but the memories of our

contact with nature, of Vasili and hunting, of fishing and hiking, of long treks through the forest following the tracks of the bears, these would stay with us for a very long time. We all returned to Ekaterinodar and life resumed some degree of normality. There were gatherings with friends; receptions, musical evenings and games of cards, and all the while, Xenia awaited the return of Ely and, hopefully, the successful results of his baccalaureate exams. Meanwhile the daily correspondence between Xenia and Prof Gerasimov was bringing reassuring news. The teacher praised his student and was hoping for a good outcome to the exams and was fully expectant that Ely would achieve his baccalaureate. One evening Xenia was standing by the card table watching an ongoing hand of whist when there was a soft knock at the door and Timote entered bearing a telegram. Xenia, not unnaturally, assumed that it was good news regarding Ely and that it would also announce his arrival back with the family within the next few days. She opened the envelope, full of joy and read: "Ely untraceable. Search in progress."

The news threw the family into disarray. Eugene immediately suggested he borrow one of the horses and set out to help Professor Gerasimov in the search for Ely, to try to establish what exactly had happened. With the memory of the threats following the blackmail demands in Ekaterinodar still fresh in our minds, the main concern was that he may have been kidnapped by the anarchists, or worse still by the marauding bandits that ran freely in the forests. A little later, further news arrived from the professor. This letter, delivered by horseman, outlined what had happened when Ely went missing. The professor explained that he had given a farewell party and combined it with a trip along the beautiful verdant coast of the Black Sea. With the weather so warm they had opted to take a boat trip and had slipped their moorings and sailed out to sea. The water was crisp and clean, the colour of sapphire blue. As they passed close to a mooring buoy Ely had asked the professor whether it would be possible to sit on it, indeed would it bear his weight? The professor explained that it would support a great weight and, to prove the point had dived of the boat and swum to the buoy. It was therefore with astonishment that, as the professor reached the buoy and began to climb aboard, he turned and watched as Ely started the launch engine and move away quickly heading back to shore! "He did at least have the decency, once he had reached shore, to send a fisherman out to rescue me," he added. The professor had not unnaturally assumed this was another of Ely's practical jokes, and had gone straight home fully expecting to see Ely. But the house was empty. Ely had disappeared! The professor's initial searches had proved fruitless and he had quickly sent a telegram to Xenia informing her of what had happened.

It took a week of searching before Eugene found his brother Ely in Novorossiysk, about a hundred miles away, at the home of a group of young revolutionaries, who it appeared were now his friends. He had abandoned his own clothes and adopted the style of those around him – coarse peasant clothing – and now saw himself as a political agitator, a firebrand, and a demagogue. They had been making speeches and holding protests amongst the workers in the dockyards but, for Ely, it was all done in vain. The term exams had already been passed and his mother, exhausted and discouraged by this turn of events, decided to leave for Prague with the children and return to her husband. However it was a cause to which Ely would return many years later in the form of the Citizens Committee for United Nations Reform in 1946.

When they parted, the two sisters, standing next to the railway carriage that would whisk Xenia away once more, looked into each other's eyes, perhaps knowing that they would not meet again for many years. Xenia would move back to America with her husband and children, whilst Sania would remain in Russia with her family. Neither could know what the future had in store for them and how things would change so dramatically. Xenia boarded her carriage and leaned out of the open window of the carriage door and held her sister's hand. When the train moved Sania squeezed the arm of her sister affectionately and then watched as the carriage carrying Xenia drew out of the station. The tears in their eyes misted their last view and the procession of carriages slowly shrank into the distance until only the tiny red dot of the rear light showed in the growing darkness. With a last sad look at the departing train our family turned and made its way back to a house that would be decidedly emptier, quieter and have a lot less laughter for a while.

Nature had begun to undress the trees, and with the sadness of everyone's departure the sumptuous summer cloak and gilded colours of the landscape now turned noticeably autumnal. In the garden the north wind stripped the leaves from the branches leaving them bare, and the cedar nuts, freed from their casing, fell to the floor, black and ugly, to be collected by the gardener and taken to the attic to dry and keep for next Christmas.

Slowly life returned to normal in the house. It was now dressed for winter with heavy silk curtains over the large windows and plush carpets covering the stone floors whilst the fire burning in the fireplace agreeably tempered the air in the rooms where family life continued. School term had begun but lessons were now held with private tutors rather than in the school in Ekaterinodar. In addition to the normal curriculum the children all took dance lessons from Professor Glovacky, ballet master of the theatre. He came every Saturday dressed in a frock coat. He was thin, tall and spare, and taught the dances of the time: waltz, mazurka, pas d'Espagne, and minuet. From the ballet he taught the pas de quatre; a repertoire which, according the girls, was more than sufficient, but not in the opinion of the professor who wanted to make them into real dancers. He laboured to teach them to dance like Salome, with veils, and although he carried out his tasks with great care, he was completely unable to generate enough enthusiasm amongst his charges, and this was soon abandoned. In the ballet lessons we wrapped ourselves in clouds of fluffy fabric and fell to the ground like dying swans, but never felt the sensation of being in front of a picture of elegance. Only the plump Olga Kozlowska, a girlfriend of Sania's, found the exercise at all valuable. Not necessarily for dance but purely as a means to an end, as she used the movements as an exercise to lose weight. Imitating exactly the final part of the fall, she carried a number of blue bruises that had to be cured with packs of chamomile. I was not, in general, a lover of dance and, even less, the dance of the master Glovacky, who was accompanied by the sound of his small and robust violinist friend, a member of a Cossack orchestra, who drew from his instrument sounds which lacked any musical value. They were merely shrill and false and, in essence, parodied the music in the way that we parodied the dance.

Time moved on and soon it began snowing outside. The flakes fell as light as feathers and covered the furrows of grey soil, dry and petrified by the frost, with a soft and shiny coat, preparing the gardens and fields for the big Christmas party.

And suddenly Christmas Eve was upon us and our celebrations began in typical Russian style. Thais and I were dressed in white, our hair loose on our shoulders and laced with blue ribbons. The boys were in sailor suits and they rushed to the windows with fast-beating hearts, their anxious faces pressed against the glass. We all awaited the appearance of the symbol of Christmas. The quiet room was lit only by the soft glow of the little oil lamp that illuminated the gold icon. Outside it grew ever darker. The boys continued to stare intently through the window, into the dark sky where, at last, they saw the birth, amongst all that dark immensity, of the first star. They immediately turned to let everyone know that Christmas had arrived, and they shouted joyfully when they saw the magnificent Christmas tree, framed by the open door of the living room, and lit by a myriad of twinkling candles. At a sign of invitation from our parents we entered excitedly and admired the trinkets and baubles hanging from the tree. We tried to distinguish the old from the new. Many had been on the Christmas tree for generations, but each year new ones were added by either parents, children or by visitors and relatives. Each had its own story and each generated its own memories of places, of people, of events; it was a magical and mysterious moment. Grandma sat down at the piano and began a medley of Christmas songs. They were songs or prayer, of rejoicing and of remembrance, and the chorus was joined by all present, including the servants.

After the prayer of homage to Christ, the gifts that had been carefully placed under the tree were distributed around the family. With squeals of delight we opened packages and boxes. Toys, books, clothes, jewellery, furs and souvenirs of the year 1907 came to light. The excitement eventually abated and calm was restored amongst the children. Toys were played with, favourites were chosen, and grateful thanks passed around. Then the younger members of the family, after assigning everyone their places in the room, explained that they had a surprise prepared for their parents. Little Tina read a poem in French, Vladimir recited a long poem by Pushkin, Thais and Sania played a four-hand piece by Mozart. Valerian, the youngest and smallest, was dressed as an angel, and I distributed the programme of entertainment. The impromptu concert was a success, the applause was gratefully received with a few blushes and exaggerated bows, both mother and father showed their apprectiation and finally it all ended with a choreographed dance, where the children attempted to show that the lessons from Professor Glovacky had not been totally wasted. The ballet was a mix of styles, stories and timing but nevertheless was completed with great grace and animation. Everyone was encouraged to join in the final dance, from my parents to the servants, and, if nothing else, there were high marks for vitality and enthusiasm and, for a while at least, the dark memories of the past year were put behind us. The announcement for dinner was preceded by a composition by my grandfather – a resounding gallop played on the piano, after which we all started for the dining room.

The Christmas Eve feast was served according to a traditional menu and included a fish pie, covered with puff pastry enclosing twenty gold roubles and a lucky charm. The dinner was a protracted family affair with much discussion and reminiscing, and talk about what lay ahead. The parents talked about their children, and the children about the gifts that remained under the tree. But when all was finished everyone rose from the table and all showed signs of fatigue. The children cast a last longing look at the parcels tucked into the tree before everyone retired for the night. The lights were switched off and, with the children in bed, the tone softened. My parents exchanged their impressions.

"It seems to me," said father, "that Thais has an authoritarian temperament and modern ideas, and is full of curiosity towards life. Beautiful as she is, I believe that she will long remain in our nest."

"Is it perhaps that you do not admit your liking of the idea of a marriage for your child?" my mother asked, "I do not think we will have enough authority to prevent it. I suspect that the forces of destiny will make that decision for us."

My father's response was that mother was always a fatalist and that he was of the opinion that each of us was the architect of our own fortune: "Take Vladimir, for example, he will be a beautiful Hussar, with the glorious reputation of his grandfather."

There was a long silence and father commented that there was some sadness in me, Alessandra. My mother was of the opinion that I was mesmerised by Eugene. She had watched me in the countryside at the dacha in Marinsk, and she had noted how I blushed when I opened the Christmas card from Eugene and read the message he had sent me. And how I had then run to my room to hide my excitement! She had noticed that on the day they had left he had embraced me tenderly and that I had held back the tears from my eyes.

With a deep sigh the conversation fell silent and my parents retired to their bedroom. I, meanwhile did not sleep. I lay there awake thinking of the card within which lay Eugene, hidden beneath my pillow.

Gushers Tinged with Sadness

Shortly after the Christmas holidays my father received confirmation from the Cossack government about the land purchase in Maikop. He read to Sania some of the more intricate and interesting paragraphs of the contract and explained the obligations that he would be expected to take on, some of which were particularly onerous.

The commitment that my father had to sign was to put into operation, every year, a new well or suffer the loss of property rights. It was a heavy and demanding condition. In addition there was a tariff to be paid on the production, which was awarded to the Cossack Government, of two kopecks for each three gallons of oil. If we did indeed strike oil then it would be a good deal for them; however my father was assuming all the financial risk. To take advantage of the good weather, my father began the hard work required in order to bring about the realisation of the company. In the virgin lands the foresters, the enormous woodsmen, set about felling trees and making huge clearings in order to establish the drilling site areas. Accommodation needed to be made ready, not only for the store of drills and machinery and spares, but also for the men who would operate them. All the machinery was transported to the site slowly, and with great difficulty, on ox carts. The roads were almost impassable, access had to be cleaved through the forests, all means of communication were difficult and the conditions meant that before long, despite all the preparatory work that had been conducted, they were falling behind their proposed schedule.

The work continued for months, hard, backbreaking work:

felling, clearing, making pathways and building. Then yet another problem arose; the access to water for the drilling rigs. The pipework necessary to deliver the water to the drilling site was delayed and, as my father marked on his calendar, despite the progress being made it was painfully obvious that the delays were mounting. Even though he had not yet finished the first well, his contract terms were such that very shortly he would have to commit to the second well as dictated by the agreement with the Cossack government. Work continued and the first rigs were erected. The ground was difficult to penetrate, the drills were primitive and expensive and the theoretical calculations from the original survey were proving to be wrong. There were now three wells; and not one was yet producing any oil. My father was becoming increasingly nervous.

For centuries in and around the Baku region there had been virtual lakes of oil. After their visit to Baku in 1568-1574, the English merchants Thomas Bannister and Geoffrey Duckett wrote: "Near the city we observe a strange phenomenon — an amazing quantity of oil comes out of the ground here for which people come from remote parts of Persia; it serves throughout the community for the lighting of homes. This oil is black and is called 'nefte'. It is transported throughout the country on mules and donkeys that you often encounter in caravans of four to five hundred. There is also another type of oil near this city of Baku, white and very valuable, and I suppose this is the same as what we call petroleum."

But for all this history the effect of the many delays led to the necessity to employ significantly more capital than expected. My father realised that he would no longer be able to capitalise the project with just his own funds and that he would now need to identify an external source for continued funding, and therefore the requirement for external shareholding. His initial search for funding, was based in Russia. Ideally he wanted to retain all interest in the business amongst Russian nationals. However the consensus of opinion at that time was that there was no demand as most Russian businessmen felt that there was no necessity to drill to the bowels of the earth for black gold when it lay in abundance on the surface and had done for centuries. Defeated in his own country my father was to make a choice between England and America in order to find the additional investment he required to complete his project. The choice of London, was made simply on expediency, the time taken to get to London being significantly shorter than going to America. After a tedious journey across Europe involving several trains, carriages and steamships, my father arrived in London, where he had booked rooms at Browns Hotel in Mayfair. Here, after long conferences and laborious discussions with the English industrialists and potential investors, there was an undoubted pessimism toward his company and his plans. All the most enthusiastic demonstrations by my father had not been enough to arouse the interest of the British to the wells of Maikop. Discouraged, he had written a telegram to his Sania: "The British do not have any confidence in the opinion of our geologists and therefore have rejected all of my proposals, even the most advantageous of them, in terms of potential return on their investment. The city is foggy and cold and has insufficient heating. I feel numb both physically and mentally and I want to return as soon as possible."

Having written the telegram, my father gave it to the bellboy in Brown's Hotel to be sent and then went out in search of distraction along Bond Street. However the frivolous entertainment that was on offer failed to distract him his worries; if he was unable to raise the finances in order to complete the drilling and find oil, then he would lose everything. He would forfeit the lease of the land and the oilrigs, and all the work he had put into the enterprise over the past year would have been for nothing. Night was beginning to fall when he decided to have dinner at Fischer's Hotel, where the restaurant had acquired a reputation of excellence not only for its cuisine but also of its wine cellar. Surely something that might finally draw my father out of his melancholy.

It was while waiting to be served that his melancholy only deepened when he noticed that his little finger was missing, the ring with the family coat of arms. It had been a gift from his father that he had always worn as a talisman. Falling deeper into depression at this further turn of events he abandoned dinner and returned to the hotel distressed by the unlucky day. Upon arrival in the foyer my father enlisted the assistance of the hotel bellboy and they went in search of the ring. The search encompassed all the rooms he had used for meetings, the lobbies and restaurants as well as the bar, all of which eventually proved fruitless. Annoyed, frustrated, disenchanted and despairing, my father prepared for bed and for the next day, when he would have to make some unpalatable decisions regarding his investment and his family. He undressed and bathed and as he took his pyjamas from beneath the pillow of his freshly-made bed, out of the folds tumbled the ring. His relief was palpable and as he bent down to retrieve the ring from the floor there was a knock on the door. It was the hotel bellboy bearing a telegram. My father, anxious to read the telegram and fearing further bad news would befall him, asked the bellboy to wait while he read the message. To his astonishment the telegram read: "Well throwing fountains of oil – twenty tank wagons a day. Please advise."

My father stood for several moments looking at the words that sprang out from the telegram but each time they remained the same. His mind was racing. He sat down at the desk and began to scribble numbers. One tank wagon was 195 barrels, one barrel was 42 gallons, 42 gallons multiplied by 195 and multiplied again by 20? 163,000 gallons! He turned to the bellboy and, giving him a very generous tip, requested him to buy, the next morning, all the newspapers that interested him. Then he sat again at the desk in the room to compose a reply and to give instructions to Maikop. The response was short and to the point. It read: "Don't stop!"

The emotion of the past few days had drained my father and now, with the news of the discovery running round his head, he was unable to sleep and unable to think. He nevertheless slept fitfully and finally awoke at dawn. Over breakfast he read the newspapers. The news reports were sensational; "Maikop – virgin soil yesterday, a liquid goldmine today" or "Maikop – a second Baku". News had travelled fast, and my father read these reports and reflected on the new plans he would now have to make to take into account the amazing developments. While he was still immersed in these meditations and thoughts he could hear, in the hallway, a hum of confused voices. He called the waiter over and asked him to establish what exactly was happening outside the dining room. The waiter, as bid, went to the doorway and opened the door and was met by a stream of people all pushing and struggling to get into the room. My father was somewhat taken aback by this rather unseemly behaviour, having always considered the British to be phlegmatic and stoic rather than excitable and garrulous! He was now surrounded by investors and industrialists who, yesterday, had declined all offers and inducements to invest in his proposals, who had belittled the findings of the Russian geologists, and who had opted not to even consider the most advantageous of terms that had been offered to them. Yet here they were now barely twenty-four hours later fighting for the privilege of being allowed to invest in Maikop. They asked for preferential bookings for the purchase of shares but, until my father had the opportunity to establish exactly what was happening at home, he was disinclined to offer too much at these early stages. In addition, the press was hounding my father for more details on the oil strike: how many wells were gushing, how many were still in the exploration stage, what was the estimate from the geologists report? In order to restore some order to the chaos that now surrounded him, my father asked for help to repel the insistent invaders, and requested that a room be made available to him that should be protected in order to stop further incursions. He could then establish exactly what was happening in Maikop and decide upon a plan of action.

The following day my father made arrangements to return to Russia and to establish the status of all the wells, both those that were producing and those that were still in their exploratory stage. This way at least he could then determine what additional funding, if any, was required, what the current and expected output from the wells would be. He could begin to draw up a plan of development and investment as well as the articles for any new investment capital. On the eve of his departure Henry wrote to bid farewell to all those with whom he had been in business contact, and invite them to visit the Caucasus should they still be interested in investing in the wells of Maikop.

The five-day trip home to Russia was significantly less harrowing than the trip to London just a week earlier. The family were waiting in Ekaterinodar, all pleased to see him home. His friends and acquaintances were congratulating him on the success achieved in Maikop, and were happy to give him a briefing of the work on the other wells that, at the moment, were giving promise of an even more brilliant success, judging by the results of the wash drilling that was being undertaken. Surrounded by his family he recounted every moment of his long journey, the carriages, the trains, the steamships and more trains. He told tales of London and of businessmen who had no interest in his venture. Of his stroll down Bond Street that was unable to lift his mood and, of course, the news brought in the telegram. He laughed as he told of the investors who only the day before had belittled his proposals, and scorned the results of the geologist, and how they clamoured to invest now that he had struck oil. The conversation lasted long into the night, buoyed by the excitement and the continuing good news of the drilling results. My mother, however, looked pale and tired. She smiled at times but looked pained and uneasy and before long she made her excuses and retired for the night leaving the rest of the family to relive the whole story of London and Bond Street once again from beginning to end.

My mother's visible suffering, however, concerned my father, and early the following morning, he took his carriage and visited the family doctor, Dr Platonov. It is there that my father learned that Sania had been unwell for quite some time, and had made great efforts to keep it away from the rest of the family.

Now aware of the deteriorating health of my mother he became desperate to find the cause and, if possible, a cure for whatever ailed her. He turned to my mother's sister, Xenia, recalling that in the past she had advised her sister to see, in case of need, the famous German Professor Roentgen, inventor of a system of rays that he used with patients in need of an accurate diagnosis for internal evils which were unrecognisable to normal listening. He implored Xenia to make an appointment with this Professor Roentgen, who was in Munich. A date was arranged and a nurse, Serella, was taken onto the staff to care for Sania on her journey to Munich, a journey she accepted without question.

All the while my father remained under siege by foreign capitalists who, attracted by the growing success of the Maikop oilfields in the Caucasus, tirelessly insisted on making an appointment with the star of the enterprise. They continued to make the most advantageous offers for the formation of an organisation or company that would ensure the extensive and profitable development of the current fields, as well as in all the other land in my father's possession under the grant from the Cossack government possession, including those close to Maikop.

Henry realised that he needed to once again employ lawyers in order to begin to draw up the contracts necessary for the creation of the Anglo-Maikop Corporation. He spent many hours in conference with notaries both for himself and for those who so desperately wanted to invest in the newly formed company. Each and every paragraph was examined with a fine-tooth comb. Both the English and the Russian versions were scrupulously examined and, of course, the requirements of the Cossacks, who also had a vested interest in the land and its return, had to be taken into account. Henry and his assistants spent many late hours poring over the documents. In the evenings the light from the study could be seen spilling over onto the lawns outside as they sat, heads bent over a table full of documents, ensuring that every 'i' was dotted and every 't' crossed. Having reached this point the thought of any more disruptions to his plans merely increased Henry's nervous anticipation. On the desk in front of him sat the culmination of three years of anxious torment, of disappointment and discouragement, and of scepticism. There were times when he thought that perhaps he had not assumed his rightful responsibilities, that he had entered a deal which had perhaps more risks than he had a right to assume. He thought of the predicament he had placed his family in and the sleepless nights prior to days of controversy, days when he had doubted his convictions, days when his nerves had been stretched to their utmost and almost, but never quite, broken. However, he had refused to surrender, he had fought against all the obstacles, all the mistrust, all the doubts, and now he was about to crown his work. The Cossack government was to honour him, he would receive high praise for his tenacity and he had written the name of Maikop in large letters.

The investment and contracts were finalised and an article which appeared in *Bohrtechniker Zeitung* in 1942 showed the true success of the investment. It read: "The drilling on new fields provided potential but seemed to lack sufficient initial financial investment. The zone of Maikop in the north of the Caucasus was particularly promising. The proposed drilling fields had been examined by experienced Russian geologists and the first exploratory drilling, although late, was crowned with success and increased expectations with regard to the overall potential of the fields. In 1909 a particularly rich gusher was discovered which led to a speculative fever on the London Stock Exchange. In total by 1913 twenty-three gushers had been drilled which, between them, had a capital value of £6,996,000."

A Proposal and a Disappointment

For a while it seemed that perhaps fate was trying to balance the books, to compensate for the agonising past few years, the earlier revolution, the strikes, the unrest, the danger the children had been in at their school, the threats and blackmail the family had been besieged by, but it would seem that amongst all this happiness another turn of the cards would reveal more heartbreak and sadness.

The return of Sania from her visit to Professor Roentgen in Munich brought the terrible news that she was suffering from an incurable disease. The euphoria of the past few weeks dissipated rapidly and was replaced by a climate of bitter despair. The atmosphere of the house was transformed and it now resembled a clinic. A nurse lent assistance to my mother, and the air was redolent with the smell of ether, and in the night the sound of prayers being offered and of tears being shed could be heard on the evening breeze. The final few months of Sania's life were a torment. In great pain, she was prescribed ever-increasing doses of morphine but, before very long, this ceased to have an effect. We all ensured she was never alone, regardless of the fact that there was a nurse to tend to her. We would sit beside her bed and read stories from her favourite authors – Pushkin was particularly preferred. We also arranged for the piano to be moved into the bedroom in order that we could play music. Even when she was sleeping we would continue to read and to play. We would place cool cloths on her brow and tenderly wipe the tears of pain, present even in sleep, from her eyes and cheeks. The youngest, Vladimir, refused to leave his mother's bedside and spent many hours talking gently to her. He would describe the gardens in the spring, the colours of the flowers, and would bring in bunches cut fresh from their beds so his mother could grasp their fragrance and, hopefully, overpower the aroma of ether and disinfectant. He explained where the flowers had come from, the hyacinths and tulips from Holland, the velvet roses from England, and lavender from France. The anguish and pain around the house was palpable.

Each and every day I prayed for a miracle, and each night I knelt by my bed and asked for help. I am sure that everyone else, both in the family and in the house, did the same. But my mother's days were cutshort, and in the late spring the same flowers we had cut to inspire and heal her were placed upon her grave. She lay beneath the earth covered in a blanket of roses, lilies, hyacinths and tulips; every flower that had bloomed in the garden now surrounded her final resting place. Our tears nurtured them.

My father was not a great believer in the philosophy that time heals wounds. He was heartbroken and began to immerse himself in work and travel, forcing everyone to adapt to his new lifestyle. I believe he felt that by doing this he would provide the family with an intermission to the play that he believed he was now living. He felt like a character who was moving between dramas, between a repertoire of comedy and tragedy that was playing itself out in his life and affecting everyone around him. He felt that by immersing himself in one element he would be able to gain the necessary respite and begin, once again, to enter a world that contained life. I was left in charge of the household and, with the help of Timote, managed to maintain some degree of order amongst both the staff and the children.

A year passed, and the following summer, at the arrival of the holidays, the family set off towards the shores of the Black Sea. My father stayed behind and left the housekeepers, Timote and myself to take care of all arrangements. We would, of course, be chaperoned by our neighbours the von Englemanns. The villa at which we stayed was situated on a hill covered by green forests, facing the turquoise sea in the picturesque resort town of Gelendzhiksaya, adjacent to the port of Novorossiysk. Big colourful tents shaded immense terraces; of wildflowers carefully cultivated flowerbeds stretched across the gardens and complemented the beauty created by nature. Wide marble steps led from the terraces to the dunes of a white sandy beach behind which, out of sight, there was the calm of the sea, enclosed by the curving headland around the bay. During the day the water seemed an endless blue, and in the evening, as the sun set over the horizon, it would turn to the most wonderful amber before, as the sun disappeared, melding with the sky.

Each morning the children were the earliest to rise and their first port of call was the beach, even before breakfast. Invariably our friends and neighbours, the von Englemanns, were present and they would organise bathing, and swimming competitions. None of the children were able to beat Miss Constant. Miss Constant was the lady companion of the von Englemanns and, despite her forty-five years, she was able, through a variety machinations and Machiavellian cunning, to consistently beat the children at any game that involved water. This in turn kept them busy as they plotted revenge and planned how they would, or indeed if they could, turn the tables on her.

I spent many afternoons in the company of Mrs von Englemann, who had been a close friend of my mother. She was educated, full of initiative and, as was my mother, a musician of great worth. We would spend many hours talking music, both classic and modern, and playing the piano. Mrs von Englemann harboured a particular affection for both of the boys, and she would take Vladimir and Valerian for long walks down the beach and in many ways became a surrogate mother to them. She would listen to them, talk to them, but never make judgements of them, and I believe that they both appreciated her compassion. The hours spent with her were full of attractions and teachings; she would cover literature, music, history and art, and she would enrapture the boys. She made even the most tedious of subjects exciting and interesting and, when they arrived back at the villa, they would be full of enthusiasm, and it would seem that some of the weight and bad memories of the past year were slowly falling from their shoulders.

We were sitting on the terrace having breakfast one morning when Mrs von Englemann came across to visit and presented an invitation to the whole family. Their son Sandro would be arriving and, for the occasion, she had planned a programme of festivities. This included visits to Novorossiysk, and a concert where we would all be able to participate in some way or another. Between our families it had been established that there were enough players to form a small orchestra. Mrs von Englemann had decided that we would be playing a Mendelssohn March as an orchestra, and also a variety of solo performances. As a result, she continued, we should with haste begin to practise, both together and individually.

The days began to follow a regular rhythm. At breakfast we would all gather on the sunny terrace across which the wind carried the characteristic smell of the sea and the sounds of the March of Mendelssohn being practised from the house to that of our neighbours. The children were excited about the orchestral rehearsals, and they also discussed the upcoming arrival of Sandro, curious to know what he was like, how he would look, how tall and how good looking. That was certainly part of the girls' conversation.

The arrival of the mail, handed over by Miss Constant, interrupted the conversation one morning. There was a letter informing us of the imminent arrival of my father and a second letter from America, for me. I recognized the handwriting as being that of Eugene and, preferring to open it and read it when I was alone, I hid it behind a large pot on the terrace. The morning was dedicated to a trip to Novorossiysk and included was Miss Constant. I made my excuses, feigning a headache, and asked to be spared from the day's excursion. As rest of the family all boarded the motor launch that was moored at a jetty, I went to the swimmers' cabin, built of solid tree trunks and providing the privacy I wanted, to read the letter from Eugene. I heard the excited chatter of the picnickers as they boarded the launch, the soft purr as the engine started, and watched as they moved quickly away on a soft silvery sheet of water. There was barely a ripple from the bow and just a long trail of silvery foam from behind.

I stood at the window of the log cabin and watched the boat disappear across the water. Remembering the letter I had hidden behind the pot on the terrace, I smiled at the happy moment that awaited me. Running to the end of the balcony I retrieved the letter and then I settled my self into the large easy chair and gazed for a moment at the pale horizon in front of me. I could just see the sails of boats, fluttering like small butterflies in the soft breeze. I felt the warmth of the morning sun on my arms and, at ease in the peace, I ran my fingers across the back of the envelope that sat in my hand and imagined the contents of the letter, sure that it would contain confessions of love and be full of endearments. Instead I read the letter with fading interest. Instead of blandishments and endearments there was a fanciful description of a stormy ocean crossing. There were no confessions of love, just an explanation of how busy America was, and how crowded the streets were. There was not a word that would reveal any sentiment of intimacy. Disappointed, disheartened and despondent, to vent my frustration I went back to the villa and started to play the piano: that always helped to soothe me. I had just finishing playing *Etude Revolutionnaire* by Chopin when a singular burst of applause greeted the final few bars. I turned abruptly and saw before me an elegant stranger, bowing, who asked pardon of the interruption and presented himself.

"I am Sandro von Englemann."

The look of those velvet eyes and the charming smile struck me, and we exchanged a few impressions on the music. Before parting, Sandro repeated the invitation of his mother to the reception the following evening. The reception took place with great pomp: arches of flowers and lighting from Japanese lanterns led along the balcony to an esplanade that overlooked the sea from the top of a cliff. There were dances, games, jokes, and a buffet laden with the most delicious delicatessen picnic.

Sandro, while doing the honours to guests, also ensured he spent time with me – so that his brother, Rodolpho, provoked perhaps by a twinge of jealousy, could not resist the temptation to mutter to Sandro as he passed "It seems the ice is melting too quickly brother!"

The ironic comment was dismissed for such as it was, and instead the spectacle of fireworks attracted the guests to the top of the rocky outcrop from which they had a splendid view of the vibrant phantasmagoria of coloured rain that fell across the bay. Falling stars, shooting fountains, Roman Candles and Catherine Wheels, all lit up the sky with an electric shower formed by the myriad of colours. They reflected back in the dark sea below like a mystical mirror. The evening over, Sandro von Englemann escorted me back home from the neighbours' villa and to my doorstep.

The following day my father arrived by carriage. Both the children and I noticed that he looked tired and emaciated, and we were more than a little concerned for his health. We assumed that perhaps it was the result of the arduous amount of work he had imposed upon himself and hoped that a few days well-earned rest and relaxation would result in his looking significantly healthier. We watched over him for the next few days but he did not appear to improve. Finally after a few more days he called us all into the dining room and spoke to us. He explained that his health was beginning to deteriorate, and that his doctor had told him that it demanded prolonged care and that there was a need for a change of climate. As a result we were all to be sent to college in Lausanne, in Switzerland. He said he had also spoken to Mrs von Englemann who had offered him the services of Miss Constant. This would ensure we had a chaperone for the girls and also that we were not so badly affected by the distance between us. Miss Constant would accompany us to Switzerland.

The boys embraced this news with a sense of excitement, and the thought of Miss Constant as their companion helped to salve the concern they had over separation from their father. They rushed next door to speak to their friends, the von Englemanns, and to acquaint their neighbours with the decision that their father had made.

Rodolfo was as excited as the boys and his main concern was that they would meet again next summer. Sandro was quiet, his eyes veiled and his demeanour melancholy. He wandered down to the seashore. I followed him and he looked exceedingly mournful. We agreed to meet that evening at dinner when my father would be hosting the von Englemanns by way of thanks for their help over the summer. I reminded Sandro to bring his violin.

That afternoon, to pass the time, we took the launch to visit the warships that were anchored in the port of Novorossiysk for an official visit. Some submarines accompanied two dreadnoughts and three cruisers, and they all swung slowly on the smooth surface of the bay in the gentle current. The still waters reflected their massive shapes, their shadows rippling with the breeze that ruffled the top of the bay. Hundreds of small and medium boats were approaching the combined navy. The occupants would watch the crews of the ships as they went about their duties, their smart uniforms pressed, their boots gleaming in the soft light of the sun as it began to droop towards the horizon, their caps all perfectly placed on their head as they awaited the arrival of the inspecting authorities. It was fun for a while and although we did admire the fleet we remembered, just in time, that we would need to make our return in order to dress for dinner.

Back at the villa the dining room had been prepared. The table was covered in a startling white linen tablecloth upon which stood silver candlesticks each of which held not only the candle but also glass bells which reflected prisms of light across the table and around the room as the candle flames flickered and shimmered. White porcelain plates with the family crest on the rim sat at the edges of the table. Beside the plate was a guard of cutlery: silver knives, forks and spoons stood smartly to attention, reflecting candlelight onto the crystal goblets and crisp white linen napkins.

Two waiters served a series of delicious courses of food, vol-au-vents stuffed with wild porcini mushrooms in a white wine sauce, others filled to brimming with turkey and ham, each vol-au-vent wearing a small pastry hat, slightly askew, giving it a rakish look. This was followed by a ragu of partridge and countless other delicacies, and finished with a pineapple parfait. All were masterpieces and the miracle performed by the cook was well appreciated by everybody.

Coffee and liqueurs were served on the lawn, to the great relief of the gentlemen, who could now relax and turn their conversation away from the small talk of the dinner table and to what they perceived as more important matters. Sitting back in the large wicker chairs animated discussions were held against the panoramic backdrop of the harbour, which was festively lit in honour of the guests and authorities. A variety of receptions were being held on board all the ships, each of which had been decorated with garlands of coloured bulbs that hung from the very top of the masts down to the furthest bowsprit. Spotlights flickered and chased each other across the ships, across the harbour and, occasionally, illuminated even the villa, much to the amusement of our guests.

The discussions of the adults were topical and ranged from the state of the politics to the standing of the Tsar Nicholas II, from Rasputin, the mystical son of a well-to-do peasant and coach driver, to Yusupov. My father confessed that the real reason he had decided to send his children to college in Switzerland was that times had changed and that these times required parents perhaps to release the brakes on the children. He felt that although tradition was good and had huge benefits, there were times when it needed to adjust, that too much tradition became a millstone to progress. However, he also believed that tradition should go hand in hand with progress and not be abandoned or cast away without a great deal of thought. It was true, he said, that young people of today no longer obeyed the old precepts blindly, and that they, quite rightly, asked the question 'why?' and would not accept the response of 'why not?'

My father regaled everyone with the rather risqué story of a friend of theirs, a lawyer, Eduardo, who had just won a somewhat tedious and laborious trial in favour of his foreign client, and had received a substantial sum of money in settlement of the claim but, more importantly, had rescued their reputation. The men looked at my father quizzically and he continued. The lawyer was invited to a party in his honour that was held in a private room of a nightclub. After having consumed a hearty meal which had been accompanied by copious libations of a variety of alcoholic beverages they were well into the night and, indeed, probably closer to dawn! The usual programme of entertainment in these sorts of clubs had been delivered and had included erotic performances by attractive women that had merely served to perhaps increase rather than satisfy expectations. As such the guests had requested some extras to be attached to the normal programme and as the early morning light rose in the sky the group saw two young and beautiful nymphs, wrapped in light veils enter their room. It would have been a wonderful vision for all had not the lawyer recognized his daughters! The poor things were on the ground in embarrassment and their father, the lawyer, was trying hard not to acknowledge them. The story may have been apocryphal, but it served my father to make a point about the changing mores of the youth and the gap that widens between them and their parents.

A light breeze stirred the sea and the faint murmur of the waves could be heard as they lapped onto the shore. The lights and bunting on the ships and the port flickered off one by one as if it was a choreographed dance. The port was fading into the night and would soon disappear into the darkness. All that remained for a while was an occasional lighted window or the flash of light as a door opened and closed. Even the moon played hide and seek, now throwing a golden glow onto the water below and then hiding behind the scudding clouds that scampered across the sky, then out again tossing moonbeams down to the damp grass and liquid waters. Sandro von Englemann and I chose this moment to celebrate the beauty of the night with music, Sandro with his violin whilst I accompanied him on the piano. The harmonies of Grieg and Tchaikovsky, cascaded through the wide-open windows and doors and echoed across terrace and houses. For a moment the guests fell silent, their eyes on the remote silvery surface of the sea, as they listened to the melodies that penetrated deep in their soul.

The calendar marked the first days of September. The visit of my father had been only for a few days, and although the party had helped to raise his spirits he still looked tired and pale. Both families were getting ready to leave their summer residences and I went to see Mrs von Englemann to wish her a special farewell and to thank her for all her kindnesses across the summer holiday. Sandro was nowhere in sight but Mrs von Englemann was waiting for me under the pergola, which was attached like a bird's nest high on the rocky clifftop overlooking the sea. It was a wonderful setting and a perfect venue for farewells but, as I sat with her in the eyrie, I felt that Mrs von Englemann was ill at ease and uncomfortable. I was unsure as to the cause of this and hoped that it was nothing that had been said or done by myself or anyone else in my family. There was an air of embarrassment about her and although she tried to hide it, it was in vain. The conversation between us was stilted and in order to diffuse the atmosphere I praised her for her help and for allowing the services of Miss Constant going forward as a companion during my travels ahead to Switzerland and Lausanne.

The sea breeze brought a pleasant coolness, and seemed to give courage to Mrs von Englemann. It was obvious that something was troubling her. After a moment she looked down at her hands, which were folded in her lap and began, hesitantly, to softly speak to me.

"Do not be surprised, dear Alessandra, with what I am about to tell you, for it is a delicate topic. My son Sandro, before leaving, told me a great secret and professed to me his love for you and how it has grown so much over these summer holidays. He has asked me to reveal to you the reasons that have prevented him from talking and explaining to you personally."

Mrs von Englemann looked up into my eyes and I could see how painful this was for her. I reached over and grasped her hands in mine, and encouraged her to continue.

She said, "Sandro's fate is tied to a pitiful incident of his youth, an unfortunate accident which resulted in the amputation of a leg. It has been replaced with a prosthetic limb. It is, as far as prosthetics go, the perfect artificial limb and allows Sandro to lead a perfectly normal life with a complete range of movements that seem practically natural in almost all everyday circumstances. However, even with all the movements, his thoughts stray to this injury and undermine his confidence and his courage and his ability to express fully his feelings, particularly for you."

The revelation deeply shocked me, my heart was pounding, and my sensitivity was shaken by a feeling of pity that drove me to accept Sandro, while at the same time, instinctively, thinking of Eugene. Confused but sincere I embraced Mrs von Englemann. However, before I could begin to frame an answer she caressed my cheek and whispered quietly to me: "Not now, but think and write to me."

I left the pergola and almost stumbled down the steep trail that ended up at the sea. For a long while I stood there, looking out at the still waters. I held a handkerchief to my eyes that were now red from weeping. I needed to cool them before I went back to the villa, before I faced anyone in my family, before I told anyone what had happened.

The train taking the family back home sped us quickly past the fields that were already changing to reflect the colours of autumn. The boys had watched through the window as the coastline retreated, and Miss Constant distracted the younger children with stories of her youth and fairy tales from literature. I was lost in thought and could not help but continually replay the meeting with Mrs von Englemann in my mind, and all the meetings and walks I had taken with Sandro. It had never occurred to me that there was anything more than just a summer friendship between us and could not understand how I, or anyone else in our gathering, could have misunderstood the situation so badly. We had practised together so many sports and Sandro had shown the same level of agility as all the others. Only now did I realised that he had always worn long trousers, and never shorts, nor had he ever been swimming with us, always seeming to prefer to stay on the shore and watch.

Miss Constant had noticed my preoccupation, and although she asked for the reasons why, I could not tell her. She tried to lift my spirits by recounting to us a true story from her youth.

"Many years ago, before you were born, there were no other means of locomotion except for the carriages, stagecoaches and trams that were pulled by horses. With the progress of time we heard of a new invention that was making its way across Russia, initially to link the big cities of the country and then, as time went by, an ever expanding network that would spread across the nation. Such was the revolutionary aspect of the railway. It would speed travel immensely and it would link cities and towns and open up parts of Russia that had never been accessible before. At the opening of the line from Ekaterinodar to Novorossiysk, among the guests, were our parents. At the station, an orchestra played hymns that mingled with the loud cries of the crowd cheering at this exceptional event. The locomotive with a loud blast of steam, and in billowing clouds of smoke, started to move, and soon after, to everyone's amazement, the train ran at the speed of 30 kilometres per hour!"

"As the journey continued the astonished travellers were served refreshments. Canapés, sandwiches and vol-au-vents made their way down the carriages served by waiters with white gloves and crisp white linen jackets with starched creases, alongside tea served from samovars. Suddenly everyone was pitched forward in their seats as the brakes on the train were applied hard, and this was accompanied by a loud, long piercing whistle from the locomotive engine. The train drew to a stop and the passengers flocked to the windows to see what was happening. The sight that greeted them was amazing. A procession of villagers in national costumes wound their way down the track, carrying large banners and icons and preceded by what must be assumed was their leader, who carried a large cross. The driver had been forced to brake sharply to avoid them. The peasants, victorious and confident of the effect of their sacred procession, began shouting at the locomotive 'Come on now, demon!' They began to sing hymns of thanks at having stopped the smoke and steam-breathing behemoth in its tracks and knelt on the railway track. The locomotive driver, however, was deaf to the prayers and invocations of the peasants and conscious only of the orders of the railroad and the need to ensure free passage for his esteemed and important passengers. The train stood there for a while, with just the gentle hiss of escaping steam to accompany the rallying calls of the peasants in the air. It was then that the driver decided that it was time to take decisive action. With a twist of his wrist he opened the cocks of the boiler and from a soft murmur there was suddenly a huge roar as boiling steam leapt out from beneath the engine and from the boiler overflows. The cloud of steam enveloped not only the engine but also most of the peasants who, having thought they had won the day, had crept close to the front of the train. The crowd panicked and terror gave them added impetus as they leapt away from the train, off the tracks and hastily made their way to a safe distance. From there they watched as the train, once more free to move, slowly picked up speed and continued its interrupted journey across the countryside."

After an uneventful but nevertheless entertaining journey bolstered mainly by the anecdotes from Miss Constant, we eventually arrived back at the station in Ekaterinodar. Carriages were waiting to take our copious bags and ourselves back to the house, and we could not wait to once again sleep in our own beds, regardless of how much fun we had had at the summer villa. Father had to stay in town for a meeting and once home I retreated to my room, a little upset at the thought of how to respond to Mrs von Englemann, and how to broach the whole subject with my father. I lay on my bed and read, again, the letters from Eugene that, although perhaps not full of declarations of love and endearments, nevertheless were from, at that moment, the boy I liked the best!

Every morning when he was home, my father would become our household alarm clock. Having finished his morning preparations he would go downstairs, sit at the piano in the drawing room and play anything from a loud and rousing march to some soft and gentle *étude* by Chopin. This was essentially an invitation for everyone to fall out of bed, and invariably ended up as a competition to see who could be the first to embrace him. I have to confess that I was nearly always the first, and this morning there was an added impetus to my desire to get to see my father at the earliest opportunity. I had already heard him getting dressed and was standing on the staircase landing the moment he played his first note. I was determined to take advantage of a few moments solitude as I knew the rest of the family would not be up for a while, awake maybe but certainly not up and dressed and ready for breakfast. That morning I flew down the remaining stairs and into my father's arms like a small tornado! Before I could change my mind I blurted out to him the story of Sandro and Mrs von Englemann and the quandary that was in my mind. My thoughts and feeling came tumbling out, my mind a maelstrom of confusion as, for the first time, I was able to share everything that had been whirling around in my head, and all the worries I had. I explained that I did not want to hurt either Sandro or his parents but was at a total loss of what to do and how to move forward.

My father listened to all of this with huge patience. He held my hands and looked into my eyes, which were by now brimming with tears, and just listened. He said he was impressed by Sandro's fortitude in the face of his adversity and that he considered him to be an eligible and friendly man, and then fell silent again as I continued to spill my innermost thoughts.

Finally I stopped, I had run out of words and was now overcome with guilt and emotion at what I had said and confessed. My father paused for a moment and, still looking directly into my eyes, simply asked: "Do you love him?"

I leaned across to him and hugged him tightly and, with my head on his broad shoulders, I whispered softly with a sense of guilt,

"No."

"So let me respond to Mrs von Englemann," he replied.

It was with great relief that I thanked him and went through the large doors from the drawing room and into the garden. I felt as if a great weight had been lifted from my shoulders, my spirits soared and it was only at that moment that I realised the toll this had taken on me. I stood on the terrace and looked out across the lawns and gardens that had already assumed their autumn robes. The leaves on the trees had turned russet and the dahlias were fading. More leaves skittered across the paths as the wind pushed and played with them, scattering them into the air and then allowing them to almost fall before catching them up again. I wandered across to the stables, that had received their summer clean. The fresh paint gleamed, the cobbled floors were damp and the horses so well groomed they looked ready for a gymkhana. I watched as the stable hands unloaded a cart of hay and stored it in the barn, and as they began to prepare the well of the icebox, cleaning everything out ready for the winter and another year of use. The woodshed was also filling up: to the back wood that needed to be seasoned, and to the front huge stacks that would keep us warm and heated throughout the winter ahead.

After my cursory 'inspection' I went toward the hill, where there was a view of the river Kuban, wide and cloudy, full of dangerous eddies. The river had claimed a number of inexperienced victims – it had merely swallowed them and spat them out into the Black Sea further down. The Kuban cut through a sad plain covered with sparse, poor vegetation, good soil only for hunters of wild ducks. A railway bridge and a brick factory with two towers stood on each side of this bleak view, "A framework of melancholy" I thought, turning back and preparing to return to the house. The subject of Sandro was never mentioned again.

I arrived home just as Miss Constant was telling us the date for our departure to Lausanne. With time at a premium, we all began to lay claim to a variety of trunks and cases, and ensure that they were safely placed in our rooms. Before long, suitcases and cabin trunks lay open in rooms ready and waiting to receive any item of clothing, cosmetics, toiletries and footwear that could possibly be required for the expected long absence. Miss Constant went to help Valerian, the youngest, who was essentially emptying his wardrobe, his drawers and his toy cupboard into every available trunk and suitcase. Every time Miss Constant took something out of the case Valerian would arrive with two further additions, which he would argue, were absolutely necessary for either the journey or his wellbeing at school. Finally we were packed. Cases had been strapped closed and labelled and the convoy of carriages made ready. With so many people and so many trunks we only required a few elephants and some cages with canaries and parrots and we would have closely resembled a Maharajah's entourage!

The trip to Switzerland took five days and was completed with no unexpected occurrences. We arrived in Lausanne with the same number of people and, equally importantly, the same number of cabin trunks, cases and valises that had commenced the journey in Russia.

Finishing School and Second Love

Lausanne was a mecca that attracted youth. There arose everywhere specialized institutes catering for all tastes and needs, whether they were educational or recreational. There were institutes for sports and institutes for learning, for languages and for science; dedicated finishing schools and schools for those with specific callings or vocations for medicine or religion. Some were located in the hills above Lausanne; others on the plains or by the lake. There were institutes with villas and parks, with gardens and tennis courts, all the details of which were taken into account by my father who read the reports of the colleges, and their prices.

Miss Constant did not encounter any difficulties in her research; she simply followed the instructions given by the head of the family. It had been decided that the girls would attend the Haute Rampe Institute under Miss Hallett, whilst the boys would be boarding at the Institute Auckenthaler in Ouchy. The programme, according to the prospectus, was very attractive, broad, full of interest and overseen by university professors. It had been designed to ensure a breadth of education, and aimed to develop and prepare young people for entry into the most prestigious of universities.

In reality things were a little different and it was only thanks to the attentions of Miss Constant that instead of having our intellectual horizons significantly narrowed by the 'professors' they were indeed expanded. It is also with thanks to Miss Constant and her demands that the experimenting of, and experience in, these institutions did not give deplorable results for our family.

However, as soon as everything was decided and we had all settled in our various classes, and with Miss Constant harrying us, we all began to show significant advances in the core disciplines. One thing that consistently puzzled me was how frequently many of my class would disappear for half a day (sometimes for a whole day), only reappearing at lunchtime. Intrigued, I asked the reason for this absence and learned that the girls where busy in the kitchen.

"In the kitchen?" I repeated with surprise, this being somewhere where I believed only the staff belonged.

"Correct, in the kitchen, we are following a course on home economics!"

I was fascinated and decided that if I could go there too, I could make a nice surprise for father when he returned home.

I applied and was immediately admitted to the course. For my first lesson, a senior cook, Mademoiselle Berthe, announced that we would be learning to prepare snails in red wine. The process of preparation was rather long and tedious, and if this was the fashion, I could understand why the girls would disappear for the whole day. However the final result was excellent.

While I had fun with lessons of culinary art, my brothers, who were passionate about sports were preparing for the championship rowing races against the Institute Jacquard from Geneva. Vladimir had been selected to row for Auckenthaler. The day of the competition arrived and Vladimir was full of anticipation and expectation. The guests and dignitaries were all waiting on the shore of Lake Ouchy, lining the course that had been divided into lanes. Preparations for the race drew ever nearer. Boats were loaded with crew and set free on the water. The guests on the shore and the rowers at the start line were focussed on the starter's flag. The students of Villa Auckenthaler were in their white sweaters; their rivals in blue. The two groups of young people, of differing nationalities, were tensed, ready to explode into action. Both were stimulated by the same fire: to reach the finish first. The crowd waiting for the flag to fall called out for their teams with cries of: 'Courage The Villa!' and 'Forza Jacquard!' The rear of the boats were held by small motor launches to ensure they were straight, and a long minute passed with the blades of the oars poised centimetres above the water. The flag fell and the oars dipped into the water, and the two long, slim, cigar boats accelerated away from their launches. Both crews competed fiercely, blades flashed in and out of the water, there was blur of white and blue as the crews strained forward and then propelled themselves back almost to lie down, then leant forward once more only to explode back again. The oars dug deep into the water and then, on their return, skimmed back across the surface. The crowd, caught in the frenzy of the moment, continued to call for their favoured teams and only inches could separate them at the finish. It was a thunderous cheer for La Villa that signalled the winner of the race. The crew, exhausted, slumped over their oars, their chests heaved, their arms ached, but they had won. The crowd continued to cheer as both boats gently came to the shore and the opposing crews gallantly congratulated each other on a race well run and a victory well deserved. The Director of Institute Auckenthaler presented awards to each of the scullers from both the teams, including my brother Vladimir. A tea dance was offered shortly after at the Chateau d'Ouchy. This hotel had originally been constructed as a castle by the Bishop of Lausanne and had seen use in a variety of guises including a prison. Now however it was surrounded by cypress trees and occupied by the guests and competitors of Institute Jacquard and Institute Villa Auckenthaler.

Later that afternoon Miss Constant collected the girls and led them from the hotel and around the lake on their way back to the Institute. As I looked around, at the circle of mountain peaks that surrounded the lake, whose tops were veiled in clouds and a very light dusting of snow, my heart was filled with memories of home. I became nostalgic about Eugene, five years had passed and I had received no news of late. Had he married, had something more sinister happened to him, had he forgotten me? The thoughts ran through my mind and I drew up alongside Miss Constant and took her arm, squeezing tenderly seeking protection. The lady with the comforting touch looked into my eyes and guided me gently back to the Institute.

Dinner that evening was followed by gossip and conversation in the living room with the director of the Institute. We talked about the boat race, the tea at the Chateau and the walk home. We reminisced about home and wondered what the winter would bring, and where we could go skiing. Punctually at ten, we all retired to our bedrooms.

Our sleep was however disturbed by a group of students and admirers who were serenading under the windows of the college. It was not at all unusual and regularly sent our Institute director, Mr Hallett, on the rampage. He burst onto the balcony overlooking the rowdy students and he did not spare his words. The young students were anything but gallant and merely responded by increasing the volume of their serenades, which began to lose anything resembling music and became merely a loud and unseemly noise. Meanwhile the director's wife, Mrs Hallett, stood guard and patrolled corridors of the dormitory block – the students pretended to be asleep in order to avoid a worsening situation but found it hard, against the background of poor singing and ribald comments, to hold back their laughter. The next morning, still a little light headed from the limited amount of sleep, I arrived at the refectory for breakfast and was met with a most agreeable surprise. Beside my place setting there was a telegram that read: 'Arrival Monday at 17.00 in Lausanne, Hugs, Eugene.'

Correspondence by telegram was habitual and preferred by the Russians. It avoided wasting time and, given the vastness of the country, a letter to reach its destination, particularly from one end to the other, could easily take anything from a week to ten days. I was astounded and found it hard to believe the reality. I re-read the telegram text several times and then ran to the phone to tell Miss Constant the news, and begged her to ask the director to place me 'off-duty' for the day so I could be ready to meet Eugene.

The morning hours passed quickly with purchases in the dress shop and a long session at the hairdresser. Having finally returned to the college it was time to get ready to go to the Lausanne station. I dressed in the new clothes I had bought that morning, a pink shantung dress cinched at the waist, with a pleated skirt. A wide burgundy red leather belt accentuated the colour and fit. With soft cream leather pumps on my feet, a Florentine straw hat in the same colour as the belt topped the whole ensemble. A glance in the mirror and I was happy to leave and meet Eugene, alone and without a chaperone. I arrived at the station with only moments to spare and walked briskly through the underpass. I ran up the stairs and stepped out onto the platform just as the train was drawing gently to a stop. Taking a seat close to the exit I began to observe the travellers as I waited for Eugene.

I observed the men disembarking from the train and, amongst the crowd, I noticed Eugene. I watched him for a while as he walked down the platform towards me. I could see he was looking for someone, me, and I looked at him as he walked straight past me as I sat on the platform bench. I followed him on his journey without losing sight of him for a single moment, studying him curiously. He did not seem anymore the 'student' Eugene, but someone else. There was something new in his personality, almost a stranger. He arrived at the taxi rank that ran across the front of the station and went to pay the porter. I had followed him out and before he could get into the taxi I called out to him, "Eugene!"

He turned. "It's impossible, absolutely impossible!" he cried out, "I cannot believe I did not recognise you – you are the absolute image of your mother!"

I looked confused but he took my hand and kissed me fondly on the cheek. I still felt that he was a stranger; there appeared to be a certain coolness within him, it was such an odd sensation. For years I had wondered and thought about him, and yet, when we finally met again, I was unsure what attitude to take. The journey to the Institute took but a few minutes during which we engaged each other in formal conversation. We parted at the door of the Institute and agreed to meet again that evening to dine, but this time in the company of Miss Constant as a chaperone.

As soon as I entered the door of the Institute I was besieged by questions from my sisters and the other girls in the dormitory.

"How did you find it?"

"How did the meeting go?"

"Has he changed?"

I was hesitant in my response and merely replied that I would leave any judgement until this evening, and would use the time during and after dinner with Eugene and Miss Constant.

Dinner was rather like a circus. All the girls had gathered on the terrace of the hotel where Miss Constant was staying and which adjoined the dining room. All through the meal I could hear the whispered commentary of the girls as they relayed back to the others what was happening; what did Eugene look like, was he blonde or dark, light or swarthy, well dressed or casual....

Eugene and I conversed as old friends rather than a couple. He spoke of his emotion when his mother had died in America and I spoke to him of my mother's illness and my father's ill health. He told me how Xenia had never really settled in America and had badly missed her home and family in Russia, and felt sure this had hastened her end. We reminisced about Ely who was now studying at the University of Cincinnati and, as ever, was constantly challenging his teachers. Little Sascha meanwhile was travelling around the world as a child prodigy on the violin, and collecting deserved acclaim. Recently, whilst in Rome, Pope Pius X had awarded him a gold medal for his playing and virtuosity.

There then followed many memories of their childhood, by

which time it was getting late. Miss Constant, aware that the waiters and maitre'd were hovering and waiting to close the restaurant, suggested a walk along the lake which, at this time of night, was only recognizable by its contours, outlined by the lights along the roads that bordered the water's edge. Eugene took my arm and we walked a few steps ahead of our chaperone. My nerves began to jangle and, at his touch on my arm, I felt a tingle run through my body as if a slight electric current had been applied, and the hairs on my arms stood up. My heart strings where stretched as though on a highly tuned harp and I could hear, in the back of my mind a long and melodious arpeggio. It was as if the world was holding its breath, and waiting in expectation.

As we walked along the lakeside path Eugene, looking directly ahead, said that the reason he was here was not merely to stroll alongside the lake but that his father had convinced him that he should take a wife and had approved of his choice. I asked him, with some trepidation who his choice was – fearing both the possible answers he may give – either me or someone else.

"That's the reason I am here," he replied, "tomorrow I will go to the American consulate in Geneva to start the necessary paperwork to finalise our union! The procedure is very simple in the United States, I just need to confirm and advertise my decision and the rest becomes a formality that you can attend to in a matter of a few hours."

As Eugene talked, he failed to realise that I had stopped walking so astounded was I at what he was saying. I felt wounded by his cold peremptory decision, as if I was merely a trinket to be exchanged in a business deal. I felt so terribly wounded and it was with a trembling voice that I asked: "Do not you think, Eugene, that perhaps the decision you are imposing on me should in fact have been part of a discussion. Not a discussion between you and your father but more, perhaps, a discussion between your proposed bride, me, and yourself."

"Furthermore," I continued, "rather than treating me as a future mate, as one might with an animal in a zoo, would it not have been polite to also discuss this with your future mate's father. And perhaps ask for his permission?"

By now I could feel my temper rising, my sense of indignation was at its height and I am afraid I found I could not stop myself.

"I'm slowly realising that the customs of your country are obviously very advanced. However there are some things that, even in this advanced world we are living in, remain unacceptable to us."

"Customs," retorted Eugene, "do not decide our destinies. I know you love me and I take this as the foundation of my decision. I'll call you tomorrow from Geneva with the result of my visit to the consulate."

At that moment I felt the total collapse of my world. Any feelings of love or affection for Eugene evaporated; it was as if a fluid life force deep inside me ceased to exist. Eugene had, in a few brief moments, demolished my trust and our relationship, and had reinforced those fleeting moments when I had first seen him come off the train at Lausanne station. Was it really only a few hours ago? Was he now the stranger I sensed on the platform, had he changed so much over the years? Is this what America did to people?

Miss Constant had listened to this exchange and she stepped forward to me and gently took my hand in hers and turned me towards her. I had tears in my eyes as I realised how much his character had changed. I recalled how much I thought I had been in love with him and how, in his long absence, I had effectively been mesmerised by him, how magnetised. I had thought we shared the hardships we had suffered; we had both lost our mothers, we had both, for all our wealth, felt loneliness and fear and yet, today, I saw a different side of Eugene: selfish, arrogant and unfeeling.

In my mind I knew it was useless to continue the conversation and I politely took my leave from Eugene and allowed Miss Constant to take me back to the Institute, back to the company of people who I knew loved me, or at least appreciated me. I am not sure if in that moment Eugene realised that our relationship would go no further. I did, but I felt that perhaps he thought I was merely shocked and surprised by his proposal and that I would, in time, come to realise that he was right. Such was his arrogance.

Back in my room the light of the moon shone through the window, but it was cold and bare, and I lay on the bed in the gloom that matched my mood. I left the bedside lamp switched off and turned my face towards the ceiling. I ran through the preceding hours in my mind, from receiving the telegram and how my spirits soared when I found that Eugene was arriving, through the hours of anticipation and getting prepared. I remembered seeing him on the platform and how, at the back of my mind I felt he had changed, but had pushed the thought away. I now thought how strange was human nature. I had lived for so long with only the thought of my love of Eugene, his words, his writing, were enough to make me happy. I was ready to make any sacrifice, although with no offer of hope or request from him. I had been fascinated, he had seemed like a god on earth and I had held his picture next to me. Now I felt almost physically the changing of these feelings as my mind and heart fought the illogic of his thoughts. A welter of conflicting contrasts stirred in my mind, and I eventually fell asleep, exhausted.

In the morning I woke up with a sense of great emptiness in my heart. The sunshine gave light, but no gaiety, no warmth. I was sad and anxious, and felt I had to confide in Miss Constant, aware that she probably knew just about everything already, but needing, perhaps, to formalise the process and encourage her to provide me with reason and advice.

Over breakfast I poured out my heart to Miss Constant. I told her of my first meetings with Eugene and his family, of Ely and Sascha, of Christmas cards and letters and how maybe I had been expecting too much. When she asked me what he had written in the cards I realised that there was rarely, if ever, any declaration of love or romance. As I continued the story Miss Constant sat holding my hands in hers and I began to feel a little less fragile, a little less destroyed and a lot less unhappy. I retold the story of Sandro and his wooden leg and although we laughed I said I felt that love kept trying to escape from me. Miss Constant's response was short and immediate, 'sciocchezze', which in essence translates to 'baloney'.

"You are far too young," said Miss Constant, "for even considering such difficult reflections on issues that no one has yet managed to solve. Not the poets, not the romantic painters nor the authors of great love stories." She paused for a moment and then continued. "Man will always remain the great enigma in his feelings, his torments and his manner of behaviour. However, wisdom is able to adapt to every circumstance that life presents along its course and shows our ability to use our heart and our intelligence to solve these difficulties. Education and the flexibility of character often serve as universal remedies and help us reach compromises that are suited to resolving the problems".

I thought for a moment and realised what was really worrying me. "Do you not think that Eugene will go ahead with all his plans and marry me without my consent?"

"Do not worry Alessandra," Miss Constant replied, "Eugene may be American but he cannot take you away against your will. Both myself and your father will ensure that."

Reassured by her words and advice, I gave Miss Constant a long hug and returned to the Institute much happier and in a more peaceful frame of mind.

Of course, what I hadn't realised was that Eugene would not take such a simple response as 'no' as final. He had travelled that morning from Lausanne to Geneva in order to obtain the necessary paperwork and advice. He returned later that day nervous, grumbling, and complaining about the lack of consular authority. He had decided, instead, to travel to Berlin where he believed he would achieve more help and would get what he wanted, such was his arrogance. No-one protested but a few hours later the cousins, Eugene and I, went to the railway station and with no more than a handshake we parted. Just before the train pulled away from the station however I gave Eugene a letter. In it I explained the change in my feelings for him and clarified that this was a farewell.

Childhood Nightmares Revisited

One day Miss Constant invited the Kozlowski family to tea at her hotel. So it was that myself, Thais, Valentina, Vladimir and Valerian met with some of Miss Constant's lady friends, as well as a Doctor Rossi and his wife, who were about to leave for Cairo. Doctor Rossi had been treating Abbas Il Hilmi, the last Khedive of Egypt, and having taken a brief holiday in Switzerland, was now returning to Cairo to continue his work.

"We hope to see you soon in Egypt," said Mrs Rossi. "You Russians travel the world with such ease! Distances do not impress and therefore we leave you our address, hoping to see you among us in Cairo."

The doctor and his wife moved away, and the brothers made fun of me, knowing my aversion to the country of sands and recalling that long ago lesson with Professor Zaleski at the Institute Marinsk. They teased me incessantly over the course of the afternoon. They talked about snakes and scorpions, camels and Bedouins, but I simply closed my ears to them and assured them that Egypt was not exactly the top of my list for places to visit, stay or live.

How often though does destiny make fun of us at the most unexpected moments? A few days later, the housekeeper of our dormitory received a communication from my father marked urgent, which read: "Because of my health, the doctor recommends care in Egypt. I want to leave as soon as possible in the company of my daughter Alessandra. Deal with the necessary departures for the Caucasus. No reply."

I could not believe this turn of events and my emotion was great. My brothers and sisters tried to console me, and helped in making the preparations for the trip back home. I could not understand why I had to leave the Institute and accompany my father to Egypt: why couldn't he take a nurse, or even Miss Constant? But in the end I realised I was being selfish and that, if the doctor felt his health was such that he needed to be in a warmer climate, I should help him as much as possible.

A tearful farewell at the station in Lausanne was followed by two days and two nights spent in a sleeping carriage. After at least three customs controls, the train finally reached Volochysk, where the Zbruch River formed the Russian frontier. It was here that I left the comfort of the European sleeping car and embarked upon the less comfortable Russian passenger train, although still travelling first class. With three loud strokes of the bell the train moved away and began the long and monotonous journey across the huge expanse of Russian countryside, passing quickly through a myriad of small stations that at night were dimly lit by streetlights fuelled by turbid oil.

I awoke late the following morning, and had plenty of time to check the route before we arrived at the next station, where we were due to stop for a little while before continuing the journey. I disembarked here to find something for breakfast. Thus far the only fare on the train had been mediocre at best and invariably consisted of cold salads and sandwiches. It would seem that many had the same idea and I marvelled at the number of passengers who, like me, wandered around the station in search of better fare. The station restaurant, also, must have been aware of the paucity of good food, as its menu was diverse in terms of ingredients and ethnic origin. Hot dishes were served in a variety of ways and presented on anything from silver chafing dishes to plain white china plates.

Cold dishes were also presented with refinement and good taste and over them all towered an enormous silver urn of caviar on ice.

Although severely tempted by such delicacies, I am afraid I was dictated to by my nostalgia for a more common Russian recipe, and certainly a much more peasant cuisine. My father had always told me not to get too close to people on long journeys, and I therefore sat down and, eschewing all the other delicacies, settled for a steaming bowl of Russian borscht, a dish that I had missed for so long. At the end of breakfast I bought books and newspapers for reading on the train, as I knew well that I would still be held prisoner for another twenty-four hours before arriving home.

When the train finally drew into Ekaterinodar railway station, I was tired and a little dishevelled, but grateful at last to be back in familiar surroundings. As I alighted from my carriage I saw our old faithful, Timote, standing on the platform, and he immediately ran toward me. I knew that my father would not be there for he hated railways, railway stations and all the scenes of farewell that accompanied them. Timote arranged for a porter to collect my various cases and escorted me to the exit. Imagine my surprise when, instead of our old carriage and horses I found instead a shiny Adler limousine and a driver named Jose holding open the rear door. Even more of a surprise was the fact that my father was there, sitting relaxed in the leather of the rear seats, his arms outstretched to welcome me home. The journey home was swift in comparison to the carriage and horses, but noisy as well. "It's the latest model," confessed my father.

Back home I spent the first few moments standing in the

hallway reacquainting myself with the house, listening to its sounds, taking in its sights and appreciating the scent which, as always, was of flowers, and scented candles and perfume. The smell of polished wood in the hallway and the dining room, the smell and feel of leather and cigars in the drawing room. After a few moments my father took me by the elbow and led me upstairs to my bedroom. He went before me into the main room and then through the door that connected to a small boudoir. He held the door open and beckoned me through. As I passed through the door I saw that there, in the middle of the room, stood a Bechstein Mignon. The black ebonized wood gleamed and I lifted the lid to expose the keyboard beneath. The white keys stood against the black sharps and flats; it was magnificent. I turned to my father who merely shrugged his shoulders and said. "A present for you. I thought that in the large living room it will be too cold, and it will be far more pleasant for you to practise in your rooms.

The fire in my room had been lit and spread a warm and pleasant heat. I stood by the bedroom window, facing south toward the garden, and realised how really fortunate I was. My father quietly closed the door behind him as he left and, alone, I began to observe with affectionate curiosity all the objects inside my room. I examined them closely and each kindled memories that were dear to my heart. The two old armchairs, close to the fireplace, once served my mother who would sit there and recount fairy tales to the children. I held the pillows of my bed to my face, feeling the softness of the fabric and my fingers stroked the lace and ruffles of the bedspread. In the bathroom was a small box encased in red silk. I opened it and found, nestled within the bottle of perfume, left by my father, my favourite 'L'amour' by Houbigant.

How was I going to repay all this loving care of my father? At breakfast I presented him with a collection of photographs that I had taken in Switzerland. I introduced him to my friends and to the staff to the facilities and, of course, to Lausanne. My father was gripped by curiosity and asked a never-ending series of questions about everyone and everything. The housekeeper, Mrs Smirnov, intrigued him and having judged her by her severe looks realised his mistake when I told him how kind she had been to me during my time at the Institute.

My father then took me for a walk around the house and I saw that he had made a few changes now that the children were no longer at home continually, but I noticed that the changes had been made with much sympathy to the house and in harmony with all the other rooms which remained the same. When I entered the large living room, which had been furnished to the taste of our mother, I found that everything was the same as before: French tapestries hung on the walls, heavy silk curtains with a blue fleur-de-lys motif, beautiful crystal lamps, antique mirrors and paintings, including some by Aivazowski, who had been a favourite of mine. 'The Storm' and 'Sea Mist' caught my eye.

Soft carpets muffled our footsteps, and an atmosphere of warmth spread from the large tiled stoves. Happy to be back in that house where peace reigned with such serenity, I felt overcome by a feeling of reverence for the principles that had been inculcated, right there, by my parents during childhood. I believed that the house was my castle, a safe refuge from every disappointment and all the adversities of fate, a help to overcome daily difficulties, a guide to some higher ideal.

Driven by these thoughts, I turned to the holy icons that hung on one of the walls and quietly made a vow in front of them. I vowed that I would ensure that my family, my children, my husband, would absorb all of those feelings and intentions that had formed such an environment.

Not long after my arrival in Ekaterinodar I awoke one morning and was greeted by the first fall of snow. Soon the whole city and its surrounds were cloaked in a white blanket. The temperature fell rapidly and the cold grew far more intense; and my father began to feel the effects of the chill air and his health declined significantly. As a result he decided, with the advice of his doctor, to hasten the preparations for his departure to Egypt.

It was 30th December 1909 and we were on a late night train that passed through the recently opened Brenner pass, the 'Egyptian Express' Berlin – Brenner – Naples, which connected with a steamer to Alexandria and then yet another train to Cairo.

After what seemed an endlessly long journey we arrived at Naples Central Station. It was raining outside and our passage to the hotel for the night was through poorly lit damp streets. It was this atmosphere, coupled with the perceived heaviness in the air that influenced our first impression of the city – which was rather dismal. Tired from the trip we went immediately to bed, foregoing dinner and only sparing time to bathe before retiring.

The following morning I was rejuvenated. I awoke to find the sun shining into my room, the clouds and rain having been dispelled. I jumped out of bed and rushed to the window, and felt the caressing warmth of the sun. I opened the window and was intoxicated by the view. Our trunks and suitcases having already been dispatched to the port to be placed on board the ship for the next part of our journey, my father and I took advantage of a small carriage to get around the city. We passed through narrow streets and were amazed by the character and originality that manifested itself in this beautiful place. It was a city whose population was amiable, smiling and with a soul that warmed you. We came across the melodic singing of dreams of love, fabulous villas with hidden gardens, picturesque stairways, fountains and palaces all overlooking the blue Tyrrhenian Sea. I think it was at that moment that I fell in love with first Naples and then Italy.

Arriving at the port of Naples my father and I embarked upon the *Prinz Eitel Friedrich*. She was a German passenger liner which would later see service in the First World War as an auxiliary cruiser of the Imperial German Navy. In 1917, on the US entry into the war, she would be seized by the US Navy and put in hand for conversion as a troopship. For now though she was charged with the responsibility of ensuring my father and I reached our destination safely. With the final formalities over, the mooring ropes were cast and with a loud blast of the whistle she broke away from the dock. Behind us the once placid waters erupted as the propellers turned and strained against the bulk of the ship and began the slow and arduous task of pushing us out to sea. On board we watched in the company of an old friend of my father's, Mr Teraszkievicz, a travel enthusiast, whose adventure stories always amused father.

The next morning the ship passed through the narrow

Strait of Messina. From a distance you could see the city of the same name, which only two years before had been destroyed by an earthquake. Tens of thousands of lives were lost from both the earthquake and from the tsunami that followed shortly afterwards. Many of the passengers had gathered on deck and introduced themselves to each other as they used their binoculars to peer at the ruins of Messina and the cliffs of the strait as we passed. A variety of nationalities were represented on the steamer, Dutch, German, Italian, and a number of the travellers were elephant hunters, fans of big game, people who got bored during a peaceful journey and yearned for some excitement in order to raise their emotions. One of the most voluble, but nonetheless amiable, was Baron Otto Pollak of Trieste. The Baron was traveling with twenty hounds and, to distract traveling companions, took great delight in showing his photographic albums where there were collected many, many photographs of his four-legged companions; he added a comment that the collection of photographs of his dogs was significantly more extensive than that he had of humans! Suddenly he turned to me and asked if I would favour him with a pose that he could photograph. The joke went all in good spirits throughout the journey as to which album would preserve my image.

On the last evening, while my father played cards, I relaxed amongst the friends we had made in the luxurious lounge. I had dressed for the evening in a pearl grey chiffon dress with a corsage of roses. The calm sea and the setting sun throwing an amber glow over the water gave everything a fairy-tale atmosphere. Music played softly and I was surrounded by admirers and travel companions in the lounge which had been decorated with flowers and bunting. This poetic atmosphere, coupled with rounds of waltz, made me quite dizzy.

The following day the steamer dropped anchor at Port Said. My father and I left our friends and admirers and went down onto terra ferma once more. The train accomplished the last leg of our journey. It was as if I was back in that classroom with Professor Zaleski, with drawn curtains and the light from the lantern. As we travelled my window reflected all those pictures he had shown, the immense golden desert, the oppressive monotony without a trace of life, and finally the canals of Suez. When we arrived in Cairo I thought we had been dropped into a fair, with the noise of the merchants, the deafening shouts of the hawkers, the huge variety of languages, some guttural and harsh, others smooth and romantic. Small traders who offered their wares besieged the foreigners. We struggled through the crowds and could hardly ascend to our carriage. We were persecuted endlessly, even when we were seated and moving through the crowded bazaar. Hands grasping silks and satins, baubles and beads would push their way towards you, thrust through the carriage windows and disembodied voices would call out, moving from language to language as they tried to find the common ground. We eventually reached the city centre and our destination. Rooms had been reserved for us at the Shepheard Hotel and upon arrival we where taken immediately to our suites, which overlooked the Ezbekieh Gardens.

Our first night in this exotic, chaotic country was memorable. The mosquito net was bothering my father who would continually get caught in the flimsy material. To distract him, I spoke to him of the friends he had in Cairo and suggested that perhaps we should arrange to meet them, in particular Dr

Rossi and his wife Lua. It was all I could do to stop my father from calling them immediately and we came to a compromise that he would call first thing in the morning. He began to anticipate the surprise he would hear in his voice, but also he wanted to ask his advice on his convalescence and treatment of his illness. We all met for lunch the following afternoon and while my father discussed his treatment and condition with the doctor, Mrs Rossi offered to take me on a guided tour of Cairo.

The weeks passed and my father's health did not appear to improve and Dr Rossi suggested a move to a clinic based in Helwan. When Khedive Abbas, who was being treated by Dr Rossi, learned about the sulphur springs at Helwan he ordered the School of Medicine to study them and, when they were discovered to have healing powers, he ordered the establishment of Helwan's Sulphur Baths. It was here where my father would take further treatment for his condition. Perhaps he could also take advantage of the recently built observatory there and catch a glimpse of Halley's comet as it passed.

My father's friend, Mr Teraszkievicz, promised his assistance during the course of his care at the new clinic but a new problem now arose. Moving from a hotel in Cairo to a clinic in Helwan, what would they do about me? My father's opinion was that the atmosphere at the clinic would not be conducive to his young daughter and that he now had two options. The first was to leave me in Cairo, which was only 30 kilometres away, under the patronage of Doctor Rossi and his wife, and the second was to return home to Ekaterinodar. Not surprisingly I chose the latter option, thus resolving the dilemma and initiating new headaches related to our departures. Mr Teraszkievicz very kindly organised everything and arranged for my passage to be booked on a Russian liner that would travel to Novorossiysk. Although it would not perhaps have the comparable luxury of the German liner and was well below in terms of tonnage and comfort, it would certainly offer the protection of his countrymen and a greater sense of safety.

The return to the Caucasus was worth, to me, all the sacrifices of the trip. I set about preparing our luggage which now had to be separated into that which my father would require and that which I would need to take home, and what would be required on the voyage. As I was entering the hotel and about to go upstairs to my room I noticed, on the floor of the hotel withdrawing room, some musical scores and the lip of an open piano. I looked around and, seeing no one, I picked up a sheet of music and sat down at the keyboard to play. I started tentatively with a piece by Debussy and then, feeling braver and having taken a few more sheets from the floor moved on to play the études of Scriabin, and finished with the Prelude in G flat major of Rachmaninoff. I was so absorbed in the music that I did not hear the soft footsteps approach behind me and it was only when I stopped that I heard a whispered compliment from the doorway of the withdrawing room. I turned, slightly embarrassed that I should have been heard playing, and an elegant lady of middle age bowed before apologizing for her intrusion and confessed her extreme astonishment at hearing, in Cairo, those melodies. The curiosity to know the player of these studies had overcome her and she now entered the room and introduced herself.

"Allessandra Falz-Fein. Are you Russian?" she asked.

I nodded, still a little embarrassed

"Then please pardon your compatriot," she said.

Three things happened in a very short space of time. First, her husband joined us; second, the gong sounded for breakfast; and third, I saw my father coming down the main staircase. They all made their presentations and my father invited everyone to his table for breakfast. The conversation not unnaturally centred around not just our business in Cairo but equally on various aspects of life in Russia. My father recalled that the name Falz-Fein was well-known in the Caucasus, and in particular for an estate in Askania which was famous for its magnificent zoological garden adorned with artificial lakes and exotic flora and fauna. He mentioned the last visit of the Tsar and his court to this wonderful park and asked if he, Falz-Fein, was its proprietor. Falz-Fein admitted he was and the lively conversation continued for the duration of the meal. When breakfast came to end, a cordial friendship had been established. Falz-Fein and his wife had only recently arrived in Cairo on their honeymoon, and they had planned a trip to the pyramids for the next day.

As an Egyptologist Falz-Fein, was interested in the ancient Egyptian monuments, whilst his new wife, on the contrary, was bored with his scientific expeditions. To take advantage the friendship that had now been created, Mrs Falz-Fein asked my father's permission to take me with them to Gizah. I would accompany Mrs Falz-Fein, and we would await her husband's return, who would now have more time to explore the pyramids. My father cast a quick glance at me and could see the excitement of such an adventure in my eyes. Permission was granted. Shortly after, we left in a carriage pulled by a horse that seemed already exhausted by fatigue, even before he began to travel the long road leading from Cairo to the pyramids. After an endless series of bumps and jerks due to the uneven cobblestones, the carriage stopped in front of the shelter at Gizah. Mrs Falz-Fein and I were perfectly happy chatting in the carriage so Mr Falz-Fein left us and, in the company of an escort of Bedouins and camels, departed to explore the pyramids.

Hours passed and as night began to fall we became concerned about the prolonged absence of our esteemed scholar. As the sun went down the contours of the majestic constructions of the pyramids became blurred and indistinct, and they slowly began to melt into the surrounding desert. Mrs Falz-Fein and I decided to take our courage into our hands and, leaving the safety of the carriage, took a few steps into that sea of sand, scanning the vast expanse ahead of us and each wondering what we should do. In the distance I saw a figure, similar in shape to that of the Bedouins with their hooded robes. The figure headed toward us with a slow and heavy tread, it gestured with its arm and we heard a feeble and barely recognisable voice. Mrs Falz-Fein cried out: "It's my husband," and we ran forward to catch him before he fell.

The amateur Egyptologist collapsed exhausted into the arms of Mrs Falz-Fein and between us we managed to drag him into the rear of the carriage. Mr Falz-Fein took more than just a few minutes to catch his breath and then explained to his agitated companions, Mrs Falz-Fein and I, what had happened.

"After a difficult climb, but with the help of guides, I reached the summit of the pyramid. We were completely alone and the Bedouins immediately seized me by force, stripped me and left me almost naked. Then they abandoned me with the gift of this Bedouin robe. The climb downhill from the top of the pyramid was hellish, the blocks of stone are some two metres high, and without knowing the direction, I was almost despairing of ever finding my way back. Only the instinct of self-preservation has given me enough strength to drag myself up to you."

"You were wise," he added turning to his wife and caressing her hand, "that you did not want to follow me. I think I am being punished for my snobbery, for wanting to give preference to travel à la fashion, instead of going to our villa at Cap Martin, by the sea!"

Mr Falz-Fein laughed as he confessed that he thought of the yellow sand of the desert just a mangy piece of memorabilia and that the smile of the Sphinx merely mocked his vanity.

"Well then, we shall all do Cap Martin" I said. "In the meantime let us go back to our hotel – I wish to play a little more Rachmaninoff."

The next day the couple left Egypt – I assumed on their way to their villa in Cap Martin. I was also getting ready to leave, and my father accompanied me to Alexandria from where the ship would sail and take me home. That day a tumultuous storm raged, and the violence of the wind howling across the quay made it difficult, if not near impossible, to keep upright as we headed towards the ship. The shaky footbridge that led up to the covered deck also put at risk the lives of passengers who ventured on it, threatening to drop them in the water as it shook with every new gust of wind. With the help of the sailors, however, we scrambled on board. My father asked to speak to the captain and explained that he was entrusting him with the safety of his daughter and would hold him personally responsible if anything happened – such was my father! The captain was a man of good looks, and equally good manners, and he hastily and energetically assured my father that he would delegate his wife to assist me.

I was impressed by the violence of the storm, and asked the captain if the time of departure was as scheduled or if we would be delayed. The captain declared that as long as the weather did not deteriorate any further we would leave the port on time. Thus reassured I suggested to my father that given the bad weather it might be prudent for him to return immediately to Cairo, particularly if it should take a turn for the worse. We said our farewells with more than just a few tears of emotion, and as my father went down the gangplank to the quay I watched him from the deck. At the corner of the dock he turned and with a final wave he disappeared from view, and I retreated to my cabin to prepare for the long journey ahead.

I had not yet had time to get comfortable when there was a knock on my cabin door. I opened it to find a ship's officer standing there, his cap tucked under his arm, with an invitation to join the captain up on the bridge of the liner. On the enormous bridge the captain offered me a pair of binoculars inviting me to observe a small white ship, flying the Romanian flag, which was trying to break away from the quay.

"That poor man," said the Captain, "is under the illusion of being able to go out in this hurricane with a ship that small."

I watched with interest and mounting fear as the small Romanian ship was tossed by the waves like a cork toy. Now sinking by the bow, and then moments later the bow reared up and the stern was awash, then the bow was again plunged under the water.

"He will turn in a moment with his tail between his legs like a beaten pup," predicted the captain.

But the small ship fought fiercely against the waves, being swung from one side to another and then she was sailing between a huge moustache of foam.

"Pitiful," said the captain as his derisory gaze swept over the unfolding scene in front of us. "You cannot imagine what will happen when she gets out to sea – she will sink," he declared dispassionately.

But the Romanian ship broke free of the cover of the port and continued her journey. She was already at sea and had now moved away enough to disappear over the horizon. The captain, ever emotional, beat his fist against the railing at his failed prophecy, and declared that a Romanian will never teach a Russian the meaning of courage. He gave the order to sail and I hastened down to my cabin to start this hellish voyage, and to commend my soul to God in the event of a disaster!

Not long after the ship had sailed the gong sounded announcing the arrival of lunch in the dining room. Not wishing to be seen as anything other than brave in front of my Russian captain, I left my cabin and ventured out to make my way to the living room. At this precise moment what can only have been a huge wave rocked the boat sideways and threw me to the floor of the corridor. I was rescued by a passing nurse who gently and compassionately accompanied me back to my cabin. She wisely suggested that, until the worst of the storm had passed, I might be better served by lying on my bed. She even offered to fetch me some straps that could tether me if I so wished. I, of course, declined!

The journey from Alexandria to Piraeus was extraordinary.

The storm continued unabated and progress was painfully slow. The ship pitched and dipped, sometimes the bow under the water and the propellers above the sea, whining as they had no purchase and the vibration through the hull was quite unnerving. Then moments later the inclination was reversed and it was the bow that leapt out of the water. Coupled with the sideways rolling of the liner the storm managed to force most passengers to remain in their closed cabins and it was in this condition that we arrived, five days later, in Athens. The arrival of the ship in the port of Piraeus was comparable to the landing of Noah's Ark after the flood, with the difference that the Ark had at least sent on ahead a dove, and the Russian steamer was landing a man.

Within moments of being anchored offshore the liner was surrounded by a multitude of fishing boats that competed with each other to disembark any passengers who may have been scheduled to leave. The ship's crew began to lower a covered companionway that sat from halfway up the hull down to almost the level of the sea, and the fishermen in their boats watched with interest, all ready to pounce on an unsuspecting source of potential income. At the top of the gangway appeared the first, and only, passenger who was to disembark. It was a priest, of medium height, thin, pale, with long hair and a sparse beard. He held up the hem of his cassock with one hand and in the other held a small cloth carpetbag. For a moment he paused at the top of the companionway and looked up at the sky, then painfully slowly he began to make his way down the still rocking companionway to where the boats awaited. He had only two steps to negotiate when suddenly the frenzy began, fishermen's arms reach out trying to grasp his hand, or cassock or better still his carpetbag, which meant he must follow. The priest struck out and caught one of the fishermen on the neck, but they were all now trying to haul the only fish of the day into their boat. One particularly aggressive sailor grabbed the priest's robes but his gritty opponents were made of sterner stuff. Seeing his prey about to escape, a large sailor with swarthy arms harpooned the priest with his strong fingers and literally hauled his catch into the boat. The priest, exhausted by the fight, lay in the bottom of the small boat; carpetbag clutched to his chest and merely thanked the lord for some degree of safe delivery. He lay there stretched out on the bench, exhausted, with his head hanging down – looking for all the world like a model for the Pietà of Michelangelo!

An hour later our ship resumed its course for Constantinople, and here we were greeted with relative calm by both the sea and by the Turks. The Bosphorus appeared to passengers as coloured by the most various shades of pink, under the fire of the setting sun. The warm air now intoxicated passengers on deck, who were resting with eyes closed in deck chairs. I learned from the confidences of the doctor and nurse, that some of those travellers, pale, bright-eyed with fever, were in a worrying condition. Many of them had gone to Egypt, as had my father, for convalescence, but were now weaker from the cure and the hot sand of Egypt. The final blow had been the terrible storm that had unleashed itself upon the ship.

We passed through the Dardanelles, that linked the Aegean Sea with the Sea of Marmara, and then to Constantinople. From there the route would take us into the Black Sea and on to our destination, Odessa. As we ventured further north the temperature fell significantly and once again the weather began to flex its muscles. With every mile there returned the anxiety of the past days. A storm grew and was soon at its height, the icy wind diminished visibility and at times all one could see was a grey mist in which echoed the klaxon calls let loose from the ship by the captain on the bridge. The long whistles of sirens served only to give the passengers the feeling of impending danger. Those days and nights passed with infernal sluggishness, painfully slowly. And, at the time when despair was reaching its greatest height, the captain gave the news that the arrival in Odessa was imminent.

Finally the ship docked, but disembarkation offered a miserable show, for no one could really hold on to his or her legs. I was exhausted and was waiting in the dining room on board to see the captain, to greet him, and thank him for his courtesy. He appeared exhausted by fatigue, taking leave affectionately he said: "I did the best to bring you to safety through the storms, but I assure you, never in all my travels, have I seen anything like this storm."

I came down with the last of the passengers. My father had had the foresight to book me into the London Hotel. My large cabin trunks had already been removed from the ship and were on their way there. Meanwhile a carriage waited to take me to join them.

On my arrival eight athletic porters in white aprons and shirts met me. They were lined up four on each side of the large entrance door and, greeted me respectfully, which meant a significant amount of bowing. They had already unloaded the baggage from the first carriage, and my first duty was to find the concierge and ask him to send a telegram to my father to let him know of my safe arrival in Odessa. Then I checked my onward reservation on the train from Odessa to Ekaterinodar the following day. Then with duties all completed I was able to retire to my room. It was large, well-heated and overlooked the park, but most importantly for me at this moment of time, was the attached bathroom. This convenience, rare at that time, allowed me to stretch out, to soothe my nerves, battered by so many vicissitudes, and soak my body in a tub full of hot water with the fragrant aroma of Lily of the Valley bath salts. A white bed was waiting, its cotton sheets and deep pillows inviting me to collapse into the warm and fluffy feather quilts. I fell into a deep sleep.

Meanwhile outside a strong wind was beating against the windows overlooking the sea, which was made invisible by the fog of darkness that also served to mask the heavy snow that was falling. The city, abundantly powdered, changed quickly. It no longer looked grey and sad but now had the white covering of a beautiful wedding dress. Odessa was completely whitewashed, the quiet streets were covered with a soft carpet and this seemed to accentuate the sound of the church bells that sounded bright and crisp and delicate in the cold air. After the storms, the town deserved respite and the port was now quite calm. At the front desk the captain had left a floral tribute with best wishes for the continuation of my journey by train, and as I passed through the streets to the station the newsboys were announcing that the port of Odessa was frozen and that a sled race would take place the following day on its frozen waters.

Sadness and a Whirlwind Romance

Once again back safely at home in Ekaterinodar I could relax. I had not realised how worried I had been about my father's health and how it had affected me emotionally, coupled with the most awful of journeys to Odessa and the storms. I was now in a place over which I had control. At peace and in the company of friends, I spent several evenings retelling my escapades and the discomfort of the journey. Then, to help to forget, I immersed myself in all manner of social activities, and in the company of Mrs Smirnov and other friends we attended the theatre, the opera and numerous concerts that Mrs Smirnov suggested.

The list of artists was like a compendium of excellence. There was a series of concerts which opened with the pianist Alexander Brailowsky, followed by the young Josef Hoffmann, whose interpretation of Chopin was greatly appreciated. The audience were further spoiled by Leonid Sobinov, young, beautiful and thin, whose voice penetrated the arcane nuances of the souls of the listeners and elevated them to sublime heights and allowed them, momentarily, to forget the worries and realities of everyday life.

During the interval the lights dispelled the gloom of the theatre and I was able to look around the auditorium. It was as if I had been transported into a magazine. Beautiful women in large dresses adorned by even larger jewellery occupied the boxes. Their hair was perfectly coiffed into curls of brown and black and gold. The fineness of the lines of their faces, the transparency of their complexion, gave prominence to their eyes, which appeared shadowed by a certain melancholy that perhaps betrayed their deeper secrets. It was a magnificent sight, these fabulous creatures accompanied by their husbands or friends, many of them officers of the most brilliant regiments, in full uniform, resplendent in colour.

Among them I noticed Ivan Savicky, a giant almost two metres tall, wearing the Cossack uniform of the Imperial Guard. He was wearing a *cherkeska*, pink laced with the gold insignia of the adjutant of Tsar Nicholas II. He was the most prominent in a group that included his girlfriend Marussia Lozinskaya. She was wrapped in a cloud of white chiffon, her diamond earrings sparkled, and she had the eyes of a gazelle as she addressed herself towards the attractive boyfriend in a display of her happiness.

Near them Sergey Bursak, a Knight of the Imperial Guard, a beautiful man, an Apollo, bowing to kiss the hand of the wife of a colleague, Lidoczka Borsyk, who looked up. Sweet, dressed in burgundy velvet, her hair a mass of black curls entwined with jewellery of diamonds and rubies, her profile like a cameo. Lidoczka's eyes followed the widow of General Domanovicz, rightly proud of the company of her three sons, who were on holiday with her, the cadets George and his twin brothers Sergey and Boris, all wearing the dark navy blue of the Uhlans, the Polish Light Cavalry, based in Warsaw. Next to them were the Baroness Annemarie Stengel and her son Boris, and his inseparable friend Efim Vidny, who vied with each other to get my attention. That rare assembly of company gathered in the concert hall impressed me, the attractiveness of such beautiful women, the luxury and colour of the uniforms. At that moment it was a colourful garland that crowned the audience in such a picturesque setting; it was, in my imagination, a picture that would remain in my memory. The title of this tableau: Concert of the year 1910.

The latest news from my father revealed the gloomy outcome of the care in Egypt. With no improvement being seen he was, as a result, being transferred to Menton on the French Riviera, that was one of his favourite places to spend holidays. He had, for some years, the use of a villa there and was hoping that he would recover enough to make a trip to the Caucasus and to visit his children who were still in Switzerland. My father had promised them he would be home by Easter.

Lent was fast approaching and it was wonderful to wake up to the sound of church bells that wafted their chimes in the clear, crisp morning air. Some sounded so close and yet others were rendered faint by distance. But all had the same message; it announced to the faithful the start of morning mass, and I was preparing to leave for the private church at the Institute Marinsk where we had the privilege of a reserved seat. I entered the church and was overwhelmed by memories of my childhood, recalling as a child when I had sat at my mother's feet, when I had knelt and copied the others in an attitude of prayer. It was at this moment that I realised how much I missed my mother. I sat and listened to the service, the hymns performed so admirably by the students of the Institute, their faces raised to the symbolic icons that hung around the walls of the church, the candles twinkling in their candelabra and the blue clouds of smoke that arose from the incense burners swung by the altar boys.

In the last few days before Easter, the family was finally reunited. Thais, Valentina, Vladimir and Valerian awaited with excitement the celebratory party. My father had returned from Menton, although to my eyes he still looked extremely pale and weak. However he insisted he was much improved. From the house there emanated a variety of different aromas: the scent of stuffed roast veal breast twisted and mixed with cooked ham, roast lamb, turkey, guinea fowl, all prepared according to traditional recipes. There was paté and game, pierogi and sweetbreads, sauerkraut and borscht. While Timote filled the lamps hanging in front of the icons with oil, the other servants brought from the kitchens a large extra table which was placed down one side of the dining room with its back to the wall and then covered in a fine damask tablecloth, that fell to the ground forming a fresh white skirt all around. They then began to prepare for the Easter buffet, exercising all their imagination and skills. The final laden table was a vision in colour and preparation.

All manner of panettone, some of which were half a metre tall, sat next to platters of lamb gingerbreads trimmed with colourful sprinkles. Further along the table were crystal bowls containing asparagus, and a variety of cold dishes. Then there were silver cups lined with fresh moss in which crowded eggs coloured in every hue of the rainbow. Finally there were cakes and sweets of every kind and colour, wines and spirits and liquors, and so many other good things that brightened up the festive table.

On the day of Easter Eve the whole family went to celebrate midnight mass in Ekaterinodar. Father, though, remained at home. We congregated in the unlit church in total darkness to symbolise the despair of a world without faith. Just before mid-night, and with the church still in darkness, the Archbishop gave a sermon. When he had finished the brilliantly robed clergy and the entire congregation went outside to walk around the church, holding candles, singing and shouting that Christ is risen, and all the while the church bells pealed out the glad tidings. This symbolised two things: the search for Christ by his divine mother, and the disciples running to tell others that Christ had risen. The Archbishop led the procession, followed by the authorities in full uniform. Having circled the church the Archbishop hammered on the church door with his stave. In the silence it was like three rifle shots. The doors opened to reveal the splendour of the church, now fully lit by candles. The Archbishop announced to the faithful: "Christ is Risen", and the crowd responded: "In truth and risen."

The Archbishop celebrated the mass and we stood in the nave of the church, for there are no seats. The choir was formed by a group of Cossacks and under the huge arched dome of the nave their voices were like a religious chant. It was a mystical atmosphere; thousands of candles in gigantic candlesticks of gold and silver had been placed in front of the icons, the reflected light shimmered and glowed and lit the temple. The mass ended with another Russian tradition. Everyone looks to their right and extends their best wishes to their neighbour for the feast of the resurrection. They embrace their friends three times and every person, friend, neighbour, relative or stranger exchanges the greeting "Christ is risen".

It is also on this occasion that lovers take the opportunity to steal a kiss, a theft that cannot be refused. At last, we all returned home, excited from the sacred tradition, intoxicated by the night and by the approach of spring, soaked in the fragrance of lilies and violets that were sold in the streets. My father was there at the door, waiting for his children. For each of them there was an egg, inside of which was always something precious. The occasion was doubly solemn as we remembered Sania, our mother, and my father perhaps because of the sadness that weighed upon them, spoiled the children.

On the third day of the Easter festival, Thais and myself, accompanied by Mrs Smirnov, went to watch the horse show, and it appeared that our western elegance attracted the attention of the public. During a break, while the knights were arguing about the horses that had to play the next game, a group of friends went into the stands to greet us. One of these, Monsieur Michael Arnout, asked permission to present a foreign friend: Monsieur Perutz. Mrs Smirnov explained the protocol surrounding such events and that without further knowledge with regard to the stranger, and reflecting on the strict rules imposed by my father, the request was politely refused.

Monsieur Arnout, who already well knew the principles of my father, and also knew that very few suitors had managed to cross the threshold of his house, had warned Monsieur Perutz in advance that his request would be rejected. Nevertheless, Monsieur Perutz was made of stern stuff and had obviously taken this as a metaphorical gauntlet thrown to the floor. He was going to take up the challenge.

When the show finished we began to return to our carriages and prepare for the journey home. A long queue had formed outside of the venue as the spectators waited for their carriages to arrive and my father's car, in order not to frighten the horses harnessed to the carriages, was moving extremely slowly behind the column of transport.

We were waiting with Monsieur Arnout when our car arrived, and as Mrs Smirnov opened the door an envelope fell at her feet, which she picked up. Surprised, we entered the car before opening the envelope and were already driving through the crowds when we saw what was inside. Mrs Smirnov took out from the envelope the passport of Monsieur Perutz to which was attached a short note. The passport registered Monsieur Perutz as having been born in Lviv, Galicia and his occupation as 'Mining Engineer'. The note simply said: "May I introduce other cards if necessary?"

In the meantime, although we were driving slowly, a quick glance around showed that Monsieur Arnout's car had moved away and was not to be caught! The question now was what was to be done with these documents?

We all arrived home in a state of high excitement, and whilst Timote served tea on the terrace our discussions were centred, not around the horse show, but around the various happenstances with Monsieur Perutz. In the middle of these animated discussions we were surprised by the sound of the bell at the front gate. Timote went to attend and returned a short while later to announce the visit of the Engineer Monsieur Perutz!

My brothers, Vladimir and Valerian, knew my father would disapprove greatly of this behaviour but he was upstairs resting, and thus emboldened by his absence they instructed Timote to bring Monsieur Perutz into the living room. They then requested the housekeeper to fetch the passport, and set out to greet our caller.

Mrs Smirnov addressed the unexpected guest and reproached him on the manner of his behaviour. However, she had not even finished the sentence when the living room door opened and there appeared my father. I have to confess great admiration for Mrs Smirnov at that moment. With hardly a pause in her sentence she presented the engineer as an acquaintance of hers passing through Ekaterinodar, thus saving the situation for the time being. My father turned to the young man and offered a few words of welcome and courtesy, and invited him to take tea with us!

Thankfully, Engineer Perutz, as he was continually referred to, revealed himself to be a fine conversationalist, extremely affable and of extremely good humour. He revealed that he had a professional interest in the Maikop fields and it was this that had prompted him to make the trip initially. He expressed his views about the land from the point of view of an engineer. It was unfortunate that his opinions and views on Maikop differed from those of my father and, furthermore, these views were given at some great length that served only to fuel my father's annoyance. He rose from his chair, gave a peremptory goodbye, and went out of the living room. Engineer Perutz left very shortly after and in our minds it could be said that the episode with Monsieur Perutz was now closed.

Warm days and birdsong announced the arrival of summer and Mrs Smirnov proposed that I accompany her on a trip to her house, which sat on a low hill on the outskirts of Ekaterinodar. A small coach was harnessed to the horse and we proceeded at a fairly sedate pace, exchanging views and conversation on a variety of topics. Mrs Smirnov raised the subject of Engineer Perutz and it was obvious from her comments that she had only admiration for the young man and his behaviour. In Mrs Smirnov's opinion it was merely the fact that he found me to be so beautiful that prompted his rather unique approach in order to gain my acquaintance. I could now understand her actions on his visit when she had told my father that Engineer Perutz was an acquaintance of hers rather than a potential suitor!

"So here we are," I exclaimed, "is it possible that every young person who comes close to me will be in love with me?" I was about to list my suitors on my fingers but realised rapidly that only one hand would be needed! "And beside, his behaviour was more than a little rude."

The small carriage arrived at the top of a slope that led down to the small house, and whilst Mrs Smirnov went about her business there I was left alone to enjoy the serenity and peace of the country, taking in the scent of the linden trees, which were in bloom, and the views across the vast green fields that were dotted by spring flowers.

I stretched out on a hammock slung between the terrace and a large old tree and began to observe the industriousness of the bees, in continuous flight collecting the nectar and then returning to their hidden hives in the shadows of the forest. Intoxicated by the aroma of nature in bloom, in this haven of peace, my imagination took flight. I daydreamed of a handsome prince who would declare his undying love for me. It was a romantic dream that was prompted by a memory from my grandmother who, as a girl, lived on a beautiful estate of her parents', near Kiel. One day my grandmother, then young and beautiful, had the opportunity to meet and get to know a young officer who was handsome and a fine connoisseur of music and poetry. Those worldly attributes allowed him to open the heart of my grandmother, and there was born between them a shared aspiration. Her father gave permission for marriage and life for the two was a the cherished dream: playing the piano, composing, and writing poems. The years went by in a whirlwind that seemed almost unreal.

It was shortly after the outbreak of the Russian-Turkish war that the young officer was called to serve at the front. He returned as a hero, but also badly injured. His bravery at the defence of the fortress of Sevastopol was recognised by his regiment, they remembered it by holding every year a parade of his regiment in the park as he and his comrades who had also been injured, watched from folding chairs. Regardless of this appreciation he gradually turned inwards and he slowly died, on the inside first and finally on the outside; and his young life was extinguished. My grandmother was broken-hearted.

Mrs Smirnov interrupted my memories as she finished her chores and informed me it was time to leave. I had not realised that almost the whole day had gone in either amiable companionship or through romantic daydreaming.

That evening, as I arrived back in Ekaterinodar, Thais rushed to greet me to deliver both a wedding invitation, and a note from Engineer Perutz. The note merely said: "TP takes leave and begs you to accept his gifts." My first question to my sister Thais was to inquire whether my father was aware. She assured me that he was not, and that Timote had exercised his usual discretion in handling the letter.

During May, Mrs Smirnov and I had to leave for Rostov, a city some twelve hours away by train. For Russians used to the large distances of their country, the journey did not represent any inconvenience. Where possible we would ensure that it took place at night, and we would soon fall asleep and then arrive at Rostov the next morning. On this occasion Rostov station was unusually animated following the apparent collision of two trains that had unfortunately been travelling in opposite directions, but on the same piece of track. However we had soon managed to load our various baggages onto a carriage and set off for our hotel.

Our arrival gave us a rather unpleasant surprise. The hotel was closed as the result of a massive conflagration the previous night. The unfortunate effect of this, combined with the train collision, was to ensure that every other hotel in the vicinity was now overcrowded. Mrs Smirnov spoke to the concierge who, although there was now no hotel, still took his role particularly seriously. With a few judiciously directed enquiries he was able to find a suitable hotel which had rooms available, and we therefore got back into our carriage and wound our way through the narrow, twisting streets which defied any logic of direction. I was aware of a carriage following us, but paid it scant attention at the time. However, when eventually we arrived outside a small private guesthouse in Sadovaya Street, and whilst Mrs Smirnov watched carefully the transport of suitcases from the carriage, I realised, with astonishment, that the carriage that had followed us not only stopped behind us, but also proceeded to disgorge none other than Engineer Perutz!

After the usual, rather surprised, greetings it appears that Engineer Perutz had also reserved rooms at our earlier hotel and was therefore in the same predicament. He had relied upon his coachman to locate alternative lodgings and it was he who suggested that we should follow his colleague, our coachman, as this would provide the best solution to the crisis of accommodation.

It appeared that Engineer Perutz had a series of business meetings scheduled that, by happenstance, coincided with my visit. We said au revoir and the manager of the guesthouse welcomed Mrs Smirnov and I and took us upstairs to our rooms. They were modestly furnished, but had the benefit of large windows that opened onto a balcony, through which the morning sun streamed.

We ordered breakfast in the room and a robust waiter soon brought a selection of fragrant sandwiches, butter, cheese and ham whilst his aide came armed with a fresh, large, white tablecloth and a shining samovar. The cloth was laid, the table set, and Mrs Smirnov and I sat to partake of a small meal. As we ate the food and sipped tea Mrs Smirnov was in high spirits. She teased me constantly about Engineer Perutz and his fortuitous arrival in Rostov and at our hotel.

I was rather obliged to commend prudence to Mrs Smirnov regarding this event, especially in view of our scheduled meeting with an uncle and aunt with whom we had an appointment for lunch. "Remember," I explained, "that if father came to hear of the name Engineer Perutz we would be engulfed in unnecessary complications given first, his last meeting with the engineer, and second, the explanation we would have to give regarding our meeting in Rostov."

Around noon Mrs Smirnov and I decided we should not waste an opportunity to go shopping in the beautiful shops of Rostov and in front of the window of a milliner we stopped to admire a wonderful chapeau created from Parisian Georgette. With the consent of Mrs Smirnov we entered the shop and the proprietor, obviously an experienced saleswoman, took the opportunity to show us her complete collection of millinery. One after another the entire collection of original designs passed across to me and, in front of the mirror, were placed on my head. Mrs Smirnov and I spent much of the time pouting and posing in a coquettish manner. Our lunchtime appointment was approaching, and Mrs Smirnov urged me to make a decision and counselled that the model in the window, which had first attracted me to the milliner's shop, would be perfect. The proprietor lifted the creation from the window model, and placed it on my head. Blue Parisian Georgette, garnished with spring flowers, it complimented my dress, which was a shade darker blue in colour, perfectly.

We left the shop, and after a short walk we reached the restaurant of the hotel for our lunch appointment. As we entered the large room, luxuriously furnished in baroque style, we saw my uncle, waiting, staring at the entrance with his eyes half-closed, my aunt beside him. He was so badly affected by strong myopia that he was unable to recognise us and inform the *maitre'd* to direct us to his table. Nevertheless the meeting was very cordial and the conversation covered the events of recent years. The description of my trip to Egypt greatly amused my uncle, such that he was wiping tears of mirth from his eyes. We were so engrossed in our stories and reminiscences that neither myself nor Mrs Smirnov noticed that at another table, across the restaurant, sat Engineer Perutz, throwing long, meaningful glances to us, and me in particular.

Eventually, however, his attitude was noticed, more by the waiters and *maitre'd* than ourselves, and both my aunt and uncle rose indignantly and changed places with myself and

Mrs Smirnov round the table. As we circled I took the opportunity to throw Engineer Perutz a withering look that, in most instances, would have electrocuted the recipient.

After our lunch my uncle and aunt accompanied Mrs Smirnov and myself back to our hotel. My uncle made it clear that he was more than a little concerned at the clear interest that the 'foreigner' had shown at the hotel. He recommended to Mrs Smirnov that, as he would be unable to take time off in Rostov to ensure our safety, she should be extraordinarily careful for the duration of our stay.

Back in our rooms Mrs Smirnov wondered if, perhaps, she should have informed my uncle as to the identity of the 'stranger', but decided that maybe it was not the best course of action. Mrs Smirnov allowed herself a little rest, and I went out on the balcony and, plunged in deep thought, casually followed the passage of the clouds and watched their ever-changing forms. Sunset began to approach and, slowly, the sky faded to pink as the sun slipped down behind the horizon.

As I stood and watched the final rays of the sun, petals began to fall onto the balcony. Soon a profusion of colours lay across the floor of the balcony as they rained from the sky, and finally a small nosegay fell to my feet accompanied by a card. Bending down I collected both the posy and the card that read: "Please excuse this new and uncivilized practice, but the desire to see you again surpasses my education. I beg you to allow me to take you to dinner tonight. T.P."

Embarrassed, I went quickly inside and woke Mrs Smirnov in order to ask her advice. I should have realised, of course, what her answer would be knowing full well how she sympathised with the young man. From the moment of our first meeting Mrs Smirnov had been more than a little partisan for Engineer Perutz, and suggested that perhaps the meeting should take place, chaperoned of course.

We had dinner that evening and there was certainly a feeling of friendliness that hovered over our table. There were several large windows in the restaurant that opened onto sweeping gardens where an orchestra performed Tchaikovsky's first symphony. The comfortable environment, combined with the uncertainty that such a chance would happen again, pushed the young Engineer Perutz to give his 'curriculum vitae'. It transpired that although Polish-born, he held an Austrian passport. He had studied engineering at the University of Freiberg, where he obtained his laureate, specialising in mining. He had gone to Grozny to practice, but primitive life in the middle of nowhere amongst the mountains of the Caucasus did not correspond to his cheerful and light demeanour. Seeking to enliven his existence, and in particular to satisfy his craving for art, he had sought distraction but had found none, and was 'bored to death'. To avoid falling into a state of acute melancholy, and opting to explore the country, he'd spent Easter in Ekaterinodar and Pentecost in Rostov, "Where our meeting makes me think of a preordained destiny," he finished.

At that point, Mrs Smirnov, with a discreet nod, warned me that it was time to return to the hotel. A dark blue sky strewn with twinkling stars, a soft breeze saturated with the sweet smell of rose and lavender emanating from the garden and from the boulevards, accompanied the young couple and their chaperone along the narrow streets that were almost deserted at that hour.

Few shops were open at that time of night but those that were sold a bewitching variety of newspapers, magazines and delicacies that attracted the attention of the chaperone, who frequently fell behind to buy her favourite delicacies. Absorbed in the task of choice, Mrs Smirnov had let the two 'children', engaged in animated conversation, move ahead of her. Engineer Perutz, realizing her momentary absence, interrupted the conversation and, with the natural kindness and the impulsiveness of his character, asked me: "Do you want to accept me for your husband?"

Embarrassed, I smiled and, believing that the question was a joke, evaded the answer.

We were now nearing our hotel and Mrs Smirnov, having fully satisfied her appetite for delicacies, did not afford Engineer Perutz any further opportunity to return to the subject of marriage. The following day was dedicated to a final opportunity to go shopping, and to attend to our departure. I have to confess I did rather regret that we would not have time for any further meetings with the likeable Engineer Perutz, also now known as Thomas. Thomas was equally sad that the time of our departure was fast approaching, and had considered a multitude of options that could perhaps prolong the moments he could spend in my company. He learned that our trains, although going in differing directions, were both leaving at approximately the same time from Rostov station and Engineer Perutz proposed that we meet at the station, Yaroslavsky.

Happy to have found a solution to his desire to delay further the time of parting, we met the following evening in the gathering dusk at the railway station and, once again Engineer Perutz asked me if I would consent to be his wife, and pleaded with me to agree. I explained that I could not give any consent because, regardless of any decision I would wish to make, it would have to be discussed with my father first, and therefore I was unable to give approval. Mrs Smirnov then added that, given the late hour and that the couchette had been prepared, we needed to board our train, especially given the habit I had of going to bed as soon as the train moved. Disappointed and sad, Engineer Perutz left the platform and set off to catch his train. I watched him disappear into the growing gloom of the evening, and after a short interval Mrs Smirnov and I set off for our own train.

We boarded and arrived at our carriage. The sleeping car was comfortable and well prepared; both bunks had been made and were now ready with crisp white sheets and soft blankets. Once we had deposited our overnight valises we decamped to the restaurant car, where Mrs Smirnov and I exchanged views and impressions of our visit to Rostov, our lunch with relations and, perhaps more importantly, our fortuitous meeting with Thomas Perutz. After a few minutes though, we were overcome by tiredness, and arriving back in our carriage we were very quickly asleep. The train, like a ghost, ran quickly through the dark. The window whistled softly and the wood that covered the walls of the car creaked gently, but nothing disturbed the passengers; the closed compartments in the carriage gave no signs of life.

Suddenly, the silence was broken. Initially I thought I was dreaming, but where a moment previously there had been a respectful silence now a strong voice resonated down the corridor outside. I struggled to wake and realised that the voice was calling my name: "Alessandra Kozlowska". Bewildered and trembling I hurried to open the door of my compartment and found myself confronted by the carriage superintendent who, after confirming my identity, delivered to me a letter.

I looked nervously at the writing on the envelope but saw no clue as to who had sent the letter. Nervously I opened the envelope and read the contents, which were a moving and passionate declaration of love from Thomas. In the letter he repeated his earlier request and asked for my permission to contact my father in order to ask for my hand in marriage. I was unable to sleep any further that night. The figure of Engineer Perutz occupied my mind. With closed eyes I meditated on the distinctive traits of his character: lovable, sincere, cheerful, elegant. There was a lightness about him, a wonderful naturalness allied to his serious love of all forms of art, be it music, painting or theatre. He was good caricaturist, and a singer of quite some class. Admittedly he was small in stature, shorter than I, but nevertheless very interesting. The train was running in the dark, and the rhythmic sound of the wheels on the track and the beat of the engine reverberating through the carriages, muffled the pulsations of my heart. I was experiencing a new sensation, and it was not an unpleasant one. From what I had perceived to originally be a frivolous statement, we had moved to a more serious intent, and I was not unhappy with the state of affairs. And I suddenly found myself thinking of 'Thomas', rather than 'Engineer Perutz'.

The letter on the train was a nice prelude to a match between two lovers, but once we reached home in Ekaterinodar life continued its normal pattern. We took a short holiday with the whole family to the beach, and then began once again to prcparc for a trip to Switzerland where my father was to receive further treatment. Thomas, meanwhile, wrote to propose his next idea. This was to exploit our trip to Switzerland, in order to arrange a meeting with his parents at their house in Lviv. Thomas argued that our journey to Switzerland would be arduous at best and that a brief sojourn in Lviv could be recommended. Our itinerary did indeed pass through Lviv, and this somewhat forced my hand in finally confessing my feelings and situation with my father.

My father was by now suffering with what were suspected to be severe heart problems. It had already been recommended by his physician that he be kept away from all emotion, and this had discouraged me from raising the subject immediately upon my return. It was therefore with great concern that I went to see my father who was waiting in the study, sitting behind his desk.

I opened the study door and approached him timidly. I took the chair opposite him and, noticing his hand on the desk, covered it with mine. I looked down and noticed how thin his hand now was, how the strength that I had assumed would always be there had dissipated. I looked up into his eyes and began to talk to him about Thomas. I started from our first meeting at the horse show, through our coincidental meetings in Rostov and my feelings for him. I talked about his love of art, his character and his personality. My father listened without interrupting and when I had finished he was quiet for a while. His eyes closed as he thought through what I had said and what it meant to the family.

After a moment he opened them and said: "At eighteen you are still young Alessandra, and you have had the strength to accept many disappointments in life already. Before I can make any decision I first need to know a little more about Engineer Perutz and his family. I am not sure where to start looking but please be patient for I promise I will soon give you my decision." My father rose from behind his desk and took me in his arms and held me close. "You are the personification of the soul of your mother. I was hoping that you would stay at home, that I could have you always close. I had purchased the villa opposite ours with this secret intention, and hoped that each morning I could say hello from the window. But now I know that this is a dream. I am unwell and it would be unfair to cage my beautiful little bird who so badly wants to be set free to fly."

I left the room quickly with my eyes full of tears, deeply moved, and went to see Mrs Smirnov to tell her the outcome of my confession.

"... And the planned trip to Lviv?" she asked.

I confessed that I had not had the courage to broach the subject with my father. I decided that discretion was perhaps the best route for the moment and I would wait for my father to obtain more detailed information on Engineer Perutz and his family.

The following morning Timote announced that breakfast was served and the family gathered around the table to discuss the arrangement for their trip to Switzerland. Father wanted to go directly to Menton in southern France, and to limit the strains which would be experienced from the various train journeys that would be required he had decided to travel there by ship. Although the journey would take several days my father would at least be comfortable in a cabin, and would be able to rest. With the promise that he would invite everyone to

Menton whenever a birthday occurred, my father departed a few days later.

My journey to join the rest of the family in Switzerland was not significantly shorter, and it was on the third day that the train passed across the Russian/Austrian border at Volochysk, and within only a few hours I had arrived in Lviv. The last few miles were completed with ever-growing levels of excitement. The train began to slow and the carriages glided slowly along the tracks, and I watched from the window as we passed several groups of people on the platform. I strained my eyes to try to see Thomas but there were too many people crowded on the platform. We stopped and as I descended Thomas saw me and ran to catch up with my carriage. He caught me as I took the final step of the train, held me in his arms and lowered me to the platform. My cases were taken from the train and disappeared whilst Thomas introduced me to his father and his sister, both of whom had come with him to meet me.

Outside the station there was an elegant Austrian carriage awaiting us, which was harnessed to a pair of beautiful white horses. It is thus that we arrived in style at the Perutz villa, close to the magnificent Stryisky Park in the centre of Lviv.

As we arrived at the villa the housekeeper, Roman, was waiting for us, the doors of the house wide open and inviting. Thomas's mother, Misy, hearing our voices in the hall, hastened to meet us, and gave me a warm welcome. Misy and Roman, with my luggage now retrieved, showed me to my room, which was adorned with beautiful flowers.

They left me for a while to allow me to rest and refresh. I had been impressed by Thomas's father and his mother, and looked forward with quite some excitement to the conversations that were waiting. I changed from my travelling clothes into a dark blue dress with a large shawl collar in white crepe Georgette. I was preparing my purse and putting into it a small handkerchief scented with 'Quelques Fleurs' by Houbigant when there was a knock at the door. It was Thomas, who had come to accompany me to the living room where he would present me to the other members of the family who had been invited to lunch.

Encouraged by compliments and supported by the optimism always present in Thomas, I conversed at the lunch table with his parents and their guests who were curious to understand and examine the character of the self-possessed girl who came to visit from the Caucasus, in order to learn about the people and the environment in which Thomas grew up.

It was a difficult task made easy as I drew courage from the tender looks that Thomas gave during the course of the lunch. Once finished, the group moved to the lounge on the second floor of the villa, and I was entreated by Thomas to accompany him at the piano whilst he sang *lieder* composed by Schumann. His magnificent baritone voice and perfect diction was outstanding, especially in the last song, a performance of '*Im Wunderschönen Monat Mai*'. Thomas appeared deeply touched by the poetry of Heine, and in the rendition of Schumann I felt he was singing of his sensitivity and love for me, and I responded to his feelings. Our audience were also impressed and congratulated us with the assurance that we could, if we so wished, give concerts such was our standard.

The guests took their leave and we moved away from the

formality of large rooms with imposing chandeliers to a smaller family room in which there was a large fireplace with a bright coal fire burning. The atmosphere was convivial and once the servants had left the room Thomas told me he wanted to discuss with his parents a number of options regarding our relationship, and had a request should all proceed as he planned. This was the possibility of a transfer from Grozny, in Russia, where he had become extremely bored, to Campina in Romania, where his father held the post of Director General in the oil company Steaua-Romana.

Thomas had already shown me photographs of Campina and Bucharest and we were both excited by the beautiful nature of the country, its culture and its civilisations. Thomas's father promised to see what he could do to help. Thomas, sensing victory said "Any place on earth, after Grozny, to me would seem to be paradise."

So far the introductions had been smooth, but this had increased the pace of our relationship and I felt that the time had now arrived when I should gently disclose the point of view of Mr Kozlowski on the marriage to Thomas and his family. I have to confess to feeling more than a trifle embarrassed, but regardless felt I owed Thomas's parents the whole truth about the situation. I concluded by explaining that my father would need a short period of time to become accustomed to the idea not only of marriage but also of my leaving home to be with my husband. His separation from me would be a fundamental change in his life and I, also, had to take a lot of care not to cause too much emotional distress, due to his health. I asked them to please allow me time, and for them to have patience.

It was now very late and I was tired from everything that had happened that day. Thomas escorted me upstairs to my room and before I switched off the light, I cast my eyes over the magnificent bouquet of roses given by Thomas and the engagement present: a ring with emeralds and cabochon diamonds, accompanied by a matching bracelet which had been given by his parents.

It took a while for me to get to sleep that night. My mind was a whirl of emotions having met Thomas's mother and father. They had been warm in welcoming me into the house and into their son's life. They had been sympathetic to the problems with my father and their affection as well as their acceptance of all of this made me deeply happy. Thomas had not exaggerated the characteristics of the members of his family, presenting his father as a great philosopher, musician, patron of art, and a real encyclopaedia within the family. His mother, married at sixteen, seemed almost to be an older sister to Thomas. She was similar to Thomas in character, exchanged jokes *sotto voce*, but was careful not to undermine the confidence of her husband. I finally fell asleep meditating on the details of the various *dramatis personae* of this play in which I seemed to be appearing, their beautiful house adorned with art and culture, rich in traditions and filled with life and exuberance.

The three days with Thomas and his parents in Lviv passed like a whirlwind; it was like living in a wonderful dream. Gathered on the railway platform, my departure was sad for both of us. My eyes glistening with tears, I said goodbye to Thomas and his family, and boarded the train. We touched hands through the glass of my carriage and then the engine whooped mournfully and began to slowly pull away from the platform, accelerating towards its destination, Harbour Road in Lausanne.

A few months after our meeting in Lviv, I was visiting my father in Menton and Thomas wrote to inform me that his father had indeed managed to orchestrate a move to Steaua-Romana in Campina. Thomas was ecstatic with this new appointment and he wrote that he now wanted us to be together. He described the wonderful plans he had for our life, the beauty of the surrounding countryside, the opportunities to explore the arts, and the convenience, which could not be overstated. The petroleum company owned a series of comfortable houses surrounded by extensive grounds.

"Moreover," wrote Thomas, "think of all advantages offered by this locality; we would be only fifty kilometres from Bucharest and close to Sinaia, the royal summer residence. Sinaia is majestic with its white palaces of the Byzantine style, deep in the green mountains, surrounded by great parks, with views that inspired the poetic imagination of the old Queen Carmen Sylva. Not long ago, I visited and admired them with my company director, his wife and three children. I was pleasantly surprised to learn that before coming to Romania, they had spent their youth in Russia, and, although they are German by birth, they remain nostalgic for your country and show a great sympathy for the Russians. They are greatly anticipating your arrival, and particularly the idea of conversing in Russian."

Thomas was sending news daily and within these missives he continually expressed his love and admiration for me and told me, constantly, how much he yearned for me to be beside him. I would read these letters over breakfast and then, saddened and equally missing Thomas, I would go for long solitary rides on the beach and in the shallows of the sea. My thoughts would wander as I gazed over the rippling blue waters, where I hoped that the waves that rode into the shore were bringing Thomas's love to me.

My father may have been unwell but his attentive gaze did not miss the significance of my melancholy. One day returning from Monte Carlo where, as usual, he had spent a few hours playing cards with his doctor, my father came to find me. I was on the terrace attending to correspondence and my father approached and placed on the table in front of me a small leather case.

"This is for your patience and understanding, and a small token of appreciation for all that you have done for me."

I thanked him warmly and he drew a chair close to the table and sat down beside me. My father continued: "I think that the real surprise will perhaps overshadow that of the jewel inside the box. I have decided that I need to make the acquaintance of the family Perutz. All of the information I have received upon them is excellent."

My heart leapt and I leant over and hugged my father and held him close. I remember the time when he extricated me from a potentially disastrous relationship with Sandro; I recalled the episode with Eugene, and each of these made me feel closer to my father and appreciate Thomas further. There now followed feverish preparations, exchanges of letters, telegrams and long conversations on the topic in the family Kozlowski. After some laborious correspondence, my father and I departed for Vienna where we would meet Thomas's parents. The first few days were spent collecting impressions of each other as my father, conservative by nature, did not immediately reveal his opinions. Our families conducted long, probing conversations, digging deeper than first impressions. Sometimes they enjoyed the humorous stories of Thomas's mother Misy, and the gay jokes and light-hearted stories soon dissipated the stiffness and formality of the first days. However the stress and the excitement of those days took a toll on my father's health forcing the Thomas's family to call for the attendance of a specialist who, after a thorough examination, informed Mr Perutz of the severity of my father's condition, and also the fact that my father was close to the end of his life.

I was thunderstruck but my father obviously knew very well his condition. I was now astonished to hear my father say that he wished to hasten the preparations for the wedding so that the marriage could be celebrated in Vienna, and not in Menton as had previously been discussed.

Given the constraints we now faced in organising the ceremony, Thomas's parents turned to Theodore Innizer, Archbishop of Vienna, whom they knew well, asking him to ease the bureaucratic requirements to obtain permission of the celebration of the marriage rite. It was with his intervention and blessing that the date for the ceremony was set for December 10th 1912. Due to the health of my father the wedding was to be an intimate ceremony with only a few guests.

On the eve of the wedding I returned to the hotel were my father and I were staying. I was exhausted from shopping for the wedding dress and all that accompanied it, as well as nervous for the following day when I would become Thomas's wife. Mr Perutz and Misy had kept my father company during

General Rogozin

Baron Kozlowski and Sania

Baron Kozlowski

Henry Kozlowski

Kuban Cossacks at Ekaterinador, 1890

Thomas Perutz, 1910

Top. Alessandra with Thomas Perutz, 1912, and their fathers, Karol Perutz and Henry Kozlowski

Bottom. Alessandra and Thomas, 1913

The Wedding Breakfast. From left to right: Adolf Perutz, unknown, Michelina Perutz, Thomas Perutz, Alessandra, Henry Koslowski, Jadwiga (Thomas' sister), unknown

Probably taken at the time of their wedding: Thomas and Alessandra are on the right. Henry Kozlowski stands on the left, with his cane.

Alessandra, Thais, Valerian and Thomas, in Russia

Alessandra's sister, Thais

Vladimir Kozlowski, on the right

Top. Alessandra and Thomas, in their Danzig home

Bottom. The family in Italy: Gabriella, Alessandra, Thomas, Krystyna

Opposite. In Rome, after the war

the course of the day and, on our return, my father asked Thomas to show him the wedding ring. Thomas stopped in his tracks and looked aghast. There was silence in the room and then, subdued, Thomas confessed that he had completely overlooked its purchase. His father looked stunned and said: "Thomas, you do realise that it is late and all the stores are now closed!"

Thomas rushed down to the hotel manager to ask for help, who in turn spoke to the concierge. By fortuitous coincidence a close friend of the concierge owned a jewellery shop and agreed to return immediately and ensure that the wedding would not be blighted by such a trivial obstacle.

The ceremony took place in the cathedral of St Stephen, and with no honeymoon planned Thomas and I were to spend some time with his sister who lived in Davos. Mr Perutz returned to Bucharest and Campina, and my father departed for Menton. Saying goodbye to my father was the most difficult farewell I had ever made. We held each other in our arms in silence on the train station. He felt frail under his coat and the lump in my throat prevented me from speaking. I breathed in the warm smell of his cologne, I felt the roughness of his cheek with my hands and I held him so tight. We separated in a silence full of anguish and I watched full of infinite melancholy as the train slowly eased out of the station and away to Menton.

The 'honeymoon' with Thomas's sister was over and it was a cold day in late December when we finally arrived at our new home in our new country. Thomas's father met us at the station in Campina and took us to the company house that had been allocated to Thomas. On entering the atrium I was pleasantly surprised to find on a small table in the hallway a platter with bread and salt. It is a typical Russian rite and one that was more than just a little appreciated. A written card bore best wishes to the new couple, Thomas and me.

The offering had apparently been left by a couple, Mr and Mrs Meinrad, old friends of Thomas's who lived close by, and where we went to offer our thanks for the thoughtful consideration that afternoon. Mrs Meinrad, small and of uncertain age, met us on the doorstep, and greeted us with a hoarse voice. Her cold eyes meet mine. I offered her my hand by way of a thank you for the gift and she invited us into the house. In the living room there was a palpable tension in the air and the talk was strained and difficult. I was unsure what to make of the relationship, and talk seemed tight and endless despite all efforts to enliven the discussion. We took our leave after only a short while, but not before repeated invitations for dinner that same evening which we accepted.

Our journey home was completed in a strange and unaccustomed silence. It seemed that everyone wanted to avoid expressing their impressions about the recent visit and quite surprisingly Thomas, cheerful by nature, had nothing to say and seemed lost in introspective meditation. Even his philosophical speculations were missing and there appeared no answer to the seriously unpleasant and complicated situation we found ourselves in. Returning home Thomas proposed a tour of inspection around the new villa in an attempt to lighten the dark mood that had, for some reason, overtaken us.

The villa had been constructed in Byzantine fashion with a columned entrance adorned with niches and a massive fireplace in the hall. Tall windows set below a vaulted ceiling gave an impression of space and airiness. A large terrace led out from the drawing room to the substantial grounds outside, and a large double staircase rose from the ground floor circling around to an upstairs gallery landing. This led to several bedrooms, the largest of which had obviously been earmarked for Thomas and me, as the servants were already unpacking trunks and placing clothes into closets and drawers. I spent some time arranging personal items around the room, photographs and memories and perfumes and creams which created an atmosphere of being a home rather than just a house and, not forgetting our commitment for the evening, I asked the servant to lay out a dress suitable for the dinner with Mr and Mrs Meinrad.

Once at the Meinrad's house Mrs Meinrad received Thomas almost as a child. He was definitely spoiled and obviously liked, and seemed to revel in the privilege and attention he received. I meanwhile maintained an animated conversation with Mr Meinrad about Russia, and he was a gallant and pleasant host. After dinner a game of billiards provided a diversion for men whilst at the same time the ladies entertained a conversation which was relatively monosyllabic and trivial, and where any real meaningful conversation was stilted and short. I had to confess I could not wait for the end of this programme of introductions. This meeting had tainted my first impressions of the country, the environment and Campina and it had tired me extremely. For whatever unfounded reason I found myself having developed a dislike for Mrs Meinrad, and for this I felt guilty. When we eventually arrived back home I tried to explain my feelings to Thomas and to find a rationale for my emotions and opinions that would appear to have been so much at odds with those of others. Thomas was dismissive and rebuked my strange intuition, and insisted that it would merely result in a disturbed harmony with his friends.

The following morning Thomas went to review his new company and to visit the oil fields and refinery. I decided to direct my energies to organising the house and its staff and assisting in the general care of the estate. This caused amusement and puzzlement in my mother-in-law, who frequently came from Bucharest to spend a weekend in the country. Almost every evening, returning from work, Thomas had just enough time to change before we would visit Mr and Mrs Meinrad in what had become a customary and frequent invitation. Indeed so frequent were the invitations that it deprived us of any chance to enjoy our own way of leisure. Obliged in this comedy by Thomas and with little new to add to any conversation I began to feel as an extra on stage, and my lines of discussion were recited almost automatically.

Our lives continued in this manner for some while and no project was accepted or implemented without the approval and guidance of Mrs Meinrad. It would seem her hand and influence was everywhere. I continued in my quest to organise the house but have to confess my mind was frequently elsewhere, generally in the Carpathian Mountains watching the silvery streams as they ran along in search of riverbeds to inhabit, and then coursed like serpents across the green fields of the valleys beneath. It was during one of these idylls that I decided to organise Thomas's study and clear through a myriad of papers and correspondence that had accumulated over the past few months. In doing so I came across one series of letters that I did not recognise and glanced to the bottom to see who the signatory had been. I was startled to see that they were signed by Sonia, the Christian name of Mrs Meinrad. My suspicions aroused, I began to read through the letters and found that my intuition had indeed not been misplaced. Each letter sent a deeper chill through my heart, each page was turned with a hand that became less firm, each word caused a tear to fall from my eye and I sat down heavily on the chair behind the desk. The sheets piled upon my knees and I tried to analyse and rationalise what I was reading, what it meant, and more importantly, whether I had merely misread their intent because of my dislike of Mrs Meinrad.

A thousand uncomfortable questions inexorably crept up on me. What to do? Leave and go back home, or stay and fight? Expose or keep quiet? Tell Thomas and resolve, or keep quiet and steer an unknown course? Marriage should perhaps be something that is studied by young people as with any school subject. Unfortunately, these are subjects that professors, who are able to teach science, are unable to educate us in the more important and more useful lessons for our existence. I did not want to admit to the destruction of our marriage after such a short time and I recalled how, in childhood, my brothers and sisters would bring me their broken toys to repair; was this another broken toy and could it be repaired? Those childhood memories brought to mind my father and, with closed eyes full of tears, I saw him again in Vienna on the day of his departure when he told me: "When I have grandchildren their future will be ensured."

Grandchildren! I thought. I realised then that my course of action was limited. How could I destroy my father's dreams? The play would have to continue, the potential parents would remain united and I would prove to my father the patience of which he had always been proud remains within me. I was forced to play two parts in this theatrical drama in Campina, one which had been imposed upon me, and the other that I had chosen for myself. The drama would continue. I would use all my skills to repair the toys of the children, the difference being that people in the flesh had now replaced inanimate objects. Emboldened by this decision I prepared myself for a long and painful journey.

History Comes to Haunt Me

My father died in August 1913 and was buried close to his beloved house in Ekaterinodar. After the funeral the executors read my father's will to his children. His Estate, which was not inconsiderable, was put into trust for the five of us, Valentina, Thais, Valerian, Vladimir and myself. The heirs would be unable to access or take advantage of the capital amount until the thirty-first year of their age. However four guardians in whom my father had the utmost confidence would administer an annuity. Should any of the children pass prior to their thirty-first birthday, and have no further family then the capital amount would be distributed amongst the remaining children. My father, true to his word, had ensured the comfort of any of his grandchildren.

After a short stay I had to return to Campina, and I left my family in mourning at Ekaterinodar. On my return to Thomas I realised that the loss of my father had only highlighted my previous sufferings. Music filled my solitude and I would spend many hours of the day in the drawing room playing our favourite pieces on the piano, études by Brahms or sonatas by Beethoven or Tchaikovsky. One evening Thomas returned from work and I asked him to accompany me with some pieces, Schubert, Schumann, Brahms, and for a moment we forgot our usual obligation to dine with the Meinrads. However Thomas was insistent we should attend the invitation, and we were forced to cease our duet. I realised then, for the first time in our marriage, that my plea for Thomas to join me on the piano was a clear expression of boredom with an inevitable commitment. We went out, and discussion around the dinner table that evening was the discovery of a new oil well on land owned by Mr Siemens. Not unnaturally he was delighted with the success and planned to leave Campina at the earliest opportunity and move to Berlin. Already he was actively seeking to sell his property.

I was aware of the house which was, to say the least, very comfortable with large generous gardens. I drew it to the attention of Thomas and suggested that perhaps we should move away from the company house and purchase the property. Surprisingly Thomas agreed and shortly after he got in touch with Mr Siemens and purchased the complete property. It consisted not only of the country house but also a farm, stables with a chicken coop and even a goat. In the summer, wisteria grew profusely across the walls of the villa and, from a distance, it looked like a huge bouquet of flowers. Over the next few months we organised the shipping of furniture from the villa in Ekaterinodar and very soon the house was filled with memories of home. Russian furniture, rugs, silverware, china all left a legacy that adorned every room. Cotton curtains from England framed the large windows, and a British colonial desk sat in the hallway and always evoked admiration from visitors.

Once we were satisfied with the furnishing the next step was to offer our first reception. Lunch was organised and Thomas's father suggested a guest list that included Mr Emil Georg von Stauss, the vice-president of Deutsche Bank, Dr Lehner and other friends. I chose the menu, as I wanted to have choices that included classic Russian dishes as well as European ones. In essence I wished this to be an eclectic mix of people and cuisine. The meal would finish with a special dish reflecting British tastes: strawberries and cream. The cream was prepared especially and arranged in crystal goblets, placed on ice in a tub that had been put in a cool place on the balcony of the kitchen and when it was time to serve the strawberries would be added to complete the desert. However at the appointed hour it was a very different dish that appeared before our guests. The waiter, John, presented himself with merely compote of strawberries with no sign or sight of the anticipated cream. There followed a silent exchange of questioning looks between John, Thomas and myself, and John, looking mortified, bent to whisper in Thomas's ear. The next moment Thomas burst into loud laughter and was hard pressed to prevent tears of mirth coursing down his cheeks. Finally managing to control himself Thomas confessed what had happened. Apparently the cream had been prepared as ordered and placed into the ice bowls on the balcony. However it would appear that the inherited goat was the first in the queue and had, by the time John came to fetch the goblets, managed to eat all of the cream! If nothing else everyone left in very good spirits.

Every morning I would wander through the gardens and make the discovery of new fruit trees, plants and flowers. I spent time cultivating strawberries in the greenhouses with the able assistance of the friends and colleagues of my husband, all young people, all full of life and all brimming with hope for the future, and this helped me to forget my predicament with Thomas, for a while.

The month of September moved gently into October. It was a beautiful day. In the afternoon the peaks of the mountains in the distance were shrouded in clouds, and beneath the shining river basin sparkled as the sun's filtered rays touched it with delicate fingers. Thomas and I were sitting on the terrace admiring nature as she moved through autumn and began to show her wintry coat. The sky was still blue but the air was now distinctly cooler, the colours of the sunset were now russet and gold. Together we were immensely happy and grateful for having made the move.

"You know," Thomas said, "it seems to me that we have arrived at the height of our happiness." I trembled, for I was not quite so convinced about what the future held. My intuition was still highly sensitive but I leaned and embraced Thomas warmly and smiled gently. At that moment John came onto the terrace and announced the visit of Mrs Meinrad who, without waiting to be invited, appeared behind John and ignoring me. Speaking directly to Thomas, she requested a private meeting.

Thomas looked thunderous. He rose from his seat and, without even a backward glance towards me escorted Mrs Meinrad by the elbow to his study. I remained rooted in my chair on the terrace. The blood in my veins turned cold and a chill ran through me. As I waited for the outcome of this astonishing situation my nerves jangled. Thomas, at this point in time, was oblivious of my suspicions and unaware that I had seen the letters that had been exchanged between them. A thousand thoughts ran through my mind as to what was being discussed and each and every thought and supposition merely ran the gamut from bad to worse. The bold, brazen behaviour of Mrs Meinrad astonished me. Her entry without greeting, her brusqueness in demanding a private meeting with Thomas, the authoritative voice she had used to gain her entrance and the time it was now taking for the discussions behind the closed door of Thomas's study to end amazed me.

The more these thoughts went through my head the bolder I became in my preparation to respond. Finally, when Mrs Meinrad returned to the terrace, we exchanged looks that were those of enemies engaged in mortal combat. Thomas did not have the courage to appear before me and explain. Instead he had left it to Mrs Meinrad to speak.

Without preamble, and I suspect knowing full well I was aware of some degree of the relationship between my husband and herself, she said, "Today my husband became aware of all that has happened between me and Thomas. You are young, and you are at the beginning of your married life, and as a result you have the opportunity to recover from this situation and if you should so wish even re-marry. It is because of this that I ask you to divorce your husband!"

I sat in stunned silence and it took me a while to digest exactly what Mrs Meinrad was proposing.

"Are you expecting a child?" I asked

"Absolutely not," she replied.

My mind was in turmoil. I was struggling to understand what had just happened and did not understand why my husband had not come to speak to me and explain. After listening to Mrs Meinrad's monstrous speech I went in search of Thomas for an explanation. He was not in his study so I returned to the terrace and it was there that a gloating Mrs Meinrad informed me that he had gone to visit her husband.

This was the worse possible news I could have heard. I could not begin to imagine the disastrous effect this could have at this moment with emotions and tensions running so high. I needed to stop this meeting at any cost and consequently I rushed out into the street calling out loudly for Thomas. I found him just a few metres from the house but this was neither the time not the place to talk on the subject even though it tore at my heart and hot tears were running down my cheeks. Instead I told him we had just received an urgent phone call from his father and that he was to go to Bucharest immediately. I am sure Thomas was completely aware of how false this statement was, but it nevertheless gave him the opportunity to return with me to the house, and a moment of grace and introspection before launching into an activity that we could all regret.

Arriving back home I find that Mrs Meinrad had thankfully already left. In such a state that I could neither cry or move, and in the throes of great agitation I sat behind Thomas's desk and reflected on how we would be ever able to manoeuvre our way from this tortuous and horrendous situation. With my head in my hands I made an effort to follow a logical train of thought as to the cause and effect upon our situation and indeed our relationship.

I needed to have solid reasoning to assist me in making a final decision with regard to a course of action. In an attempt at innate fairness I laid out the case for each of the protagonists before me.

On the one hand there was Mrs Meinrad. A woman of forty-eight years with all the consequences and insecurities that age can bring. Allied to this was an apparent history of depression having already, as she had previously told us, suffered from a nervous breakdown. She and Mr Meinrad had known Thomas for many years; indeed the relationship between the three of them stretched back as far as Thomas's days at the University of Freiberg. So when Thomas planned had returned to Campina to work with Steaua Romana, by virtue of his father's position, the relationship as friends had been renewed. It was also a fact that at that moment Mrs Meinrad had been feeling particularly fragile and that her relationship with her husband, because of her nervous disposition, had also been under severe strain. So Thomas arrived, young, humorous, an old acquaintance with witty conversation that dispelled the boredom that hung heavily in the house. He amused them with his lively stories and anecdotes. As an example, he regaled them with the time, as a student, when he and Mr Meinrad had, for a bet from colleagues, taken a walk through the city streets with live lobsters on leashes. The escapade took a turn to the expensive when the police commissioner accused them of cruelty to animals. However, for a considerable sum of money the error of his ways was overlooked. For Mr Meinrad these reminiscences awaked memories of time long past. He had been a famous duellist and spoke passionately of the challenges he had received, accepted and won.

On the other hand there was Thomas. As would be his manner he did not miss an opportunity to compliment either the host or the hostess; exaggerating their kindness had been inherent in his character. He would thank them for their hospitality and their company, and it would seem that by merely entering the Meinrad's house he would bring with him a breath of fresh air and life and, particularly, made Mrs Meinrad feel younger and helped her perhaps to forget the gap in ages between them. The atmosphere of boredom and melancholy that existed was dispelled and became instead an assembly of light-hearted entertainment. The fun he was offering was, in essence, a theatre, which the Meinrads embraced wholeheartedly, perhaps even over-zealously.

The 'audience' would thank Thomas for his stories, for taking them away, momentarily, from their provincial roots for a brief and exciting diversion. When, a little while later, Thomas became ill with a high fever that lingered and he was grudgingly confined to bed, Mrs Meinrad, to repay Thomas's kindnesses, and appreciating that he would be alone, offered to treat him during his malaise and subsequent convalescence, an offer which Thomas, perhaps unwisely in hindsight, accepted.

There are times in life when reason and logic and emotional feelings make uncomfortable bedfellows, and, in essence, this was what happened between Thomas and Mrs Meinrad.

All this happened prior to our engagement, and in reality was really a continuation of Thomas' bachelor conduct for the past twenty-eight years, although it remained no excuse. This, coupled with circumstance, exacerbated a situation that should and could have been avoided. The meeting with my father in Vienna, the unexpected seriousness of his illness, the hastily arranged wedding and our return to Campina sooner than might have been expected, left Thomas unable to resolve the situation with Mrs Meinrad.

Finally my thoughts turned to Mr Meinrad. I did not know much about his character but I could assume that his pride was severely wounded, and this in itself did not promise anything good. Coupled with Mr Meinrad's predilection for duelling my concerns were further raised: surely this was the pastime of someone who wished to settle scores with a degree of finality.

Having turned over all these elements in my mind I decided that the first course of action was to telephone Mr Meinrad, who had been made cuckold by my husband! I called and reached his housekeeper. I could hear her call Mr Meinrad and heard his retort as she told him it was Mrs Perutz calling. I patiently listened to his furious outburst against Thomas, the viper in the nest, and heard his death threats. The threats were made in a quiet voice; he demanded a duel to settle not only his honour but also that of Mrs Meinrad. He obviously believed that the entire escapade was the fault of Thomas and that Mrs Meinrad was merely an injured party and had no part in its entire instigation. I felt that the threats of a duel were not idle. I took the opportunity to tell him that I could not talk about my feelings and emotions over the telephone, and I was sure neither could he. I asked him to accept an invitation to meet in my house when we were both alone. In this manner we would be able to talk freely, as two wronged parties, without witness and without the possibility of revealing, to a larger audience, the scandal that was engulfing us. There followed a moment's silence. I knew he was still there, I could hear his breathing. Then without protest Mr Meinrad agreed. We would meet that evening, at my house, at eight o'clock.

Mr Meinrad arrived promptly; I met him at the door and we moved to the living room. I wanted to ensure we were well away from anything that may have brought him directly to Thomas, which is why we did not meet in the study, even though it would have been more private. His first words were that he required a duel with Thomas to satisfy his honour, that he believed had been besmirched. Having said his piece he sat upright in the chair, his hands folded in his lap, his knuckles white with the tension he felt. At his words my blood ran cold. His eyes were dark and his lips pursed into a tight thin scar on his face. We were both touched by the guilt of others and for a short while there was silence and a reticence to meet each other's eye. After a few moments I looked up and began to speak and ensured he was looking straight into my eyes. I wanted to see his pain, but I needed him to see mine as well.

"There is no one better than me, right now, who can understand the state of our emotions and what we are going through. The two of us, we are suffering the same pain, the same torment, and the same anguish. For you it is the pain of ruining your years of happiness that have suddenly come crashing down around you both. For me it is the collapse of a trust that I had in my husband whom I thought loved me and would be faithful to me. I fully understand your reaction to these events but also realise that, at this point in time, these reactions, these emotions, do not allow you to be rational in your analysis of your feelings. The difference in our ages prevents me from giving advice but does, perhaps, allow me to speak to you as a daughter."

At this point I paused to try to gather the words I needed to express my thoughts and bring this ugly, unedifying episode to a close without any further disasters. Then after a moment I continued.

"In my opinion, a vulgar, simple killing, although authorized by custom, in a word – a duel – is still a murder. I would not, could not, come to the man who could attempt such a course of action, whether he was the winner or the loser. The intent would accompany me through life, and I would not wish the perpetrator to accompany me also. I do not wish your children to have the burden of a father involved in a murder, or for them to have the drama that upsets your family, which could, in the worst outcome, leave them without a father to guide them through life, and to be tainted by the stigma that will accompany any outcome. The joy of revenge has a short existence, the pain of conscience lasts a lifetime. Do you not think that a duel, as satisfaction of honour, is in reality a theatrical farce?"

I paused for a moment to allow my words to register and to ensure that Mr Meinrad was still listening. I had not taken my eyes away from his for a second. I then continued, "I offer our departure from Campina, within twenty-four hours. In return, prove your generosity because within me there still remains a little confidence in the human race. Let time heal our wounds."

I looked into Mr Meinrad's sad blue eyes and, shaking with emotion, I touched his hands and begged him to accept this proposal.

Mr Meinrad stood, and I waited for the explosion or the acceptance. Would he turn and walk away or would he accept the proposal, however difficult and against his pride? He stared hard into my eyes for what seemed like an eternity. I could see him weighing up the result of the various actions and the impacts it would have on so many lives. Then he took my hand, kissed it and muttered: "I accept." He turned and left the house.

The next day we left Campina as promised. We went directly to Lviv, accompanied by Mr von Tappe, a good friend who would commission the necessary arrangements for the transport of our goods.

Assassinations and Declarations

After a two-month stay at the Hotel Imperial in Lviv, we moved into an apartment that had only recently been constructed. The outside was still surrounded by wooden scaffolding and, in order to attempt to dry the external plaster in the humidity, the constructors had placed large braziers on the scaffolding, particularly at the rear of the building. On the day of moving I remarked to Thomas that leaving the braziers unattended on the dry wooden beams of scaffolding could be a serious fire hazard. Thomas, jokingly, offered to write to the architect and construction engineers on my behalf and advise them of my concerns which, obviously, were based on my years of experience in the field. With that final comment he closed the windows, turned out the lights and we retired to bed.

We were rudely awoken at five in the morning by the incessant clamour of bells and shouts of "Fire! Fire!". The noise reverberated through the whole building and the loud knocks on our apartment door were unnecessary as we were already awake and clothed in dressing robes. The corridors outside were awash with people as the inhabitants of the building rushed either to the elevator or down the stairs in an attempt to escape from the flames as the house began to burn. Outside the temperature had fallen to twenty degrees below zero and it was snowing. The tenants stood around in small groups of confusion, dressed only in whatever they had managed to find in their haste to get out of the building.

Thomas wandered round bemused, looking for a means that could take us to his parent's house. His search for a cab was in vain, and shortly after the fire fighters were able to douse the flames and we were allowed to return to our apartments; the fire, it seemed, was not as bad as perhaps we had envisaged. It was later certified that the cause of the fire was indeed the result of burning coal falling onto the wooden scaffolding. The work to repair damage caused by that wayward burning ember commenced immediately, and after only a few months everything returned to normal, and we were able to once again see something other than scaffolding from our windows.

One day I received a call from a modern Polish composer Karol Szymanowski, asking permission to bring along a young pianist, Arthur Rubinstein, who had come to Lviv to give a series of concerts. I followed, with great interest, the discussions of those young artists on the subject of modern music that for me seemed incomprehensible. It was not for lack of trying, and each of these young musicians had patiently tried to explain the spirit of the new technique. The day following the call from Karol Szymanowski I went to Arthur Rubinstein's concert and was reminded of my convictions and enthusiasm as I listened to his execution of the works of Chopin.

Not long after the concert our first child was born, Gabriella Inestia Perutz, and with the approach of spring further changes were in the air. Thomas spoke to me of a number of new projects that he had been asked to manage on behalf of Galicia Oil that would require us to change location to be closer to the work sites to monitor progress. As a result we left Lviv and moved one hundred kilometres south to Truskawiec. Famous for its mineral springs, the town lies in an attractive little valley in the Carpathian foothills and was served by a railway station that made returning to Lviv to visit friends a simple task. Housed in a quiet hotel we thought we had found the most peaceful place in the world. The area offered fresh air and beautiful walks that I alternated with the thermal baths, to pass the long hours of enforced idleness. This state of bucolic serenity was rudely interrupted by the news of the assassination of Archduke Franz Ferdinand, heir to the Austrian throne, and his wife Sophie, during their visit to Sarajevo on the 28th June 1914. The assassin, Gavrilo Princip, was one of a group of six assassins (five Serbs and one Bosniak) coordinated by Danilo Ili , a Bosnian Serb and a member of the Black Hand secret society. The political objective of the assassination was to break off Austria-Hungary's South Slav provinces so they could be combined into a Yugoslavia.

With a distinct lack of newspapers the population of Truskawiec gave itself to gossip. Rumours spread like wildfire such that soon, in the eyes of the recipient, this hearsay became fact not fiction. The Austro-Hungarian government waited three weeks following the assassination of Archduke Franz Ferdinand, heir to the Austro-Hungarian throne currently held by Franz Josef, before issuing its formal response. This delay further fuelled speculation and fabrication. Seizing the opportunity presented by Ferdinand's assassination the Austro-Hungarian government decided to settle a long-standing score with near-neighbour Serbia. They made a long list of demands and presented an ultimatum on the 23rd July 1914. The Serbians conceded to virtually all the demands made but, regardless, war was declared on the 28th July 1914.

The news reached Truskawiec by way of large posters attached to the wall of the hotel. Groups of agitated people ran along the terrace as they realised the import of what they had just read. War had been declared.

In no time at all the life of the country was paralysed; the government requisitioned everything and the trains no longer stopped at the station in Truskawiec. By lucky chance Thomas's father had managed, under the pretext of needing to remove commercial machinery that would be needed by the government, to send heavy transport accompanied by a small car, ostensibly for security. The heavy transport was left behind in Lviv and Thomas and I began a journey which, although only one hundred kilometres north, filled us with fear and anguish. We were sure that our car would be requisitioned before we had got very far and indeed, as soon as we arrived in Lviv, we were stopped and the government forces commandeered the car. Our arrival in Lviv coincided with a huge influx of refugees from the border with Russia who were fleeing the Tsarist troops. It meant that, unknown to us, the Russians had entered the war on the side of Serbia. Not unnaturally it also meant that these fugitives from the Russian forces occupied all the hotels, though we were fortunate enough to find shelter in a guesthouse run by a Mrs Panazek.

Unexpectedly the agitation of Thomas's parents surpassed all limits and it wasn't until Thomas told me their history that I appreciated why they were so concerned. Thomas's maternal grandfather had been one of the leading Polish insurgents during the January uprising in 1864. The uprising of the Poles against conscription into the Russian Army was originally a spontaneous protest by young Poles. However it was soon joined by high-ranking officers and politicians and, severely outnumbered, they resorted to guerrilla activities. The uprising lasted eighteen months and the toll on the Poles was huge. It is estimated that four hundred people were executed and almost twenty thousand exiled to Siberia. Others were sent to the Caucasus and the Urals and altogether about seventy thousand people were imprisoned and taken out of Poland to be deposited in the more remote regions of Russia, and one thousand seven hundred estates were confiscated.

Thomas's mother, it seems, had every right to be fearful. Russian politics has an extraordinarily long memory. She burned all the documents and anything else that would indicate her father's involvement in the uprising. Her sister Edviga was equally distressed and, having lived through the 1905 Russian revolution, was well aware of the gruesome ferocity of the Russian Cossacks. It was only when they decided to leave for Vienna that both the women calmed down.

For me the political situation was an embarrassment and a nightmare. Although I tried to persuade all my new relatives and friends of the sincerity of my feelings they saw me only as 'the Russian'.

My feelings toward Thomas grew more intense in this cauldron of mistrust and he stood by me throughout all the recriminations that were directed at me. His sense of goodness and justice were plain to everyone and were an important support and balanced the hostility that I felt, not only from strangers but also some friends, even those who knew me only in passing. Without Thomas I don't know what I would have done.

The enemy guns could be heard day and night, and after the first few weeks came increasingly close. The whole town was on the brink of panic and Thomas's parents fled. After a long and arduous wait at the railway station they managed to board a train. It was stormed by thousands who wanted only to get away from the war. Some cried, some fainted, many hung onto any part of the train they could grasp: a part-opened window, the roof, the space between carriages. Many were hurt or died as the train pulled away and they lost their balance, or grip, and fell to the floor, often under the wheels or between the train and the platform. It was a scene of carnage and hysteria characteristic of such moments of crisis. Lviv was now half empty.

The streets were deserted; only a few isolated inhabitants could be seen hurrying their way home, keeping to the shadows anxious not to draw attention to themselves. People went out only from pure necessity: to go to work, to visit relatives who may have needed help, to visit or call a doctor. There was no need otherwise; the shops were closed, and doors were locked. In the silence all that could be heard was the echo of the bombing that became more and more intense as the days crept by. It seemed now that the battle could only be a few kilometres away, but perhaps that was just the effect of the eerie silence. Our boarding house became full again, this time with young Poles forced to leave their homeland and flee from the occupying Russians.

These poor boys suffered terribly and were unable to understand why Poland had been dragged into a war that was ostensibly between Austria and Russia. I tried to explain to them that since partition, while Poland did not exist as an independent state during World War I, its geographical position between the fighting powers meant that much fighting and terrific human and material losses occurred. The partition between Austria-Hungary, the German Empire and the Russian Empire, became the scene of much of the operations of the Eastern Front. It would not be until after the war that Poland would again become an independent republic. I spoke to these youths and denounced Russia and expressed my sorrow, but I was convinced that nobody would believe me. If only they knew how much I also hated war!

It was only two months after the declaration of war on the 3rd September 1914, when the maid at the boarding house, terrified, ran into the dining room at breakfast. Her voice had been made hoarse by fear and it was with quite some effort that she managed to tell us that the Cossacks had come. "They've come for our children with lances," she cried. I rushed to the window and saw the first of the Russian patrols which would now take possession of the city. The arrival of the Russian troops was initially peaceful but what followed quickly reminded me once again of the terror we had experienced in 1905 in Ekaterinodar, a feeling I had hoped I would never have to repeat. Arrests followed, espionage of neighbour upon neighbour was rife, and hateful denunciations, whether fact or fiction, were the order of the day. It was a time to settle scores and grudges, a time to curry favour and, if possible, an opportunity to feather one's own nest.

Thomas and I were determined to remain neutral. We both would appear to have been caught in the middle of this war, Thomas with his Polish background and myself with my Russian heritage. It was best, we agreed, to maintain a diplomatic silence. Despite this desire it was always difficult to remain neutral and one day a dear friend who asked us for help, or at the very least prayers, approached us. He told us of two brothers, journalists, who although completely innocent had been arrested on the basis of scurrilous hearsay and rumour. They were now incarcerated in Lviv prison but thankfully under the supervision of the political police rather than the Russian Army. They were also under the sentence of death.

Having heard the story we were, for once, minded to intervene and at the very least have the summary sentence of death rescinded. This is perhaps a time when being Russian would be a help rather than a hindrance. I agreed with Thomas that I would visit the head of the political police, General Skalon. On arrival I was introduced to him through an aide.

After a brief exchange of pleasantries the General requested how he could be of service. I drew breath to calm my nerves and said, "General, we are both Russian and we are both wanting to conduct this occupation in the most civilised manner. By the same token I would wish to convince people, at least my friends, that the Russians are not barbarians. Among those you have recently arrested are two brothers who, based upon false accusation, are considered to be spies and are under sentence of death." I paused for a moment to gather my thoughts and to see how my speech was being accepted. The general waited. "General, please accept that there is no truth in this accusation, and that no trustworthy information exists to either justify or bolster the charges. It is because I know there is no proof and because I know that their character would not allow them to be spies, that I have the courage to demand their release."

At this moment I realised that I had not drawn breath for these last words. I stopped and looked the General straight in the eye. There was a space of perhaps ten seconds that seemed to me to be ten minutes and then the general rang the bell that sat on his desk.

The aide I had spoken to earlier came directly.

"The two brothers, they are here?"

"Yes, sir"

I watched the head of police intently as if trying to penetrate his mind and fathom out his decision.

"Release them immediately."

Touched by this spontaneous gesture I extended my hand to thank him, and at the door to his office I complimented him on his courage. I will never know what it was that encouraged the General to take that course of action. Perhaps it was patriotism between two Russians, or the need to see the occupying troops as something other than barbarians. All I can say is that I was extremely relieved and so very grateful. Despite my prayers that this episode would pass over in silence, in a city where rumour and gossip was rife, news immediately began to circulate about the release of the two brothers. As a result I began to receive an ever increasing number of petitions but was, unfortunately, obliged to refuse to take an interest in most of them, given their trivial importance, for example: "The soldiers took my lamp...", "The soldiers stole two pounds of sugar". And so on ... Meanwhile, the Russian army was continuing to advance, and in March 1915 they had conquered the fortress of Przemysl that had held out for almost three months against the invaders.

The dwindling population of Lviv was in turmoil and appalled by this terrible news, and although it was not the most favourable time to become acquainted with the Russians, the guests of Mrs Panazek's boarding house were forced to accept the company of one of them when the hostess, at breakfast, presented Colonel Yassinski. The colonel was small in stature but extremely elegant in his cavalry officer uniform and his presence had the effect of paralysing the conversation in the room, which fell into silence. The Colonel looked around the dining room and gave a sharp, crisp military salute to the occupants and sat down at his table. The guests rapidly finished their meals and were quick to retreat to the adjacent lounge where they were soon settled in their more usual daily pursuits of cards and gossip, of which the latter, this morning, took precedence.

Colonel Yassinski understood the situation. He was an educated man, had mastered the Polish language, and had, with great patience and refined sensibility, gradually conquered concerns and gained the sympathy of all those who lived nearby. His brilliant tales helped the residents forget the war, even if only briefly, and he was adept at bringing into the conversation Russian literature. He would happily argue the virtues and vanities of Russian art but at the same time had an appreciation for what he would call 'Foreign Artists'. Over card games we would discuss, extensively, music, art and literature and would spend long periods comparing and commenting on the literary heroes from the books we had read. Pushkin and Tolstoy would be compared to Kafka and Masoch and the art of Gauguin and Picasso to Kandinsky and Chagall; our conversations and subjects were as diverse as our relative situations. The Colonel was grateful for these small distractions and in return would give small kindnesses; he helped me to unravel the skeins of wool for Gaby's layette and taught me new and more complicated versions of solitaire.

Often at night he offered to be Thomas's guide in his escapades around town, allowing him, with his presence, to circumvent the curfew, and also provided a reassurance to me regarding Thomas's safety. However the relationship between our unlikely trio was beginning to blur the boundaries between what were ostensibly enemies, and there were one or two events that caused me to re-evaluate our association. It became apparent that the feelings of the Colonel towards me had perhaps passed that of just comradely friendship, and events took an unexpected turn when he sent me a letter to accompany the flowers he regularly had delivered to me. It was with some embarrassment that I realised this change in feelings, and I suppose that in hindsight I should have recognised the subtle changes earlier. The letter made me reflect upon his behaviour and how it had altered, how his eyes would bypass whoever he was speaking to and would focus on me, and the passion with which he would argue romantic art, and I began to see that he was, in reality, slowly trying to dominate me, as he would a trophy or wild animal. In the light of these discoveries and revelations I decided that I had to remove him from our proximity as soon as possible, and I suggested to him that perhaps it might be better to change his place of residence.

"Your order will be executed," he replied and snapped his heels, saluted and then, under the pretext of a call from the front turned and left the boarding house, and very soon the city.

We spent long months in Lviv, and the news became encouraging. The Russians were losing the positions they had won and were preparing to retreat. Although Lviv had not yet been liberated towards the latter months of 1915, to my amazement our friends suggested that Thomas and I should leave Austria. Their explanation was simple and brutal. "In war the ear hears gunshots, and the voice of informers lose no time in making accusations and even less time is spent checking their validity. Because of your Russian heritage we are certain that suspicion will fall upon you and the accusations will fly regardless of the good deeds you have managed. As ever, this is a time to settle scores and win favour."

I swiftly realised how accurate this prognosis might be. I recalled the early days of Russian occupation in Lviv and the story of the journalists came swiftly to mind. I became desperate to leave as quickly as possible and with the help of friends and relatives we were able to ask Count Szeremetieff, prefect of the city, for permission to move our family back to our villa in Ekaterinodar in the Caucasus. Life, it seemed had turned full circle!

The evening of our departure loomed and we took leave from our friends by inviting them for dinner at the Hotel George. Thomas was dressed in black tie and I wore a black dress accompanied by a yellow jacket, and as we entered the restaurant we passed by a group of Russian Officers who were in the company of General Ivanoff, commander of the front, and his wife. As we walked to our table, I noticed a commotion among the Russian officers and at the same time a young officer rose from the table and came towards us. He told a waiter that he wished to speak with the Count Ostrowski who was among the friends at our table and said, gravely, that General Ivanoff and his entourage were deeply outraged by the ostentatious offence that I had caused by wearing a dress and jacket that shamelessly flaunted the colours of the flag of the Austro-Hungarian Empire!

Count Ostrowski, disconcerted, blushed and replied: "I am

certain that you are mistaken. Mrs Perutz is Russian and her maiden name is Baroness Kozlowska. I'm sure that she had not intended to offend your feelings any more than you intended to offend the Baroness."

The officer withdrew quickly and apologised profusely as he re-joined his own table and spoke to the General. The following morning I received a magnificent corbeille of flowers, addressed to 'The beautiful Russian Baroness with an apology from her countrymen'. But such were the eggshells we trod upon at this moment in time!

With permission granted for us to move back to the Caucasus and the necessary paperwork drawn up in readiness for any inspection, Thomas and I left to return to Ekaterinodar. Just moments before the departure of the train a familiar figure arrived to greet and say farewell. Colonel Yassinski. Before the train drew slowly away from the platform and headed east towards Russia the Colonel asked Thomas for our address in Caucasus. Thomas gave him the details and as the train drew away we could see the Colonel motionless on the platform. I wondered just then if that was indeed the last we would see of him.

Home Again

It was early 1916 and spring in the Caucasus welcomed us home. A huge carpet of flowers covered the grounds and the air was redolent with the fragrant scent of roses and fresh flowers. We arrived at the villa in Ekaterinodar that had been left empty of family but looked after by the servants. A telegram had been sent when we left Lviv informing them of our arrival, and the journey, fraught with difficulties as we passed through the various lines of battle, took almost four days.

Life quickly returned to normal, the servants were rapidly shaken out of their inertia, and the house resumed, once again, its serene course. Timote had obviously benefited from the rest, as he looked twenty years younger, although this could have been the effect of little Gaby as he attempted to dance traditional Russian dances with the little girl in his arms. We quickly fell into a routine that seemed unchanged as the cat, Rozyk, assuming his usual place on the terrace whilst we had breakfast in the mornings. Timote sat on the steps of the terrace with Gaby on his lap, Thomas read the newspaper and I read my books. In essence we were enjoying a tranquillity that was perhaps necessary the past few years of agitation.

Life in the Caucasus appeared to have suffered not one jot from the inconvenience of war, and it was easy to forget the hardships that we had endured, and more importantly that others were enduring in Austria. In late spring Vladimir sent a telegram from St Petersburg to inform us that he had been promoted to officer in the Nicolaievsky Cavalry School, and, at the same time, of his immediate departure to the front. He asked me to visit him in St Petersburg to say goodbye. Both Thomas and I had foreign passports and it was necessary for us to request special permission from the Governor of the Caucasus to travel to the capital. It was wonderful to see Vladimir again after such a long time. He was resplendent in his Hussar's uniform, and it was sad that we only had two days before we had to say goodbye again, and he boarded the train to the front.

Thomas and I prolonged our stay in St Petersburg so I could show him the beauty of this wonderful city. We were both mesmerized by the spectacle of the white nights, where night and day become almost indistinguishable. We became immersed in the city, and the splendour of the gardens and palaces plunged in the silence of the night with the juxtaposition of day. St Petersburg is built on islands in the Neva river, some populated, some just green and dense with vegetation like sleeping shadows as they lay in the delta where the waters wound their quiet way to the sea. We left for Ekaterinodar enchanted, taking with us unforgettable memories.

When we returned home from St Petersburg we found there a family of friends from the port of Novorossiysk, which had been heavily bombed earlier in the war by the German Fleet that had passed through the Dardanelles and entered into the Black Sea. They had lost all their possessions and only narrowly escaped with their lives. Shortly after their arrival Thais appeared, newly divorced. She now sought comfort under the parental roof, and suddenly the trickle became a flood. Valentina arrived from Switzerland and, under her wing, came some Polish refugees whom she had found sheltering, goodness knows where. Finally Thomas's brother and his wife,

Beatrice, arrived on our doorstep. They had been forced to leave Austria and now took advantage of their sister-in-law's hospitality.

This sudden influx of guests caused a few concerns, as I wanted to ensure that they were comfortable in our home. We had now both family and friends accommodated, and needed to ensure that each felt safe from their various trials and tribulations. One morning, shortly after their arrival, we received a telegram announcing yet another possible guest. The telegram read: "Please do me the honour of allowing me to spend a few days with your family. Yassinski."

As I had suspected at the station in Lviv, we had indeed not heard the last of our Colonel. Those who knew him, however, greeted the news with joy, claiming this would be the perfect antidote and would provide excellent entertainment. Thomas immediately sent a response to the Colonel confirming he would be expected, but he did not ask why the colonel was honouring us with a visit. There was an expression of opposition that could have been read in my face that Thomas did not, fortunately, notice.

Colonel Yassinski arrived twenty-four hours later, with his attendant Vasili. In the evening when all we congregated in the drawing room, the Colonel was conspicuous by his spirit. His anecdotes included the times of the Russo-Japanese War, in which he had taken an active part and where he claimed to have seen the same mistakes of the government that were repeated in this latest defeat. He described the complete lack of careful military preparation, bureaucratic corruption and mistakes by the General Staff, but he always concluded with that the saying: "God and our climate will do wonders."

Meanwhile the army was set against the enemy guns in the Austria-Hungary conflict, just as they had been against the Japanese. Men fought, baring their chests in defiance against a losing battle, and to this was added the latest alarming news from the front, where Russia was being defeated. And the gossip grew around Rasputin and the Tsarina.

Rasputin's influence on the politics of the time offended all the military. His jokes were always barbed with double meaning; they had been introduced by dissidents and enemies to mock the Tsarina and her Court. The result was that every officer of the Tsarina's army would blush with shame at such blatant insults and every officer would inwardly seethe with rage. The atmosphere at the front was not quiet either, with persistent rumours circulating that Russia was betrayed by the Tsarina and her counsellors, that Rasputin was a punishment for the Russians, and that in St Petersburg storm clouds were gathering. The frequent differences of opinion between the Court and the aristocracy further widened the chasm that divided them, putting Russia in grave danger on so many fronts. Something had to cede!

For the time being the Caucasus was a paradise away from all this ferment, a peaceful oasis and refuge for those seeking tranquillity, hospitality and balance. Colonel Yassinski enjoyed this hospitality for over a month and took advantage at every opportunity to express his feelings toward me, which I tactfully ignored. Every morning the maid, entering my room to wake me up and open the windows, carried a large bouquet of flowers combined with a note of homage. However the Colonel seemed to believe that this then allowed him to continually stare at me, to pay exaggerated compliments, and offering, at every moment in the day, to accompany me to the city, to the gardens, to dinner. Indeed after a while I realised that the Colonel was losing his originality and that his conversation and anecdotes were becoming banal and repetitive, and frequently merely reflected the words and views that I had offered only moments previously.

As was the case in Lviv, the Colonel's devious behaviour was, as I was now aware, in full accord with his character. He reminded me of a spider trying to encourage the fly into his web, an invisible network which would trap the unwary and where struggle would only encourage the spider to renew his cunning. The beautiful autumn days gave way to the first cold snaps of December and I was comfortably ensconced by the fireplace in the library. Having declined an invitation to accompany Thomas and members of the family to the cinema, I had taken afternoon tea with a dear friend followed by the preparation of a list of recipients and their gifts for the coming Christmas. We had just finished when the Colonel appeared at the door of the library with a copy of a Russian novel that he ostensibly wished to replace on one of the shelves. As if taking a cue from the book he began to recall his memories of Lviv and in particular his first meeting with me at the boarding house of Mrs Panazek. Of how he had immediately noticed my beauty and how, ever since he had left, he had missed seeing me and indeed longed for the moment we would meet again. I did not respond to these tales of woe and, as if in agitation, he turned to my friend and said: "And all this in vain! Women are capricious and prefer to spend all their affection on those who do not deserve it. I am content to appear on the list that women betrayed."

By the light of the fireplace I could see, on his face, a devilish grin that made me despise him even more. Outraged by such atrocious behaviour, and not finding words to respond in kind, I left the room followed by my friend, and together we withdrew to my boudoir. While we discussed the Colonel's behaviour a clear gunshot was heard which reverberated through the house. We flew downstairs and were met at the bottom by the servants, in a great state of agitation, who were standing by the library door that had been locked from the inside. Just as we were about to go outside and enter through the large French windows the lock turned and Vasili, the Colonel's attendant, emerged, his hand injured and dripping blood. He explained that there had been an 'accident' due to his carelessness in handling of a gun that had released a round into his hand. He apologised profusely for the noise and the incident in general but refused any offers to call a doctor. Thankfully my companion was an experienced nurse and was able to clean and dress the wound which was not as serious as first feared, and, in the confusion, the Colonel was able to walk away quietly from the scene of the incident, and of his embarrassment, through the garden windows. Later that afternoon I found a letter that contained only a few lines and which read, simply: "My passion obscures reason. I think I am crazy, please do not judge me wrongfully or too badly."

Revolution Déjà Vu

An avalanche of criticism rained down on the upper echelons of St Petersburg spreading to all the territory of Russia, and with it a deep discontent at the front as the battles continued outside Russia and the discontent fermented inside. It was not only soldiers that suffered in the war; by the end of 1915 the strain of wartime demand had had huge impacts on the economy, with food shortages and rising prices, allied with inflation which rapidly dragged down incomes. The shortages were a problem especially in the capital, St Petersburg, where distance from supplies and poor transportation networks made matters particularly bad. Shops closed early or entirely for lack of bread, sugar, meat and other provisions, and queues lengthened massively for what remained. It became increasingly difficult both to afford and actually buy food. The volcano was ready to erupt and the population followed with feverish attention the warnings, rumours and the threatening roar that came from its mouth. The murder of Rasputin in December 1916 by Prince Yusupov was like a careless lighting of a match near a powder keg. Rasputin's death would not be a solution for Russia.

In February 1917 demonstrators clamouring for bread took to the streets in St Petersburg and, supported by huge crowds of striking industrial workers, the protesters clashed with police and refused to leave. The strike spread amongst all of St Petersburg's workers, and irate mobs destroyed police stations. In March troops of the St Petersburg army garrison were called out to quell the uprising. In some encounters, regiments opened fire, killing demonstrators, but the protesters kept to the streets and the troops began to waver.

Every day there was terrifying news: "The Tsar abdicated", or "The entire royal family has been arrested", or "The soldiers at the front have laid down their arms and are fleeing". The provisional government, without strength or prestige, was unable to crush the insurgency that broke out in the North and which spread inexorably. Despite the best attempts of their opponents the Bolshevik party assumed power.

The revolution triumphed when regiment after regiment of the St Petersburg garrison defected to the demonstrators' cause: the Imperial Government was forced to resign. On March 15th Tsar Nicholas II abdicated the throne in favour of his brother Michael whose refusal of the crown brought an end to the Tsarist autocracy.

The Caucasus was literally invaded by refugees from the North. They told of terrifying episodes and an indescribable chaos that had taken control of Russia. Ekaterinodar became increasingly crowded and the authorities threatened to seize houses and apartments for the accommodation of refugees.

The authorities in Ekaterinodar asked us to offer hospitality to General E.A. Wolkoff, Chief of the Imperial Cabinet of the Tsar, and his consort. One day the General presented two guests, whom he had brought for lunch, they were the president of the Duma, Mikhail Rodzianko VI and his son Nicolai. Conversation at the table that evening was somewhat stilted as we had been advised that, for obvious reasons, we should not discuss policy. Most around the table were conservative and felt that Rodzianko was to blame for being the power within the commission that had forced the Tsar to abdicate. Similarly the army recognized him as a member of the Provisional Government which had published the enactment of a law that abolished every discipline in the army and ordered the return of soldiers to their barracks. He remained President for just three days before he was forced to flee from St Petersburg to Ekaterinodar, where friends accommodated him.

With a singular lack of any efficient communication with the capital by telephone or telegraph, news was transmitted orally. There was talk of heavy fighting between the Bolshevik Red Army and the Tsarist White Army. Although the White Army was larger, they were suffering significant defeats despite the strong support of the Kuban Cossacks. Ekaterinodar was filled with people coming from all over to join the White Army. The city was transformed into a military camp; men equipped with all kinds of weapons began to take orders from General Denikin and left for the front towards Rostov.

My sister Thais, Vladimir and Valerian followed the General. It was now the last days of autumn 1917 and the fighting was coming ever closer to the city. We could hear the roar of the cannon in the distance and Thais returned from Rostov with demoralising news on the White Army. She said that there was an complete lack of food and no organization among the fighters, and this had led her to create a mobile kitchen. She had managed to commandeer a wagon of supplies and then organize an expedition with the express objective to prepare for the exhausted soldiers, who were suffering badly from both cold and hunger, the much-appreciated borscht.

With all the commotion and excitement of Thais returning home, no one noticed the furtive departure of General Wolkoff and his wife. Events were beginning to overtake us, and as the news continued to arrive of the beatings the White Army were taking, nerves were not surprisingly on edge. One evening the sudden sound of bells jolted me from my sleep and Timote announced the arrival of Nicolai Rodzianko, the son of the President. His face was crumpled in despair and it was obvious that something was seriously amiss. I dressed quickly, asked him to sit and offered tea and waited....

"Thank you," he said. "We are desperate. Our friends refuse to accommodate my father and me any longer and now we are in the street and do not know where to spend the night."

Without hesitation I offered him the room that had been so recently vacated by General Wolkoff and his wife.

"Really? Can we come now? I'm going to call Papa, he is waiting outside by your gates." Nicolai went out hurriedly and shortly after the two men took their place in the spare room.

One evening, which was memorable for the disastrous sequence of events that rained down with the force of a storm, the son of Rodzianko arrived at the front door on a cart overloaded with hay. Disguised as a peasant, sitting in the driving seat, he waited for his father who came downstairs shortly after, also dressed as a peasant. Giving no explanation he took a seat next to his son and I watched from the doorway as they disappeared into the night. I was did not know of the reasons for this hasty and clandestine departure, but I was aware that something was seriously amiss.

An hour later and another commotion in the entrance hall! Thais, Vladimir and Valerian were at the front door saying goodbye. Thais explained that they had received a call with orders from the commander, and they were to present themselves that night at the railway station. The moment of parting was swift and the three of them set off accompanied by words of encouragement and a last goodbye. Valentina, Thomas and I lingered again at the front of the house as they, too, disappeared into the gloomy darkness. Inside, with friends and relatives, we gathered around the dining table and exchanged thoughts about the fate that may befall our families and loved ones. Exhausted by the subject and its potential outcomes, and to hide our growing misery and discomfort, we fell into a deep silence. Within moments, though, the silence was once again broken by a loud knock on the dining room door. In the doorway appeared the officer who had long ago requisitioned two rooms in our house. We had obviously left the front door unattended and he had walked directly into the house. At first glance we welcomed the officer into the room until we noticed that the insignia on his uniform had changed. Those of the Revolutionary Red Army of the Bolsheviks had replaced the badges of the White Army.

With a wry smile and ostentatious indifference he asked: "Allow me to raise the flag of my Government on the door of your house. I also want to introduce myself as Minister of Foreign Affairs of the Caucasus: Vasili Trachtenberg." It wasn't a request, it was an order, and with that he turned and left the room. For a moment the blood in our veins ran cold. We were awestruck and the reasons for the hurried departure of Rodzianko and his son, and the orders to Thais, Vladimir and Valerian now became clear. With that understanding came fear and anguish; the Red Army was not just winning, it was now in our house.

From the entrance, meanwhile, came the happy voices of the minister and his wife, accompanied by hammer blows as they set the new flag. As soon the standard had been raised, Trachtenberg, his wife and his troops left. The hours passed slowly and eventually Thomas and I retired. We were unable to sleep and before the sun had even begun to rise we went down to the dining room. There was no respite from the troubles, and as we entered the room Timote presented us with a sheet of paper he had collected from the courtyard. It had dropped from the sky he explained but, of course, he was unable to read it himself. I scanned it quickly and then read the contents out loud for all in the room to hear: " We ask all your forgiveness for having abandoned you at this time. May God help you and bless you in our absence."

It was the last farewell of the White Army, launched from an airplane. With that piece of paper in my hands I looked out of the window. I stared at the dark road that almost symbolically seemed as dark as our future. It was an effort to control my emotions. Timote looked ashen and then looked at me quizzically. "Give me your jewellery box," he said, "I shall put it in a safe place and when this is all over I shall return it to you." My heart went out to him at that moment; he knew there was little he could do for us but nevertheless was prepared to help us at least salvage something from this terrible situation. I told him where to find everything and then left him alone.

Slowly the hours passed and the pale watery sun arose giving the first light of the new day. I thought it would be better if that day had never begun. It was seven in the morning when, on the corner of the deserted street, I saw appear a group of shadowy figures, hard to distinguish in the early morning gloom. As the mist lifted and they came closer, I realised it was a small group of soldiers who, with excited gestures, were pointing to our house. They headed resolutely toward us and hammered loudly and incessantly on the front door. Timote, looking through the peephole, could see a small group of soldiers but had little idea as to whether they were from the Red or White army as none seemed to be bearing any insignia. The band of men was dirty, unkempt and unshaven, and looked severely in need of baths and showers. Their boots were covered in thick mud and I tried to direct them to the servant's entrance at the back of the house in order to protect the carpets. The response this elicited was screams, protests, louder hammering on the door and threats that they would shoot through the door if we did not open it. I told Timote to go into the kitchens and then when he had gone, I opened the door.

Outside were fifteen young soldiers, whom I think would be better described as bandits, pillagers or plunderers. The moment the door swung open they pushed past me and into the house and began to go through every room in search of valuables, preferably small. I was grateful that I had taken Timote's advice and given him the jewellery, but fearful that they would perhaps realise and question everyone in the household in search of more valuables. They stole everything they could fit into pockets and bags, and roughly pushed past everyone in the house. They turned out drawers, bags, cupboards, purses and handbags. They emptied Thomas's briefcase and threw the contents of his desk drawers over the study floor. They tipped the books from the library shelves and tumbled them to the floor seeking hiding places and anything of value. They found the two racks of British shotguns and relieved us of them, and all I could do was stand and witness this wholesale destruction of our possessions. After two hours they left with the warning that they would be back later and that, if they had not found the guns, the whole family would have paid dearly. I shudder to think what these gangsters would have been capable of.

We gathered in the hallway and started to take stock of what had been stolen, and began to tidy up at least one room to make it habitable. We had, perhaps, been working for twenty minutes when Timote called from the hallway that another group of men were coming towards us with the same vagabond look, ruffians every single one of them. We had no choice but to let them in the moment they reached the door. The robbery started all over again, this time we were questioned as to where the valuables were, Timote remained conspicuously absent and for good reason. We explained that not long before another of their band of brothers had visited and left behind this havoc. This did not satisfy them and they gave vent to their frustration by ripping curtains, slashing pictures and trying to burn papers and books in the library and study. We followed behind doing our utmost to ensure that the damage was minimised but nevertheless some items were destroyed and lost forever. They had little regard for anything other than an item that could be turned into money. Gold, silver, jewellery, guns, all were fair game and our concern was that we would be the next things they would use to take their vengeance. We were able to show them where two more shotguns had been stored and that seemed to appease them, and with pockets full of looted items they left the house as casually as they had entered.

It was ironic then that as this second band of marauding pirates and wastrels left the house who should they come across but the first group returning, as they had promised, to see what other goods, valuables and trinkets they could steal to further bolster their ill-gotten income. The returning group realised that this second group had also robbed the house and moreover had pockets full of valuables. Timote quietly closed the door and we retreated upstairs to watch the outcome. The first group had decided to lay claim to all the booty and there ensued a fearful argument that escalated as neither group would concede either ground or contraband. Loud words and bloody insults were exchanged as the two leaders of the gangs began to push and shove each other, and when this failed to provide either side with any form of satisfaction blows were exchanged. I noticed one the men, I am unsure to which group he belonged, slip his hand into his jacket pocket and I watched, horrified, as he pulled out a large revolver. Two loud shots rang out followed by a silence that was absolutely total. Then there was the sound of running footsteps along the boardwalk and voices calling. The end result of this was two dead and both gangs fled.

Around noon came a third visit, but this time as it was Red Army officers and their troops. This new situation was a little more worrying. The thugs would make do with jewels, bangles and trinkets, the officers were more interested in establishing if we were Russian aristocracy and at this point our lives were truly at risk. They would have had no compunction if they had to murder us; such was the colour of war between Red and White Armies. The senior officer asked to see my passport. I handed him the documents, which thankfully I had managed to prevent being destroyed by either of the gangs, although both Thomas's and my passports were singed at the edges.

The front of the passport bore the insignia of Imperial Austria on the cover. The officer made great show of inspecting the passport and of looking through each of the pages. He then held it out to his colleagues for them to examine. I realised that none of the officers or soldiers could read anything except Cyrillic and that the language of the passport was completely beyond them. I waited to see what would happen. This could either be a total disaster or possibly a blessing in disguise.

"You are English?" the officer said looking straight into my eyes. I did not answer and, trembling inside, took the passport from his hand as he held it out.

"Too bad" he continued. "The English, we cannot touch them but your house is now requisitioned. We will give you permission to cohabit in order to cater for us." I glanced down at the passport and, for the first time I realised that he had merely seen the coat of arms on the cover and assumed it was British. I was not going to be the person to disillusion him.

In the space of half a day our lives had been turned upside down. We had been robbed twice, and three times we had managed to avoid any serious personal harm. But we knew that it was not yet over. We had gone from being masters of our house to virtual prisoners. We also had to be aware that one small slip of the tongue could cause the soldiers to realise that we were not English, but that I was indeed Russian aristocracy. By the afternoon eighteen high-ranking officials from the Ministry of Finance were living in our house. This new situation raised fresh problems to be resolved. We were left only with Timote and after a request for further staff to help attend to our 'guests' the Chief of Police very kindly sent us some prisoners of war; a cook from Karlsbad and two Viennese waiters. All three performed their duties to perfection but being unable to speak Russian they were incapable of communicating with the rest of the staff in the house. This led to frequent misunderstandings as to duties and requirements, and even more frequent arguments from being quite unaware of what the guests required.

The installation of the Bolsheviks in our house took no time whatsoever. Within a day there arrived two lorries from which the soldiers unloaded hundreds of sacks. I later learned that the sacks all contained money, freshly printed, which would go to pay the soldiers of the Red Army. Our days stumbled between alarm and anguish as news arrived from all parts of the country. Because of the ranking of the officials in our Finance Ministry we were frequently privy to fresh news that was overheard, generally by Timote who, because he was unable to read or write, was treated as simple-minded. His ears however were as sharp as any and his memory excellent.

At a rally of 'comrades' held near the station, Timote learned that Evgeny Vaqueret had been sentenced to death in absentia. His crime? Having the title of Senior Official of Railways was enough for him to be condemned. Another time, for a whole day, I could not take my eyes off a man, the Director of the Lyceum. He remained motionless, from early morning through to late evening, on the corner of our street. Staring into space, he was waiting for his son of eleven who had left the house to go to the library. The next day, the poor father found him in a ditch, massacred and tortured. Again the news begged the question 'why?'. To what end? What would it achieve? We would never find out, it was just the effect of the war and the impact it had on innocents. It wakened the cruellest passions in a human being, it exacerbated the loss of our dignity, and pride became a misplaced commodity. My belief in the fundamental goodness of Russia and in the feeling of being Russian began to falter, and not wanting to lose it, I tried to explain and rationalise to myself what was happening. I had to believe in the fact that most of the brutal cruelty was committed on behalf of special groups of men, men who had scores to settle, however trivial, and would stop at nothing to sate their appetites. As with most atrocities they were committed by a small minority of people whose voice would become so loud it was deafening, and others would be sucked into the vortex of mayhem, murder and execution. We had to believe that good would eventually win over evil. As much as at points in time we might not believe so, we should never lose faith.

At the orders of our 'companions' we were forbidden to lock the doors of our rooms during either the day or the night. The rationale was they might have had orders that need to be carried out. We slept fully clothed. Our senses were so heightened that the slightest noise would awaken us and eventually Thomas and I would take it in turns to sleep whilst the other would sit in the chair and watch over Gaby. During these hours of night I would absorb myself in embroidery. By the light of a small lamp I was embroidering a tablecloth that was decorated with drawings of my imagination; drawings of better times and of memories of my family and Russia as she used to be. I gave it the name of the 'Bolshevik Tablecloth,' and every morning it would be carefully hidden, a different place.

Two weeks passed and the officers decided to organize a reception. The servants were ordered to arrange the chairs in a semicircle in the large drawing room and, it was announced that everyone had to attend the ballet organised for the evening. The chef Bruno appeared to perhaps know more than others and wandered around for most of the day with a mischievous smile.

With the approach of evening, and the hour of the party, the anticipation reached fever pitch. Long tables had been laid in the corridor outside the drawing room and were now laden with food prepared by Bruno, and a large number of bottles of wine and champagne taken from my cellar. Towards sunset the performers of this ballet arrived, a cheerful company of women, scantily clad at best, virtually undressed at worst and poor Timote, so shocked, was probably the only man, apart from Thomas, who did not partake of the bacchanal that night.

The debauchery finally ended at dawn with a target practice for rifles and pistols against the solid wall of my room. Suddenly the door opened and there appeared a soldier, bloodied, with clothes torn, and wounded in the shoulder. He asked for help and, while the housekeeper cleaned and bandaged his wound, we listened to his explanations on the incident. "I have been hurt because of my insubordination, by the officer and my cousin."

There was a certain irony that was not lost on us; they now turn upon themselves? The wounded man was bandaged as best we could and his companions spent most of the following day asleep and nursing many a sore head. Once awake they asked, with genuine curiosity, what would be the impression if we were to tell our countrymen back in England of their behaviour. Imagine, they said, what would you tell your English neighbours. Understandably we maintained a tactful silence.

Days passed nervously and any good news was scarce. We appeared to be simply lurching from one piece of frightening information to the next. One day there arrived an invitation from the Government. It was addressed "To the owners of buildings and land", and requested us to meet in the hall of the Lyceum to discuss a number of matters that would be of general interest to us. I read the full content of the circular to Thomas and said that I had no intention of going. I later learned that the theatre, once filled, had been surrounded by Red Army soldiers and all those attending had been arrested. No one knew their fate, as they were never heard of or seen again.

After a prolonged period of house arrest we began to observe changes in the behaviour of the 'comrades'; they showed themselves rather prey to nervous agitation. In April 1918 the sound of cannon fire betrayed the secret they were harbouring. A new battle was raging and the Red Army faced the White Army at Kuban. The Revolutionaries against the Volunteers, the Bolsheviks against the Tsarists. One morning, taking advantage of the distraction of our warders, we took to a nearby hill and, armed with binoculars, followed the battle that took place right in front of us.

The combatants of the two sides were divided by the Kuban River and attacked each other's points of defence. I focussed on the red brick factory occupied by the White Army on the left bank. They were firing against the Revolutionaries, the Bolsheviks, who defended the right bank, on the edge of the city. It was noticeable that the Bolsheviks had a significant lack of precision in pointing their heavier guns, their shells and bullets going astray. This incompetence allowed the White Cavalry to wade across the river and initiate an attack which forced the Red Army to retreat to the borders of the city. We were so engrossed in following the actions of the moment we failed to notice the approach of a group of Red Army soldiers who gave the gruff order to "Get out of here!"

We left quickly and on the way back to the house we marvelled at the great mass of Red fugitives who, overcome with panic, littered the streets with horses and vehicles loaded with their belongings, trying to reach the bridge over the river. Splinters of shells and machine gun bullets fell like hail from heaven, forcing us to find shelter in the house. However the eagerness to know the progress of the battle won over our fear of mortal danger. We continued to observe the unfolding of events from the upstairs windows, careful to ensure we would not be seen by trying to keep below the sills. We saw the Red officers give some orders to a group of soldiers who were manning the heavier artillery. Prisoners, who were shackled to the guns, quickly replaced the soldiers. I recognised their uniforms as being two Hungarian officers and their Czech aides.

The aim of the Hungarians was far more satisfactory to the Red officers. They pointed their gun and fired at the brick factory scoring a direct hit. A volley of shots was returned whilst the prisoners reloaded the gun. A second shot was fired and again the hit was direct. But what followed was silence. No returned fire, no shells no bullets. It was inexplicable and continued for many hours. Not knowing why was intolerable, and we ventured out onto the terrace in search of an explanation.

There was a change, the flow of refugees from the Red Army had not only been stemmed but also reversed. Faces now seemed soothed and they were flowing back into the city. We remained completely disoriented; we had no account of what happened and could only assume the defeat of the White Army. What had felt like a success and freedom now rang with the truth of continued captivity in our own home. The answer was soon known. In an extra edition of the Bolshevik newspaper it was announced, not only their victory over the White Army, but also the sensational news the General Kornilov, head of the White Army had been killed. He had recently joined General Denikin and was in the tower of the brick factory that had been chosen as the observation point for the battle on the river. Initially, no one believed the version of events published by the newspaper because it clashed with logic. Why would a Chief of Staff, such as the General Kornilov, have placed himself in such a vulnerable position so exposed to the cannon fire of the opponent? However that argument tried only to console rather than reassure. The bitter truth was that the General had indeed been killed.

The battle was over and for a while we were beguiled by beautiful spring days. I spent a lot of time on the terrace working on my Bolshevik Tablecloth and thinking about the recent events that had shattered our faith. Apart from the defeat by the Red Army at Kuban I had heard no further rumours regarding the White Army. Looking around I noticed the figure of a woman trying to enter through the small wrought iron gate that led to the garden. I watched her efforts quietly and as she succeeded and came closer, I recognised her as the daughter of a well-known local lawyer. She looked around suspiciously, and furtively came beside me. She leant down and, with a last glance around, she whispered, "Do you know that a train will arrive tonight at midnight. It brings with it the wounded from the latest battle and among them you will find your sister. She has had both legs amputated. I bring you this news because the Bolsheviks will allow relatives to care for their wounded as long as they themselves pick them up from the station."

I tried to hide my excitement at the news that my sister Thais was alive and my dismay at the severity of her injuries. As calmly as I could I asked the girl. "Is this true? My sister has, for many years, been living in Switzerland." I did this as not to admit that I was Russian and aware that there had been many suspicions and tests over the previous months, and to fail now would have disastrous consequences for my family and me.

"I saw her a few weeks ago, as a nurse of the White Army," she replied.

"I am certain you are wrong," I replied in return. "None of us have reason to go to the station to receive my sister who is, I am certain, in Switzerland."

The girl stirred and became aggressive, "You will regret your refusal." And with those words and a last glance around she scuttled off towards the gate, never looking back, seeming to be in fear for her life.

I was in a quandary. I recalled the abortive attempt to invite us to the theatre and the consequences of that action to those that attended. Was it possible to believe that the Red Army would transport the wounded White soldiers or was it just another sham in order to lure the more wary Russians out into the open? I discussed the whole affair with Thomas and some friends and accepted the second assumption, as painful as it was. Nagging doubt tormented me and every moment that passed that night pricked my conscience.

The news came at dawn. Among the wounded transported on the train, there was no Thais! From information received later, I learned that the Red Army soldiers had indeed loaded some badly injured officers of the White Army and had them transported to a state hospital where they were under the control of trusty guards. With the passage of time the injured soldiers health did improve and, despite the precautions taken, they all, with the exception of one, escaped.

The disturbing events continued. To demonstrate the magnitude of the blow dealt to the White Army, the Bolshevik newspapers announced that the body of General Kornilov would be displayed on the Cathedral Square, the central point of the city, to the population. Surrounded by Red soldiers and curious civilians the coffin was left open for identification. A Bolshevik commander turned to the collected soldiers and screamed, "Company, which of you can give precise details on General Kornilov?" One of the soldiers, a sergeant of the late General, claimed, "the General has false teeth and two gold teeth."

The mouth of the corpse was forced open to ascertain the truth. The General's identity was confirmed amidst horrified gasps from the civilians and soldiers alike. The crowd then began to behave as animals; the body of the General was grasped, lifted from the makeshift coffin and tied to the tail of a horse. It was dragged around the city behind the steed, surrounded by a baying mob of soldiers and civilians. Someone had found a large hand bell and all this was accompanied by the din of the ringing bell. The ghastly unsavoury episode lasted for almost two hours and then, once into open country, they threw the remains of the body to be food for the starving stray dogs. Excited by the spectacle, the fury of the men broke out and their ferocity was not contained to just that night. Over the next few weeks hundreds of people disappeared, the wounded and dead were thrown together onto wagons and were transported on their last trip to the Kuban River to be drowned. Their cries and their prayers went unheard, or if they were heard, unheeded. There were rumours of making a night of St. Bartholomew where the privileged classes would be systematically destroyed in the city, neighbourhood by neighbourhood.

We knew from the Minister of Foreign Affairs, Trachtenberg, which night that fate would be coming to our neighbourhood. There was little we could do to prevent any slaughter and the best we could hope for is that the hordes would, perchance, bypass us and move onto to different pastures. Our course of action was no more complicated than congregating on the terrace in the dark and awaiting our destiny. No one spoke, and at every little noise there was a sharp intake of breath and then silence as we dared not breath. Gaby was sitting on my lap and at each reaction I hugged her tightly to my chest. I knew it was a vain attempt to comfort her but somehow it made me feel less useless. From a distance we heard the clatter of horses galloping in our street, they approached, entered our driveway but passed on by, stopping instead at the property of the widow of General Domanovicz.

We heard the excited barking of his dogs, German shepherds, and the plaintive cries of the disturbed peacocks followed by series of gunshots, a crash of glass, and then silence, interrupted occasionally by a harsh voice giving orders which we could hear but could not quite distinguish what was being said. We sat on the terrace, with not a solitary light around us, our hearts gripped by terror. Quietly we asked ourselves, would this be our day, or would they pass us by? We spent long hours in this nightmare, none slept, every nerve was taut, we were stretched to breaking point. Then we saw the first rays of dawn and light crept slowly over the horizon. We heard the sound of a wagon, its wheels crisp on the ground, and then it came into sight, loaded with goods and next to it Mrs Domanovicz. She passed by, escorted by the cavalry and they walked away from us. We gave a deep sigh and made the sign of the cross. Last night was not for us, but tonight, tomorrow night, we could not know. We had to take each day as it came.

When the sun was full and dawn had broken, and we were sure all the soldiers had left, Thomas could not resist the urge to see what had happened. He returned within moments, with news. "Imagine the effect of a terrible hurricane," Thomas said. "The house is devastated, windows smashed, doors ripped off hinges, every drawer had been emptied on the floor, every cupboard cleared and ransacked, books thrown on the floor, wooden panels smashed and pictures and bookshelves torn from the wall." Outside they had dug into the garden and Thomas suspected that these excavations were seeking the legendary treasure that was reputed to include the General's sabres, decorated with gold and precious stones. They had been given by the Tsar in recognition of the General's service in the war against the Turks. I heard later that

Mrs Domanovicz, with the help of her servant, had been spared her life, but had lost her mind.

One evening, while I was busy putting Gaby to bed, Timote came to tell me that Minister Trachtenberg had announced that he wanted to see me as soon as possible. I felt uneasy but was in no position to refuse the request – or was it an order? – and I left Gaby in the custody of Thomas and made my way to my Aunt's house, where Trachtenberg had requested the meeting. I found Minister Trachtenberg sitting at a table examining his stamp collection. He and his wife, with huge catalogues in hand, were assessing the value of the collection, many of the stamps were apparently extremely rare. He told me that the value of his collection was matched only by one other, that of the Tsar. He held forth on his collection for a while, how the value was incalculable and how this value is improved by imperfections, sheets and overprints, and the fact that, given the quantity of his collection, it will guarantee him an income for life. I waited patiently for the end of that speech, for an explanation of the urgent call.

Finally, without looking up and as if he had just realised or remembered my presence in the room the Minister said, "I wanted to warn you of your situation; you are in grave danger. This morning, during the meeting of our General Staff, we received a letter that proves that you are suspected of hiding in your home the former President Mikhail Rodzianko VI and his son Nicolai."

It was fascinating to watch the Minister as he performed this miraculous turnaround: he knew very well that both had been staying at our villa, for he had met them there!

He continued, "Did you not know that my Government

gave orders for his capture, offering a reward of 300,000 gold roubles for his head? As a consequence you can expect at any moment the order of your arrest."

The moment he finished talking he looked up briefly into my eyes and then went back to his work of evaluating his stamp collection. I waited to see if he had finished for I felt that there was still something he wanted to say and he would say it when he was ready. Then as if analysing his thoughts, and still looking down at his stamps, he suggested that I might wish to hide in the house of his faithful friends.

I refused. I told him I refused for two reasons. First, I would not let my little girl and my husband suffer because of my actions, which they undoubtedly would. Secondly, if I were threatened with death for hiding President Rodzianko and his son I would not want to put his friends into the same position for harbouring a fugitive from the Government and from justice.

"So thank you for your warning and I assure you that I will just have to put myself at your disposal."

I was exhausted and I wanted to take my leave but then the Minister, yawning, asked me: "What day is today?"

"Tuesday," I replied.

"Oh I forgot that today Major Timoschenko went to the front and therefore your arrest cannot be executed tomorrow." He looked up, smiled and then dismissed me.

We parted; I went home, it was four in the morning.

The absence of Major Timoschenko dragged on from day to day and with it the agonizing wait continued. After a few weeks the Minister came to me to announce that he had finally been able to convince his colleagues that to base a judgment with such a severe sentence on an anonymous letter was not a civil procedure. Apparently his opinion had been accepted, and the incriminating letter had then been destroyed.

While the Bolsheviks occupied the city little or no communication between friends and acquaintances was possible. Many had been thrown out of their homes and were now in hiding. I was therefore very surprised to receive a visit one day from one of my Guardians, a lawyer and his wife. Although they had been strangers, I was aware that their leanings were contrary to mine and Thomas's, and also that they were very much more concerned with self-interest. Nevertheless, given the experiences of late, I tried to welcome them with cordiality and listened to their story.

"This morning," began the lawyer, "the spring air had lured us out of our hiding place, for the first time, leaving my mother alone in the house. On our return, we found that she was missing, and a note on my desk, in my mother's hand, which said: 'I beg you not to come looking for me. Your children need you, do not try to save me if you please.' There was also a communiqué that we should immediately report to the Military Command."

"On this point," the lawyer continued, "my ideas conflict with those of my wife. I find that my mother was right and we have to follow her wishes."

His wife interrupted, crying and protesting: "How could I live, knowing that you sacrificed your mother? What lives would we have, what pride would be left with such a weight on our conscience? Please do not protest Sergio, let's not waste time, we should go to the Command."

Turning to me, they asked if they could leave their children in my custody. Moved, I pledged to help, and we parted with long hugs. I watched them through the window as they made their painful way to the Military Command villa, which had been established in their own property. As soon as they had gone I contacted Minister Trachtenberg and, informing him of the incident, asked what had been the reason for the arrest of their mother. He listened to me and he said: "This matter will take some time. While our interests are focused on issues of war, civilians, unfortunately, will have to wait."

Returning home I resumed my embroidery, wondering how long could I be in control of my nerves, living in this chaos? Living life one day at a time, with no thoughts of tomorrow, and each night as we went to bed we did not know if we would meet again in the morning. It made the goodnight kiss for Thomas and Gaby even more poignant. It reminded me of a quote from Blaise Pascal, "Evil is never done so thoroughly or so well as when it is done with a good conscience." It seemed to me that this was exactly where we were that day. I was looking for comfort in the past for I felt we did not have too much future. I looked at the small chapel in front of the house and was reminded again of Pascal: "Belief in God is a wise wager. Granted that his existence cannot be proved, but what harm will come to you if you gamble on its truth and it proves false? If you gain, you gain all; if you lose, you lose nothing. Wager, then, without hesitation, that He exists." The fact that we were still here, and that Thomas and Gaby were by my side was, for me, proof enough that God existed, and I had faith that there will be a tomorrow. My faith might be tested but it would prove true.

The church might have seemed to be a sad mausoleum with a crucifix outside, and it might no longer be open for worship, but how much consolation had been gained by attending a mass on a Saturday evening, the lights of countless candles lit in huge candlesticks, glittering on the golden altar and on the icons, the heavy aroma of incense swung from burners by altar boys, the voices of the students in the choir, angelic. For a moment I was transported to another world, excited by the ritual and my soul was, momentarily, at rest. I entered the room of my little Gaby, to attend to her meal. I gazed at her in admiration, her golden curls, big almond eyes tinged with green. She was the realization of my dream. To hear her speak in innocence with kittens and dogs took me away from some of the usual concerns.

It was November 11th 1918 and a day that would linger forever in my memory for it provided some light at the end of our long dark tunnel. Thomas came into the dining room, breathless and brought the news that Poland had been granted its independence and that in St Petersburg Count Ledohocwski was acting as attorney to issue passports for Poles who wished to return home. We got in touch immediately and waited anxiously for a response. It was a hope, a shining star in a dark sky that we had watched for so long.

Amongst all this hope I had not forgotten the fate of my Guardian lawyer, his wife and his mother, and continued to pester Minister Trachtenberg on their fate, although all I received were evasive answers. More weeks passed until one day I saw the lawyer and his wife again. They had grown old, they looked totally lost and their hair was grey and unkempt. They seemed like different people. With a timidity that had not existed previously the lawyer broke the silence and in a low sad voice said: "I have no right to live; I have been forced to witness abominable scenes committed on my wife and mother by drunks and murderers." His wife promptly interrupted him and begged him to forget things that were part of the past. He should remember his children were safe, while so many others were lost, and that as long as he remembered the atrocities she could not forget them.

A few hours later I arrived to see Minister Trachtenberg. After accepting my thanks for the release of the lawyer, he asked me point-blank: "The lawyer has money?"

"The last objects they owned," I replied, "were their wedding rings and the lawyer's gold watch, all of which were taken when they were arrested."

The minister paused, steepled his fingers and looked at me: "You have not heard," he continued, "that the lawyer possesses a valuable collection of stamps? And is it not strange that this was not found in his house at the time of the occupation?"

"I did not know that the lawyer was a philatelist." I said and I realised at that moment the reason for the lawyer's arrest. The Minister saw my embarrassment and simply said: "Do not worry, I will speak to him personally." It was not long after that the Minister's collection of stamps was significantly enhanced by way of a very generous 'gift' from the lawyer and his family.

The months that were consuming our nightmare seemed to be endless and our inertia, coupled with our inability to influence any event, seemed to double the length of time passing. Then one day we heard that Minister Trachtenberg was preparing to travel to the Crimea. He boasted of now owning a magnificent motorboat, comfortable, he said, and large enough to transport the crates full of albums containing his collection of stamps. After several days of noise due to the packing that was required to secure his precious cargo the house fell suddenly silent. Thomas went and found that every room visited had been completely emptied and that the Minister and his wife had obviously left permanently. Almost simultaneously we were surprised by a violent cannonade and learned, with astonishment, that the White Army had again attacked the Bolsheviks and were approaching the city.

We stayed in our rooms upstairs, the doors closed and the curtains drawn and all lights extinguished. The streets seemed deserted, silence reigned and the atmosphere was one of torment whilst we waited to hear the outcome of the battle.

The chef Bruno came and, informed by a particular witness, told us that in the last few hours many houses had been looted and the women raped by gangs of bandits on the run. Curious, I asked him if he knew what the Bolsheviks were doing downstairs in our house, and he replied that they were busy preparing bags of money which were being hastily transferred to waiting trucks standing by the gates with their engines running.

The cook had not even finished his story when we saw one of the bands that was talked about, composed of sailors on horseback, armed with hand grenades and machine guns, ride close to our house, jump from the saddle and rush to the entrance screaming: "Open the doors – death to you all!"

We stood in the hallway, paralysed with fear and saw, at that moment, the door of one of the occupied rooms open and one of the Bolsheviks, pale and uncertain, headed to the besieged entrance. He opened the door and quickly slammed it shut again, and for a moment the clamour outside subsided as the band was surprised by this course of action. There was a sudden shout from outside.

"Vassica my cousin, is that you?"

The Bolshevik who had opened the door stopped in his tracks, turned and opened the door again.

"Vassica, how many years have passed since we last met?"

The two men warmly embraced each other and to everyone's amazement they exchanged words in secret and then the Bolsheviks jumped into one of the trucks and drove away with an escort of bandits! I can only assume they were now rich beyond their wildest dreams. God can do miracles.

We closed the front door and barricaded it, and did the same with all the other doors of the villa. Once we were secure Timote went to inspect the rooms that had now been left empty. Going into the living room Timote found laying on the ground the body of a Bolshevik who had been left seemingly dead. He came running to me, to give me the news, advising me to act as soon as possible. I agreed we did not need the serious consequences that would occur if he were to be discovered in our villa. I had no doubt that if either bands of brigands, White Army or Bolsheviks found the body we would be accused of killing him. With Bruno's help Timote managed to transport the body of the dead man from the living room to where there was a large disused well that was used as an ice store in the garden. I had recognised him as the young soldier who had been beaten after the bacchanalian party. He was laid in the bottom on the ice, then the lid was closed and we walked away.

Having just recovered from this shock when there was loud hammering once again on the front door. Not trusting whoever was on the other side we looked through the peepholes but our slowness to open the doors only unnerved our visitors further. Impatient they cried: "For God's sake, open soon. We are your friends!"

We removed the barricades and two officers of the White Army entered quickly, greeted us and asked if there were Bolsheviks in the house. After receiving a negative response, they gave us the order to go down in the cellar, feeling that our house was in the line of fire. They then jumped on their horses and galloped away to the next house. As we hid down into the cellar, and while bombs exploded covering the terrace and the garden with splinters, one thought worried us: "This time will the White Army be able to liberate us?"

Towards late afternoon the shelling subsided. The chef, Bruno, went out into the street in reconnaissance and, returning, reported that he had seen the White Army enter the city. We went out in the yard, and carried on the wind, we could hear the peal of the majestic bronze bells of the cathedral, desecrated and closed during the occupation of the Red Army. The first group of brave inhabitants emerged from their homes and ran directly to the town centre to greet their heroes. We awaited the return of our loved ones who had been away for so long, Vladimir, Valerian and Thais. Timote and I prepared everything for them: their rooms, clean clothes, baths and food.

Family Reunion

First to arrive was Thais. She had lost weight, looked so gaunt, and had changed a lot. In the uniform of a Red Cross nurse she was trying to hide the wounds that marked her face, neck and hands. First she gave comforting news of Vladimir and Valerian, both were safe and well although, like her, could probably do with a bath and some good warm food. After a long rest a change into clean fresh clothing, Thais began to tell of her long odyssey.

"After our separation from you, due, as you know, to an evacuation order, the small army of General Denikin was defeated and retreated towards the mountain and forest territory of the Caucasus, where we hoped to be able to stop and to join forces with General Kornilov. This meeting was important for the purposes of planning our counter strategy, where to attack the Red Army and when it would be at its weakest. We needed to regain lost territory."

"The wait stretched from days into weeks and all the time the Bolsheviks were pressing in on our positions and eventually they succeeded in encircling our depleted forces. Without food or supplies, and low on arms and ammunition, we began to despair of being able to join with General Kornilov. We were trapped, condemned to death. Earlier in the campaign President Rodzianko had visited with his son and had spoken to us about his passion and pride in Russia. Deeply touched by the words, we decided to follow his proposal, to accept death as the final duty and with the Christian spirit. We gathered together and we knelt in prayer. Under the guidance of those words of the President, thousands of voices, in chorus, raised their last prayer to God. Looking up at the sky the stars symbolised for us a thousand candles, and the hymns we sang rose up to meet them and they flickered as though touched by the wind of our words, a last celebration of our lives."

"I do not remember how many hours we spent in desperate song, but I do know that it was our salvation. Our opponents became confused, they thought this was a manifestation of joy stimulated by the meeting of our army with that of General Kornilov. For that reason, much to our surprise, they retreated, changing their strategy, and at the same time we were offered the chance to break through. We seized it with both hands and we prepared for a new march in search of supplies, of food, of arms but more importantly, of General Kornilov and his army."

"In that moment of exultation an officer named Sniegekow approached me. He told me that he had been ordered to give me some important and highly secret information and beckoned me to a point away from the rest of the troops and hidden behind some trees. In the dark of the forest, and with the continuous movement and noise of troops in carts and on horseback I realised his plan was not to give information but to rob me. The noise, the movement, the darkness of the forest, merely facilitated this. As soon as I understood his intentions, I fought him in a desperate struggle; he held a Kindjal knife to my throat. I managed somehow to grab the knife but suffered cuts to my hands and arms in the process, I tried to walk away from him but he reacted so violently, he threw me to the ground and put a gun to my temple and fired saying: 'This is for my safety'."

"The rest I was told by my friends. After the breaking of

the siege, and moving from camp, they noticed my absence. Their calls and appeals remained unanswered and they began to search for me. They found me on the floor, just a few paces from the Red Cross cart."

"They called Doctor Platonov who, after examining my wounds, declared that I would probably not survive. The cuts to my arms, hands and wrists were relatively superficial, but the bullet, fired to kill me, and gone through my skull, the roof of my mouth and lodged in my throat. With no instruments available surgery was not possible, and the doctor proposed that I should be left where I was; it would be pointless to take me with them and I would only slow down the retreat. The officers, however, had other ideas. They remembered the sacrifices I had made for all of them and refused to leave me to die on the ground, to be food for wild animals. They gently lifted me off the forest floor and lay me in the Red Cross wagon so I could be buried in a nearby cemetery. The convoy began to move and at daybreak came near a village where I was to be buried. As they removed me from the wagon the officers noticed with amazement that I had regained consciousness and rushed to give me as much care possible. To provide some relief from the pain I was administered morphine from the reserve of the doctor. My wounds were cleaned and bandages made from torn strips of cotton obtained from the skirts of the peasants in the village. For a long time morphine was the only medicine I had to release me from the pain that ravaged my head and face."

"We continued our journey and joined forces with General Kornilov, who was moving ever closer to Ekaterinodar with the intention of claiming back the city for the White Army. In full hope and expectation of victory we approached our assigned positions for the battle and we were camped in the brick factory on the Kuban River."

"In the beginning, the inaccurate shots of the Bolsheviks favoured our plan to pass the river Kuban. Our patrols saw the stampede of Bolsheviks as they tried to leave the city and the White Army continued to push across the river to the outskirts of the city. At that same moment a volley of artillery fire from the Bolsheviks rained on the tower of the brick factory which had been chosen as an observatory by General Kornilov, killing him instantly."

"The panic this provoked amongst the soldiers meant that General Denikin was forced to order a retreat. It was rapid and brutal. No painter could ever capture the tragic scenes of our flight. We left behind our wounded comrades, among them boys of fifteen and seventeen who cried for their mothers, and prayed for us to take them with us, or at least provide a coup-de-grace to stop them falling into the hands of the Bolsheviks."

"The place where we buried General Kornilov remained unknown to the soldiers. A committee was selected and, after taking a solemn oath, had the task of finding a suitable place. It was to be as hidden as possible because they did not want the burial site, or the body, of General Kornilov violated. I would expect that in the next few days there would be a solemn funeral for this hero of the White Army.

"The march back to Rostov was long and arduous and after several weeks of walking I was admitted to hospital and received surgery on my wounds. They removed the bullet, which had damaged the nerves and prevented me from chewing. Although it was removed, it took longer to wean me from my dependency on morphine, but now you can see me in all my goodness" Thais concluded her story with a sad smile.

After the victorious entry into the city, the first thought of the army was for the funeral of General Kornilov. President Rodzianko and his son Nicolai returned from exile and were once again my guests. The President gave orders to the same committee that had provided the burial of the General to locate the temporary burial site, exhume the body, and bring it to Ekaterinodar for a full military burial. The whole White Army was waiting for news of the arrival of the body, scheduled for noon, but the wait was longer than expected. The flowers that had been arranged for the tributes were beginning to wilt and I was begged to make available the facility of the old icebox. I asked Timote to take over the preparations and ensure that the floral tributes were transported to the icebox in the garden.

Poor Timote, having brought the flowers to the villa, lifted the lid of the icebox and suddenly heard the ghostly echo of a voice calling from below. Frightened out of his wits he ran to me in the drawing room shouting at the top of his voice, "The dead speak lady, come with me and hear it. The dead speak!"

We both gingerly peered over the edge of the now open icebox. I leaned right down in order to better hear whatever it was that Timote heard and then:

"I beg you, do not betray me, ma'am," we heard. "My companions have tried poison to get rid of me. Save me! I will never forget your good heart and your generosity."

He was crying and trembling from the cold, after spending three days on the ice, lying on the straw that was put to keep it fresh and cold. I recognized the soldier we had found in the living room when the Bolsheviks had fled the house. I gave orders to Timote to bring civilian clothes and a coat for him. After a few minutes, the dead was transformed into the living and was out of hiding in the icebox, but, perhaps, reduced instead to hiding from the White Army. We said goodbye and he kissed my hand and promised that he would, at once, return to the White Army and help in their fight against the Bolsheviks. I will never know whether or not he held that promise, but as Timote closed the gate behind him, I felt very relieved and I turned to my old servant and friend and made him promise that this incident would remain a secret between us. He nodded, smiled and went about his business.

Meanwhile, the commission in charge of the exhumation had arrived back and were in deep conference with President Rodzianko. It was obvious, given the animated discussions being held, that the report they were giving was serious. Bearing in mind what I had witnessed, I suspect I already knew what had happened. Suddenly President Rodzianko, looking extremely concerned, came into my room and asked if I still had the Bolshevik newspapers that reported the description of the funeral of General Kornilov. I tried feverishly to remember where I had put the newspaper (the state of excitation of the President troubled me) and I found it in Thomas's desk and gave it to the President. From his uneasy glance I sensed the tragedy that upset him, the coffin of General Kornilov could not be found and the fate that had befallen the General, at the time described in detail in the Red Army papers, was unfortunately correct.

My nerves were shattered and the events of the past few days made me worry for my family, and what would happen in the war between the Red and White Armies. Thomas, also, was feeling the strain; he had not heard from, or spoken to, his family from which we had been separated for so long. With no news, the absence was keenly felt. After what seemed like an eternity the Polish passports arrived courtesy of Count Ledochowski. We began to prepare for the lengthy and precarious trip to Poland, one that was frowned upon by President Rodzianko, who envisaged that this latest victory was the final nail in the Bolshevik coffin. He based this belief on his rejection of the proposal of help from the Germans who, at that time, occupied the Ukraine and part of the Caucasus. They had offered to clear the entire Caucasus from the revolutionary threats, and, in return, they asked the supply of grain necessary to feed Germany.

"If I accepted the German offer," said the President, "what a miserable figure I would cut for Russia at the peace conference, in the guise of an ally of England and France!" The topic was sensitive and I found myself in agreement with him. The Russians, by nature, are not speculators, and alliances bear the consequences that often weapons are turned against themselves.

On September 4th 1918, my relatives and friends, including President Rodzianko and his son Nicolai, gathered at Ekaterinodar railway station. We said our emotional goodbyes on the platform and entered our carriage. The train slowly began to move away and detach itself from that group of loved ones who, excited for me, waved farewell. It gathered pace and the increasingly rapid motion was matched only by the tears that flowed down my cheeks. My eyes were dimmed as, through the window, I watched the familiar landscape pass by. There was no doubt I loved my country, I just did not love where it was at that moment; but I was sure that as always, it would balance itself and all would be well. Night fell quickly and outside the darkness covered the view like a funeral cloak and took away all that I had seen.

The following morning we arrived in Rostov and had to break our travel with a visit to the German High Command, in order to obtain a special permit to continue the journey on the territory occupied by German troops. We believed the meeting would last only a short while and were looking forward to continuing our journey the next day. However as with all the best laid plans the trip was postponed when Thomas fell ill with Spanish flu.

Meanwhile the political situation was worsening by the day. The German defeat was accomplished and with the cessation of the war began the movement for the return of the military. Indescribable chaos reigned across all ranks and all nations. Travelling in this atmosphere of extreme excitement was a very dangerous and difficult proposition and one that we were going to have to accept. With Thomas recovered we finally left Rostov. The train was packed with refugees. Every available seat and space was taken, luggage racks were full and refugees were sleeping on floors, in toilets, in any free space, even standing up!

We arrived, at night, in Kharkov and now faced an equally daunting set of difficulties. With the influx of soldiers and refugees a place to sleep would be impossible to find. The German military had requisitioned the hotels, pensions and private homes of any size and our driver told us it would be impossible to find anywhere free. Thomas, however was made of sterner stuff, and refused to accept the situation. Trusting his good fortune, he must have visited every hotel, boarding house and guest house in Kharkov without success. Eventually our driver, moved by our despair, proposed we make one last attempt to seek asylum with one of his acquaintances who was a caretaker of a villa. It was then that Thomas recalled that Mr Toplitz, a friend of his brother's, lived in Kharkov but as he unfortunately did not know the address he would have to accept the kind proposal of our carriage driver.

Fatigued by the hours spent dragging his carriage through the avenues, the streets and the dimly lit alleys of a city unknown to us, made even more mysterious by the dark night, we finally stopped in front of a wrought-iron gate. Thomas lit a match, looking for the bell: he read the name of the owner – Toplitz! We heard the bell sound beyond the gate and a light flickered on. A waiter came out of the door of a splendid villa and approached to open the gate. We told him of our situation and about Thomas's brother and, apologising for the absence of the owner, he invited us into the house. Mr Toplitz, he explained, would return soon from his club. We did not hesitate to accept his invitation and follow him into the villa. We passed through some beautifully furnished rooms and up to the first floor where there was a large, well populated, library. It was here that we sat and waited for our potential host.

We sat for a few hours, fighting the onset of heavy eyes and trying to stay awake. Then we heard footsteps approaching and, reanimated, we composed ourselves, trying not to seem too overcome by fatigue, and prepared to welcome our host with a broad smile. We wasted a torrent of words expressing our sincere apologies for the invasion of his privacy as the gentleman who entered, having listened patiently to our explanations replied, "I'm not Mr Toplitz, I am in a similar position!"

Mr Toplitz eventually arrived and we will never forget the unconditional and sincere hospitality shown to us. Having heard our story he arranged for his servant to reserve train tickets for the next day, in itself no easy feat. He also assured us that the housing situation in Kiev would be exactly the same as in Kharkov. In anticipation of this he offered us the address of a room that had been reserved for his secretary on a business trip in a small, rather charming, hotel. Our time in Kiev could have been worse than that of Kharkov if it had not been for Mr Toplitz and his address.

Another long train journey and another arrival at night, but we did not need to waste any time seeking accommodation. We went directly to the hotel recommended by Mr Toplitz and were immediately offered a small room, with two folding iron beds and a coffee table, together with a servant's room for Gaby. The next morning we woke once again ready to continue our journey. I was feeling a little unwell and Thomas looked at me with a worried frown.

"Your face is flushed," he observed and went downstairs to get a thermometer. My temperature had risen to 40 degrees and Thomas immediately called a local doctor, who confirmed the diagnosis we had already suspected: Spanish flu. Doctor Rusczyc said it would be impossible to fight the illness in the room we had and recommended we seek alternative rooms. Thomas went out with the doctor in search of more appropriate accommodation and I sat with Gaby, feeling absolutely terrible. As they left the room Gaby woke and asked me to tell her a story. I looked at her and tried to smile, already I was finding it hard to speak.

After two hours Thomas returned, accompanied by two nurses. They laid me on a stretcher and carried me to an ambulance, essentially just a cage with iron bars in a window, which reminded me of a box for dogs. It was pulled by a horse so weak that, to move, they were forced to ask some curious passers-by, who had stopped to watch the spectacle, to push the vehicle to the point where the road went down a slight incline. Arriving at our new home, not far from the small hotel where we had spent the night, the owner, seeing my serious condition, refused to allow us in, fearing that we would be the cause of an epidemic she apologised by saying that having lost her daughter the previous week she did not intend to witness yet another tragedy.

Thomas and I tried to calm her, assuring her that my illness was due only to a slight weakness caused by the strain of the long journey from Russia and to prove the truth of his assertions invited me to sit up. With the best will in the world I knew this would be impossible and all I could do was turn my head and plead to her with my eyes. She looked at me for a moment then turned and opened the door. Crying I was taken and put to bed in a large, bright and airy room, and promptly fell asleep.

Thomas left me in the care of the nurses and was returned to our original hotel to collect our bags. He was just passing through the centre when, to his great surprise, he met the Timofiews, a couple we had known well in Petersburg. They were passing through Kiev, bound for Siberia, in order to join the army of Admiral Aleksander Kolczak. They told Thomas where they were staying and arranged to meet the following day, and for days after each time they asked about my health.

There came a point of crisis in my illness and Dr Rusczyc, fearing for my life, suggested Thomas should look for some particular medicine. He explained it would not be found on the free market for all medicines had been requisitioned by the German Military. It was, though, available on the black market but he would need contacts, as the sellers were notoriously suspicious of strangers. Thomas went out in search of this precious product and, after a long search, managed to get the required amount from a dealer. The price was that of the underground, a bracelet with emeralds and diamonds: money had no value.

The Germans, preparing to return home, had transferred the government of Ukraine to Hetman Skoropadsky. This resulted in exposure to constant threats by revolutionaries, be they Ukrainians, Vynnychnko or Petliura, and that, after the liberation of the territory from the Germans, they all progressed in their efforts to wrest Ukraine from Russia.

I was beginning my recovery, but still in bed, when our friends the Timofiews arrived. They were extremely agitated and after a few moments they asked us if they might shelter in our room for the night. The reason for their audacious request, they explained, was a rumour that revolutionaries had threatened to blow up the temporary hospital at midnight. It was where injured officers of the White Army had been admitted and the hospital was in the same building as their apartment. The fear of death and the lack of beds in Kiev significantly outweighed the possible contagion of Spanish flu, and the inconvenience they would cause to a sick family, but we were, as far as they were concerned, the last resort.

All this happened in the hallway outside my bedroom and

Thomas came in to tell me of his decision and discuss practicalities. We had to accept the imposition, he said, they were friends and many friends and acquaintances had been extraordinarily helpful and kind to us. I agreed but was more concerned about the sleeping arrangements we owed them a debt of gratitude in finding us rooms.

It was decided that Ms Timofiew would sleep in my bed and Mr Timofiew would share with Thomas. And so it was, Mrs Timofiew went into my room, undressed and rested in the custom of our mother Eve. That was apparently her habit. The two husbands stripped in the hall and in the dark, groping, they reached the bed of Thomas. A quartet of voices intoned the wishes of goodnight, although were all convinced that we would be spending the most miserable night imaginable. In the darkness and silence, pretending to sleep, actually we heard the beat of hours by a nearby bell tower.

There were twelve beats – midnight.

That's when the explosion shook our walls, rattled the windows and I leapt from my bed completely forgetting our lack of clothing. The noise of the explosions continued to echo in the air and I was afraid to ask the fate of the wounded soldiers who were lying in hospital.

Sleep was now a far distant memory and Timofiew ventured out into the street to try to establish what was happening. He returned shortly after with rumours of the revolutionary army approaching the city with the express intention of bringing down the government of Hetman Skoropadsky.

"We must not lose time," said Timofiew. "We have to escape the hell that awaits us if we linger. I sincerely hope that you will also take recourse to the same action."

After breakfast that morning the Timofiews took their leave of us and began their preparations for their return to Siberia to join Admiral Kolczak.

I was still recovering when Thomas met Prince Chervaschadze and was invited to eat with him to celebrate the opening of a new club. We ate a great lunch, well served in a large room furnished with taste and elegance, adjacent to the game room. Here, sitting already at the tables were several players, bourgeois and military. The majority was composed of German soldiers, including a colonel whom the fates had treated particularly well that day, judging by the money accumulated in front of him. Thomas could never resist the attraction of the game and, leaving me in the company of friends, moved away to take a seat at a table by the door of the restaurant.

Still feeling quite weak, my health would not let me do the small hours so, at midnight I went to the dining room to look for Thomas. The curtain separating the two rooms was opened and at the same instant I saw, come forward from the door opposite, Ukrainian soldiers, machine guns shouldered and shouting. During the momentary confusion as the players at the tables reacted, I managed to pull Thomas inside the restaurant and to escape. The director of the club, seeing what was happening, and realising we were looking for refuge, pointed to a cellar door and accompanied us down. At the bottom was a small room where he kept a huge amount of fine wines. Other customers, realising we had found a place to hide, rushed in behind us, *en masse*, to safety. Things were now more dangerous in the cellar than upstairs in the gaming room. The pressure of the crowd in such a small place caused bottles of wine to rain down from the shelves as they tipped and began to fall on our heads. In the ensuing panic I again managed to grab Thomas, open the door and flee outside. On leaving I saw through the entrance of the restaurant, German soldiers, armed with grenades, had arrived to face the Ukrainians.

A command rang out: "No one moves from here!"

On this occasion only our perfect knowledge of the German language allowed us to sneak out into the hall where, helped by a German soldier, we could get out of the way and into the night. Outside it was freezing with a full moon. We breathed a huge sigh of relief; the cold air so pleasant after the overheated atmosphere of the club, and we blessed our salvation. God must have been with us, again.

Given our recent uncomfortable incidents, although I was not fully recovered we began to make preparations for the continuation of our journey. We paid large sums of money to black market speculators for our railway tickets and managed to procure places on the last train that would leave Kiev. We arrived at the station in the evening in plenty of time to board the train and mingled with the fugitives who could not hide their excitement at leaving, and their nervousness about the uncertainty of their departure. We spent almost two hours waiting and the tension rose to its climax when a voice over the tannoy system announced: "Travellers to Warsaw please have your tickets ready for inspection and boarding."

A mass of people rushed toward the entrance, fighting desperately for places on the train. I hung grimly on to Thomas's arm as he pushed and wriggled his way through this desperate surge of humanity with Gaby in his arms and myself being dragged behind. Eventually we managed to get into a carriage and sat there, relieved, with Gaby on our laps, watching the hysterical free-for-all outside as refugees clamoured to get onto the train. Because of the proximity of the front line there was no lighting on the train, so we sat in the dark, silent, in a state of apprehension, fearing that the battle for seats on the crowded train was not yet over.

The wait for the train to commence its journey seemed endless, and, as the time passed, we marvelled at just how many people were now in the carriages. At the back of our minds was always the risk that everything would be cancelled and we would be back at where we started, but at last, with a sudden jolt, the locomotive nosed to the front of the train and coupled to the carriages. Moments later came another jolt as the engine started to pull its load, slowly at first, away from the station. There was a squeal from the protesting wheels as they began to turn, metal against metal, and with effort as if the track itself was an obstacle. We were moving at walking pace, the platform only slowly receding, faces moving in and out of focus outside the smoke begrimed window. This slow pace continued for several kilometres and it seemed that it would take forever to reach Warsaw. I overheard a fellow passenger explain the reasons for this slow progress. The train was due to pass over land that had been mined to thwart the offensive of the revolutionaries. Thomas held Gaby a little tighter and we thanked heavens we are not at the front of the train. Nevertheless the fear in the carriage was palpable.

Beyond the danger zone the train began to move at a more regular speed. At every station at which we stopped, a mass of people assaulted our carriages, seeking to find space to sit, stand, lie, anything to get away from the conflict around them, and that which was expected. The crowd was now like animals in a barn, the atmosphere hot and sweaty, the odour appalling and there was no room to move. One could not go to the toilet; in fact I was not sure there even was one on the train! Our inhibitions had been cast aside, and at this point humanity was no different from animals.

At our arrival in Warsaw we received the first news of our family. Thomas discovered that his mother had died and that his father had moved back to Vienna. It was with this sad news that we realised our journey was still not yet over.

Vienna – a city in which we found so many cherished memories. At once elegant and cheerful, with unparalleled splendour, dazzling visitors with gaiety and music and kindness and the knowledge of how to live. That day we found it completely different from the friendly city we once knew. The streets were crowded with soldiers of different nationalities, and Viennese civilians with backpacks on their shoulders. Their faces were sad and worried as they wandered through poorly lit streets looking for food to feed themselves. Vienna was dying of shame. Thomas's father lived in a smart apartment, luxuriously furnished. I appreciated that we were privileged but we still suffered from the same deprivations; we spent our evening in the dark talking about the habitual lack of provisions. These conditions did not help to improve my health, which had still not yet fully recovered.

I succumbed to a deep depression that manifested itself in an exaggerated nostalgia for my loved ones whose presence I missed sharply. I wrote to them, giving my address in Vienna, all the while doubting that the correspondence would reach its destination, as all communications with Russia were more than a little problematic. Thomas's relatives suggested I tried some hypnosis sessions, and they appeared to be successful. I began to actively attend to the problems facing us rather than trying to ignore them. My father-in-law's money, converted into cheques, had become merely a pile of waste paper with little or no value. The devaluation of the currency encouraged a dangerous contempt of money. The sense of saving that had previously been inherent in every citizen was deemed pointless.

The mentality of the new generation was germinating in a red-hot atmosphere of convenience and immediacy. At the expense of almost every tradition it sought unbridled pleasure.

In this hedonistic melting pot Jazz was the rhythm that resonated in the air, obsessing men and women alike with the frenzy of its music. We felt perfectly immune from this mania; we were regulars, instead, of the symphony concerts of the wonderful Viennese orchestra and its famous soloists: Kreisler, Huberman, and Piccaver. On the stages of concert halls and theatres, their perfect execution shone for the exceptional talent they possessed. Our good friend Monsieur von Laszcz, a Polish widower, used to gather at his home a select group of famous artists of the Burg Theatre in order to distract from his solitude.

One day I had the opportunity to meet in his house the famous Raoul Aslan, who had taken over from Alexander Moissi. We had many an interesting conversation and argument in which he praised the Russian artists who had managed to escape the revolution and were then celebrated by Austrian colleagues. That evening, after taking leave of the master of the house, we went out with some friends to the 'Opera Bar', to listen to some Viennese light music, with singer Jacques Rotter. The bar cannot be compared to any other place in the world, even of the same genre. It is typically Austrian, a place where the public goes to drink the last drink of the evening to the sound of a discreet music performed by a good pianist or a great singer. It is a distinctive meeting point of beautiful Viennese society so that every celebrity passing, after the success of a concert hall, cannot fail but make a detour to the bar in order to enjoy that very particular aspect of Viennese life.

We were sitting around a table, when we saw Arthur Rubinstein appear. He entered the room and was enthusiastically applauded by all present. We looked at each other for just a brief moment and he immediately recognized us and, amazed, he approached our table.

"What a surprise!" he exclaimed. "After ten years, and still looking so young and so slim." He sat down with us and told us of his long years in Spain, under the protection of King Alfonso XIII. The meeting with Arthur awakened memories of distant and happy times, times before the storm clouds came across and inexorably made everything so dark, so bleak and so black.

My nostalgia for my distant homeland resurfaced and was made more acute with the passing of the years. Thomas's father decided to leave Vienna to return to the residence of his family in Lviv and, forced to move, we agreed to cohabitation with our neighbour and family friend, an English widow, Mrs MacHarvey. It was to this address there arrived, on a beautiful spring day, the first letter from my sister Valentina. The envelope was stamped from Turkey and, judging from the date at the top of the letter had been traveling for four months, but no address was given to which I could answer. The letter was short but nonetheless so welcome. It read:

"I am writing these lines with very little hope that they can reach you but with faith regardless. With a group of recent refugees, my husband and I arrived at Constantinople where I was admitted to a clinic. After a short while I gave birth to our first child and once we have settled we intend to come in search of you. With God's help we will find you. I have so many things to tell. I hug you. Tina."

Meanwhile the world was changing. Poland was recognised, Latvia, Lithuania and Estonia came to be, and three empires slowly sank, the Austrian-Hungarian, the Russian and the Ottoman. It would take a few more years and several more treaties before all was complete but the cost, for now, was enormous. In four years of war sixteen million people had died and yet we found ourselves living in a world where we didn't know to which country we belonged. In Russia the revolution was over but civil war would continue until the White Army capitulated in June 1923. I had realised that peace was a strange word, and was also a precarious state to manage.

We were established in Vienna and Thomas was certain that there were new oil wells to be drilled. "There has to be hope," he would say, "otherwise it is just a pipe dream." I began to believe him. I had decided that Vienna was my favourite city and I was determined to make my life there. With this in mind I sent a letter to Poland, to the friends who had been looking after our belongings and furniture, asking them to please forward them to Vienna. I was thankful that I had kept my father's furniture, as it was all now that I had left of him. There was nothing left in Russia, all was gone. It was a sad realisation.

Vienna slowly awoke from its slumber and life started again. There was suddenly a vibrancy in the streets, enough for a small charge of gas, to impress people. The streets were illuminated again, shops started exhibiting art and passers-by began again to stop and look. Old habits returned; at noon the elite found themselves in Kartnerstrasse and elegant gentlemen would greet beautiful women with 'Kuss die Hand gnadige'.

One day with Gaby, now six years old, we were walking

along the Kartnerstrasse heading towards the cathedral of St Stephen. I wanted to show her the church where Thomas and I had celebrated our marriage. We stood in front of the altar and I described the scene for her, the guests, the priest, and our parents and told her all the details. It brought back memories and as I finished I paused for a moment lost in thought. It was then that Gaby tugged my hand and asked, "And where was I sitting?" I could only smile.

Back home we ate early as Mrs MacHarvey had organised a reception for us. As we passed through the hallway she asked me to help in the finishing touches and told me the names of the guests and the arrangement of the groups at the tables.

"Miss von Call with Baron Riedl, Lord von Jurie with the beautiful Lady Quittner close, your husband, etc., etc., Then for you a very distinguished friend in whom I have a particular interest, Colonel Koschul. I would like your help in managing an introduction to the Colonel, and perhaps the important thing is to let him know the state of my finances. I think that at the moment this is the only difficulty that prevents him from marrying! With your innate skills in diplomacy I am sure that you would be able to inform him, subtly and in a few discreetly dropped sentences, my situation."

This task was not a nice one, neither was it an easy one, but I did owe Mrs MacHarvey a debt of gratitude, so I prepared, nevertheless, to hold a conversation with Colonel Koschul. At five o'clock, on time, the guests arrived. Mrs MacHarvey wore a dress of violet chiffon dripping with jewels of significant value and well prepared to make the desired impact on her prey. Finally the waitress, Olga, announced the arrival of the last guest, Colonel Koschul. Tall, of impeccable elegance, with a rich and well-groomed head of greying hair, his big blue eyes seemed to have great depth and I could imagine many women drowning in their placid pools. As he entered the living room, the ladies instinctively gave a quick glance to the big mirror placed above the fireplace, to be reassured of their perfect beauty, and then greeted him with exaggerated cordiality.

The guests, each assigned place, held a lively and interesting conversation. The Colonel was generous in his praise and, sitting down next to me, began to address a few gallant words of greeting.

"My Lady, I am happy to meet you at last; this is a wonderful surprise."

"We have met already, with my friends, but I regret it was only from a distance."

"Your appearance in Vienna was indeed an event..."

"You are Russian, I have so much interest in your language, and it is beautiful. You must not refuse me the honour of being one of your students..."

And so on. So much so that the dialogue that I had imagined, became a monologue that exasperated me. As the speech continued Mrs MacHarvey was aggravating my discomfort with repeated looks and raised eyebrows. I tried to change the subject alluding to the elegance and the refined taste of the hostess, all things which the Colonel amiably ignored, preferring instead to continue on the topic of sympathy for Russia, in which he appeared to show a great interest.

The dinner was nearly over and the time to leave was drawing ever closer. I tried to catch Thomas's eye but he was deep in conversation, and I worried about the consequences and the questions that would be asked of me by our hostess.

I felt a chill with the departure of the last guest, as a feeling of guilt seized me. Mrs MacHarvey rushed over to me, asking me to give her all the details of my long conversation with the Colonel. By what means could I explain how difficult the situation had been and yet, at the same time, reassure her of the success of my assignment, even though I had obviously failed miserably. I suggested that the Colonel probably needed a little more time in order to make a decision on a subject so important and finally, exhausted, I retreated to my room. Thomas, accompanied by his friends, was just going out for a small drink at the Opera Bar.

I lay in bed wondering for a while if I could have completed my task any differently. The answer to myself was 'no' and I soon fell into so deep a sleep that I did not even wake upon the return of Thomas. The following morning I rose unusually early, and ate breakfast alone, not waiting for the rest of my family to join me. I arranged for a taxi to take me to the Imperial Hotel. Although normally impossible to obtain rooms there, with the intervention of the director, I was able to book a room with two beds and continued on my mysterious mission.

I then visited the Institute of Nurses, chose one, and left with the order that she should present herself the next morning at the Imperial Hotel when all would become clear. I was about to return home when I realised I had forgotten one important essential: the time of the arrival of the train from Turkey. Trains were overseen by l'Agenzia Cook and I entered their offices and asked the clerk for the latest information about the arrival of the train from Turkey.

"Direct communication with Turkey has not been

restored," he said, "because of a conflict with a neighbouring country. However a train made up of wagons from different countries, Yugoslavia, Greece, Turkey comes through once a week, at twelve midday or half-past eleven at night. I have to warn you though the times are purely hypothetical!"

I was at the station at midday and it was clear that I would have to wait until the late night train arrived. I went home to have lunch in the company of Mrs MacHarvey who interrogated me with questions that I could not answer.

I turned to Thomas and proposed that we go out together that evening. Thomas, surprised by the idea, asked if there was a special reason for this sudden and unexpected request.

"You are the special reason," I said, "I am going to the station tonight to pick up my sister Tina. She arrives at half-past eleven and I did not want to go there and wait alone. So I ask you to accompany me. Will you?"

Both Thomas and Mrs MacHarvey were surprised by this revelation and once again questions were fired at me and once again I had no answers to give them. They both thought my imagination had run amok and that perhaps I was having a nervous breakdown. To prevent further discussion I retired to my room to calm my nerves which were jangling with anticipation.

That evening I went with Thomas to the Kaiser Bar where the excellent music from their pianist Ravicz almost made us forget the hypothetical time for the arrival of the train.

As soon as I became aware of the time, and because there were no taxis, I ran to catch the bus, Thomas behind me, complaining and grumbling. We climbed aboard the bus; Thomas did not speak but the expression on his face told all its disappointment and discontent. On the last part of the journey, along Prinz Eugenstrasse, the old engine of the bus refused to climb the slope and all attempts of the driver to re-start it were useless. The engine would not turn. I jumped off and ran to the station, and didn't stop until I reached the Sudbahn, just as the train pulled in. Thomas was breathless beside me as I stopped at the exit near the platform controller. I glanced quickly at those who had already begun to pass through the exit gate and then, not having seen Tina, I stared fixedly along the platform and into the darkness. Thomas joined me, furious, reproaching me, "Do you not see the result of your childish doings?" he remonstrated. "Maybe now you should see a medical specialist." Patiently asking him to calm down I continued my watch on the passengers disembarking from the train. I asked him politely if he could do me the pleasure of taking a look at the last wagon of that long train.

Bored, Thomas started in the direction of the final carriage that was way further down the station. I continued to scan the passengers leaving the train through the station exit. I heard behind me a whistle, but for some reason ignored it. A few moments of silence followed, and then the whistle again. I suddenly recognised it as Thomas's, the same whistle his father would use to attract attention. I turned my head towards where Thomas had disappeared and peered into the gloom of the station and saw only shadowy figures approaching. I looked more closely and then, into view, I saw Thomas, on one arm was Tina, my sister and next to her, her husband, their child in his arms.

I ran towards them and could not see for the tears that streamed down my cheeks. I hugged my sister tightly and a myriad of emotions ran through me, of love, amazement, happiness and also a host of questions to ask. But first we hailed a taxi to take us to the Imperial Hotel.

I could not sleep that night, and slowly and gently Tina informed me of my brothers. Vladimir had fallen in combat. Before leaving for that last mission he had removed the small bracelet I had given him many years ago as a birthday present and given it to a Red Cross nurse. He asked that she keep it safely until his return but, if he fell in battle, then it should be returned to me.

Those times had not been a friend for the White Army, decimated and exhausted by the long and continued fighting; their opponents were being reinforced and supplied from the warehouses of our allies. In 1920, at Perekop, incited by propaganda, the Red Army had massacred the White Army rearguard, which had fought heroically to cover the retreat of the last of their comrades. The survivors managed to board ships that carried the husks of men, wounded in body and soul, away from the the coast of their country. A dense fog had fallen, as if nature was providing the inexorable final curtain. The battle was a key episode in the civil war and the last act of the tragedy of the White Army. In the vastness of the appropriately named Black Sea the ships continued through the fog en route to Constantinople.

Millions of Russians, fleeing persecution from their fate, now appeared on the stage of the world to perform in the most different roles. In Paris, London and in New York we found them working as sweepers, porters, drivers, cooks and waiters. Their courage, energy, inventiveness and, of course, talent was not slow to be noticed, especially in art. Writers, painters, musicians, dancers, Russians attracted the admiration of the people that now hosted them. Even the subsequent Russian generation, who remembered little or nothing of their country felt tied by the stories of their parents. These stories were told in tears; they were of suffering and sacrifice, but always they hankered to return to their now distant homeland. The revolution and all its consequences, they said, were nothing but a new invasion of Genghis Khan, the most cruel killer and destroyer, who had occupied Russia in 1224, reducing it to a 'clean slate' and forcing the inhabitants into shameful slavery. It was sad and disheartening that our world had not found a remedy to such incursions over the past seven hundred years. Perhaps it never would.

The presence of my sister in Vienna was a great relief for me. My brother-in-law, associated with Viennese industry, had hoped to rebuild his fortune lost in Russia during the revolution. His plans, however, went badly wrong as the consequence of his poor assessment of the opportunities that existed for development. He quickly decided that it might be beneficial to move, with his family, to Paris.

Their departure coincided with a happy event in my home, the birth of the second child, Benita Krystyna. The first name was chosen for its true meaning, blessed. This wonderful small creature, born in a period of disruption and anxieties arising from the wars, could, with her innocent smile, dissipate our anxieties and replace them with happiness and relief.

Thomas was by now more than ever convinced that the Kartnerstrasse was not a suitable place for the rise of oil wells, and departed for Poland in search of work in his real job. Recommended by colleagues, he got in touch with the coal industry of Katowice and after several months of absence he returned suggesting that we should move to the city. As I watched the packaging of furniture to be shipped from Vienna to Katowice I received a telegram from Thomas. "Plans have changed, we will now be moving instead to Gdansk. Will now be a representative of Kaiser Wollheim associated with Polish Company 'Progress'. Thomas."

In the year 1921 Gdansk was proclaimed a free city under the control of the League of Nations, that regulated the passage of traffic in the port. The Poles had hoped that the city would be incorporated into Poland but the Germans still represented a majority of the population, so instead of being placed under Polish sovereignty it was declared a free city, an independent quasi-state. The Germans, not unnaturally, preferred incorporating it into Germany. The centuries-old mistrust between Poles and Germans made the mutual relations an interesting minefield which led to on-going tensions which, in turn, would come home to roost in a few year's time.

Gdansk though, is a beautiful Gothic town with delightful surroundings of green boulevards, elegant gardens and superb forests. A long avenue of trees, planted at the time of the Napoleonic occupation, links the city with seaside resorts including the famous Sopot.

My first meeting with the owners of the company, Messrs Droge and Arnold Kuhnheim, ended with a high degree of mutual respect which was to bond us in a friendship that would endure for many a year, particularly with the young Arnold Kuhnheim, heir of a noble German family, and dubbed the 'charming prince' for his remarkable resemblance to the Prince of Wales.

After so long leading an almost nomadic lifestyle and never having quite settled for a variety of reasons, I wanted our new villa to be as comfortable as possible. I was now hoping that at last we could settle and so I suggested to Thomas a few changes that could be made which would better suit our taste and also would help cement friendships for business. His easy-going manner soon won the sympathy of colleagues and he managed to convince them that, for the good of the two countries, and of the business, they had to focus on business and leave behind the political discords. In a short time both Germans and Poles became good friends and would mix comfortably in our home. We gave frequent receptions that, although challenging, were tailored to the needs of our social position. The task however was not easy and it was necessary to ensure that the staff were especially chosen and could be as good at diplomacy as we needed to be.

The exception was finding a chef. It was not easy to find one who was truly really capable in the culinary arts. I soon realised, having lunched with the various families who had invited Thomas, that the menu offered was always the same in all the houses. I finally established that its origin was from the famous restaurant on Jopengasse, 'Martin Lautenbacher'.

One day I found myself with some friends in Sopot at a luncheon at the Casino-Hotel, an imposing building on the beach with an excellent restaurant and large terraces overlooking the bay. I had the idea to ask the waiter if, by chance, he knew of a *chef de cuisine* that might be looking for work. I assured him that his interest would be rewarded and left my address. We stayed most of the day and, at the end of the evening, Thomas and his friends moved to the Casino gaming room to the roulette table that my husband felt often played favourably for him. It was hard to convince him that luck was as fragile as glass and that it takes only a moment for both to shatter! Nevertheless together with his friends, also lovers of this game of luck and chance, he paid his dues for the fun, excitement and the nervous anticipation as the ball flew round the wheel. It would run free then, as its velocity slowed, it would begin to tap the dividers between the numbers, slower still and the ball, with mesmerising efficiency, would bounce in and out of colours and numbers, one moment yours, the next not. I watched for a while, and looked around at the green carpet in the great hall, lit by huge crystal chandeliers reflecting light through the large picture windows that looked out onto the beach. Viewed from there the building was like a great beacon of light that magically attracted the fireflies to their tables, eager to fight with luck. I walked out into the night and admired the paintings of nature, the moon on a placid sea, the shadows of the trees reflected in the windows of the casino, I sighed and finally made my way home, alone.

June 1st 1931, Benita was celebrating her sixth birthday and it was time to replace the nurse with a housekeeper and to prepare Benita for the exams that would allow her to enter the Ursuline Convent. I had to confess that the end of her first week would remain vivid in my memory. This small whirlwind, a veritable tornado, blew through the door in floods of tears and ran to hug me. When she had finally finished sobbing, and could catch her breath she begged me to change her name. She could, she declared passionately, no longer be known as Benita, she renounced all ownership of it.

Stunned I asked why, and she explained:

"Every time I go into class," she sobbed, "all my classmates stand up and scream, Good morning Mussolini!"

At her baptism no one could have predicted such a possibility! However we agreed that perhaps we could use her second name in order to make life a little more pleasant at school. She declared that from this day on she would be known as Krystyna; it seemed to do the trick at school anyway.

At home we were in the middle of intense preparations for a big reception in honour of some important business personalities in Gdansk when Felix, the waiter, said there was someone at the door who, in his opinion, had not been included on the guest list. Not to commit a social faux pas I asked Felix to please bring the visitor into the library. To my amazement I saw, in the hall in front of me, a look-alike of Tsar Nicholas II. The distinct shape, brown hair, a beard treated the same way and especially the almond shaped eyes, green-blue in colour, tender and veiled in melancholy struck me deeply. He wore a well-cut dark blue suit and from a distance he saluted with a bow of impeccable style. Noticing my obvious embarrassment, my uncertainty, he turned to me saying in perfect Russian straight from the pages of St Petersburg, "I hear you're looking for a chef."

"Do you have someone to offer me?" I ask, even more amazed.

"Yes," was his reply. "Myself."

Apart from his confession that he had worked in the Imperial kitchens in St Petersburg I had no time to ask further questions or establish any of his credentials as I was waiting for the arrival of our guests but I gave him an appointment for the next day.

I went upstairs to put the finishing touches to preparations for the lunch. I lit the candles on small tables prepared in the Louis XVI room hung with green silk mignonette. The guest list was eclectic and included the High Commissioner Count Gravina and his wife, the President of the Port and wife, M. and Madame de Loess, (he, a handsome man very distinguished, she, elegant and full of spirit). The beautiful couple Posek von Ritner, Nagurski and other Polish friends completed the group of invitees.

While talking with the Countess Gravina, a woman of great race and culture with wonderfully expressive eyes, she asked if I remembered a great artist of the past, Eleonora Duse, and then another star of the theatre who was trying to increase her reputation: Emma Gramatica. We continued on the subject of art and I spoke enthusiastically of the maestro Toscanini who I had heard, years earlier, in a performance in Vienna that I would never forget. We talked also about the last performance of Anna Pavlová, that wonderful Russian ballerina, who had enthralled the Auditorium of Vienna and all the Austrian aristocracy, the year after the first war in Europe, helping the audience forget, for a while, the past cruelty of wars, revolutions and massacres. While we were intent on reminiscing, the men finally finished their game of bridge and the guests began to leave.

The next day, as had been agreed, the Russian chef appeared. I confess that, after his revelation that he was chef of the imperial kitchen, I had the impression that his claims would have been more than adequate for my purposes and also that his demands would be way beyond my means. I tried to dissuade him from the idea that he would want to work for me, explaining that perhaps the tasks would be too menial, our cookery requirements too basic, and how different the environmental and economic situation would be between working in a private home and in the court of the Tsar. The chef, however, would not yield, and even managed to dispute all the reasons that I cited in an attempt to discourage him. Now his insistence, his manifest desire to come into our home, made me suspicious. Was he a Bolshevik spy?

The temptation to make sure of the services of an excellent cook was strong but I was looking for a pretext to dismiss him. I asked him what were his claims in terms of salary, hoping they were unacceptable.

"I do not wish any salary," he replied. This was an offer I feared even more than one with a lot of zeroes.

"I cannot accept your terms, then," I replied, "but please accept my thanks for considering us."

The chef did not move, instead he looked at me with pleading eyes and, in perfect Russian that sounded so sweet to my ear he said, "And I pray you to give me the chance of a little rest, a little quiet life in a private home? It's a dream I have been chasing for many years. Can you not help me cease this wandering and accept me?"

Moved by so much sincerity I could not refuse, and I accepted. Nicolai Krylov was his name.

During his first weeks in my house my suspicions faded. Krylov was unsurpassed in exercising his profession and his character was also excellent. With a quiet dignity he impressed the staff who spent most of the day gathered around him in admiration of his abilities, ready to execute any order or his desire often forgetting their own obligations and daily chores.

We were in June, a favourable season for shrimp. I asked the chef to prepare a *soupe d'ecrevisses.*

"And what price would you want, Madame?" he asked. I was guardedly surprised by the question, but he went on to explain. "In the market the price varies greatly; it can be as little as two roubles or as much as twenty roubles." I stared at him amazed and he continued, "If we take, for example, lobsters ordered specifically in Spain, and kept twenty-four hours in a bath of champagne, and then cooked in a chicken broth coming from Tuscany, that's when the price will reach the upper limit. But if instead we take the simple shrimp from our market, which are magnificent this month, we will achieve the same desired result at a cost much lower."

I was dazzled, and simply nodded. The soup was exquisite. To complete the menu, we were served a pistachio cream, brought on a platter of gold and trimmed with red roses that the cook had collected from our garden. The guests were enthusiastic about the composition and were not sparing in their congratulations to our Russian chef.

As usual, the coffee was served in the living room as the sun's rays shone through the windows that were wide open so you could see beyond the lawn, which looked like a wonderful carpet of lustrous green, to the colourful blooms of hydrangeas that ran alongside the paths. We were listening to the latest news on the radio. President Hindenburg had died and Adolf Hitler, who had been Chancellor, declared the office of President void and, as Führer and Chancellor, made himself head of state. Although born in Austria he had moved to Germany by the age of three and now we felt he was leading Germany into a new era, one that would bring serious consequences for

Gdansk. Hopes for a peaceful future began to recede and opinions and feeling, fuelled by discontent, began to circulate.

I followed with great interest the moves of the Germans who, in my opinion, made no secret of their war preparations. There were frequent military exercises that became increasingly aggressive. The restlessness saddened German women whose husbands and children were frequently called upon after hours spent in the office, workshop or school, to attend these practices. I was reminded of an incident that took place in front of our house when the last row in the line of these marching columns of children would wear cross-belts to which were attached red lights. By an oversight that night the last of the line was devoid of these belts and didn't have the red warning lights either. A truck driver, by mistake, came at speed down the road and ran into the rear of the marching column. Five of the children were killed instantly and at least a further ten were badly injured. They were brought to our house and the cries of the children calling for their mothers still to this day rings in my ears.

For quite some time I was worried about Gaby and how we could best continue her education. The events in Gdansk were becoming more serious. The German youth were educated to use weapons and there was a brooding cult of war and a hatred for the Poles around us. The chauvinist Hitler, had formed an atmosphere that was confused, unhealthy and full of insane excitement. The need to remove my daughter from this environment was obvious, and discussions with Thomas quickly established that we would leave, once again, for Switzerland.

When I arrived in Lausanne I was struck by a sudden wave of cherished memories that resurfaced in my mind. In Ouchy we went down to the Hotel Beau-Rivage. It had not changed, I could even find the place where my father would sit as he waited for our visits after classes. From the balcony in my room I had a delightful view of the lake and the garden, but I had also to locate a college for Gaby. I visited several colleges and decided at last on the Villa Cyrano School. It was a tearful separation from Gaby but with the reassurance we would see each other very soon I left Lausanne and continued my journey to Paris, where Thomas was waiting for me with my sister Tina and our cousin Nadia.

Nadia had gone to Paris after the death of her young and beautiful fiancé Nicolai, Prince Wolkonsky, who was killed in Yugoslavia at the beginning of her wanderings. Now settled, her natural beauty provided her distraction as a model for the fashion house Maggy Rouff, that had kept her busy and led to a degree of success. Her portrait on the cover of *Vogue* and the clothes created for her were the favourite of the elegant clientele. The success of Nadia fired the enthusiasm of my sister Tina who succeeded in her desire to enter the same fashion house, for the same work.

"The Russian beauty is en vogue," the director of the house told me as she accompanied me to my place for a fashion show. I sat in the front row, entranced by the beauty that passed by me, not just the models but also the clothes they wore. The parade of exquisite women with their perfect looks and their exaggerated walk, the swing of the hips. Then, my sister Tina, with her charming smile and perfect figure, descended down the catwalk, how appropriately named. Illuminated by spotlights she slowly stepped through the room followed by the other mannequins. One by one they disappeared behind the curtain only to emerge moments later looking even more sophisticated in another creation ever more elegant and ever more expensive.

The audience was entranced by those who wore those fabulous creations, but the real price of those outfits had been, of course, paid by the fatigue of the beautiful models, before the parade, the hours and months spent standing every day, trying on clothes in front of mirrors. The show over, Tina and I went home, Tina to look after her daughter, and I to hurry back to the hotel where Thomas was waiting.

"You realise," he said, "that the chef you have hired is really quite bizarre! He came to me and asked if he could offer me a gift of sable skins! He told me he was the owner of vast lands in Siberia that are used primarily to hunt down these precious and sought after animals. However the final straw is that different people have assured me that he attends the Casino on a regular basis where he is losing appreciable amounts of money on both roulette and blackjack!" Each of these revelations left me puzzled, for who knew where he was obtaining money to gamble? I therefore sent a telegram to Aunt Kozlowska asking her to find a way to fire him in our absence.

Our time in Paris was spent visiting celebrated monuments and museums, and I tried to meet with my old friend Marussia Savickaia. Before the revolution she had married a Cossack officer of the Imperial Guard, an adjutant of the Tsar. As an aide to the Tsarina they were assigned rooms at the Winter Palace just after they were married. Located on the quay of the Neva it was a wonderful setting but, with the revolution and the civil war, they had fled the country, along with so many of their countrymen, and settled the suburbs of Paris in a charming cottage in front of an airplane factory where her husband had invested much of his capital. An interval of fifteen years separated our last meeting, which I remembered with tenderness, and I was looking forward to seeing them again after such a long time. After an interminable journey across Paris in a taxi we arrived at our destination. Marussia was the first to greet me, and she looked tormented and wrung with emotion. She introduced first her mother and then her two grandsons. They resembled their father, tall, thin, with distinctly Slavic traits. Marussia went to prepare lunch and whilst she was gone her mother took the opportunity to confide in me the pains that plagued her. She told me that her daughter, who had been working in the aircraft factory, left the home one morning, went to the factory, but never returned home. Having spoken to the managers and staff in the aircraft factory, it transpired that she did not report for work that day and, since then, no amount of enquiries or searching had provided any clue as to her whereabouts.

The years passed and the search never ceased and the hope of seeing her again never faded. Lately some friends came to visit and persuaded Marussia that she should go and see an American movie that had been recently released entitled, *The Great Caterina*. Marussia's mother was happy for this diversion and planned to pass the time playing with the children, bathing them and putting them to bed. It was with great surprise therefore, that she heard their car arrive home much earlier than expected. She had hastened to meet them and as she came out of the door saw Marussia, her face contorted with grief and staring with her large doe eyes. Our friends helped her into the house and she fell into a chair, grief stricken.

"I saw her, in the beautiful Cossack costume of the Imperial Guard. Playing the role of helper to Catherine the Great!"

It was thus that we learned she had run away to Hollywood!

I had the impression that Marussia had waited for the end of that sad story, for as her mother finished, she reappeared in the living room holding in her hand two medallions framed with diamonds on which was engraved the portrait of Tsarina Alexandra.

"They are gifts from the Tsarina to my child; she is her godmother."

I took leave of them while the tears, raised by many memories, bathed our saddened faces.

Before leaving Paris my friends advised me to see the patterns of the Maison Irfe. The founder and creator of this house was none other than Prince Yusupov, the protagonist in the turn of events that culminated in the murder of Rasputin. The fashion house was called after their initials, IR for Irena and FE from Felix. Established in 1924 and launched at the Ritz Hotel, his models evoked the admiration of connoisseurs, not so much for the originality of the cut, but for the refinement of taste with tender colours, fine fabrics, delicate lace embroidery falling in cascades and pinned by jewels that gave a wonderful effect. Fur from chinchilla or sable created visions that were worn by mannequins chosen from among the Russian aristocratic ladies dazzled the audience.

On the day of our departure from Paris, the hotel concierge gave me a letter. It was from our bizarre chef, Krylov that ended with these verses from Baudelaire.

I want to build for you, Madonna, my mistress,
An underground altar in the depths of my grief
And carve out in the darkest corner of my heart,
Far from worldly desires and mocking looks,
A niche, all enamelled with azure and with gold,
Where you shall stand, amazed Statue,
With my polished Verses as a trellis of pure metal
"This was the reason for my service"

"What a strange guy!" said Thomas.

The Lull Before the Storm

Back in Gdansk I breathed with pleasure the fresh air of autumn, the most enchanting of the seasons with its infinite variety of colours. From the forest where I was sitting, I let my eyes wander far over the sea. The wonders of nature contrasted with stark platoons of khaki Nazi uniforms sprouting everywhere during their exercises, disturbing the peace with frequent bursts of fire from machine guns. At the same time, the Poles devoted all their efforts to the construction of the modern port of Gdynia, a gigantic work that would change the strategic and economic prospects of the country. Optimistic by nature, naturally proud, the Poles did not notice the turn events were taking in Gdansk.

Doctor Goebbels, as an ambassador of Hitler, was in the city on a visit to inspect the local organization of the Hitlerjugend. He was received by the people with delusional sympathy, and cars full of the hierarchy passed by my house. The training of the Nazi troops and Hitlerjugend was perfect, their obedience unquestionable and their military panache beyond reproach, but it was really no more than a circus going through a routine. With the opening of the port of Gdynia, Poland had a truly independent port structure after ten long years. Wollheim relocated its shipping and processing to the new port, and with these changes, the role of Thomas became superfluous. We left Gdansk for Rome.

Thomas had been appointed by the Polish Government as a delegate for Italy representing Polish Carboniferous Industry that would be based in the Eternal City. With this in mind he was busy practising and exercising his skills in the Italian language, studying verbs and conjugations, and by default forcing us to do the same. He insisted that we conduct all discussions in the house in Italian, which, led to a significant amount of confusion. Breakfast was invariably a disaster as neither the housekeeper, the servant nor the chef knew what he meant. Thomas would, on these occasions, take what was given and say that was exactly what he had asked for. The fun was to see how outrageous we could be before he capitulated.

Upon our arrival at the station in Rome the real difficulties began. As we dismounted from the train we ran the risk of losing our entire luggage, as Thomas did not have the necessary vocabulary to summon a porter. He became more confused as the moments passed, and would repeat, "I would like.... I would say ... would be...". He was totally unable to construct an understandable sentence in Italian. The girls, however, with gestures and smiles were able to communicate their intent and managed to rescue our bags, call a cab and get us to our hotel.

The next morning during breakfast, we decided to make a surprise visit to our friend Tola de Rudroff, who had been living in Rome for some years. Still being rather early in the morning, and certainly too early to call, we took a taxi to Via Veneto and, starting at the Villa Borghese, we strolled the length of the street taking in the shops, the sights and the monuments until we reached the Piazza Barberini where we sat for lunch. We had just finished eating when we were ourselves surprised by Tola! The idea of living in Rome was beginning to excite me and I felt I was slowly falling in love with its sights and sounds and even the smells, of coffee, of leather, of fresh flowers. Couple this with the history that greeted you on every corner, and Rome became irresistible.

We settled temporarily in a furnished apartment belonging to the Countess de Martino on the way to Santa Sabina, and began once again to set down roots in yet another city. Having lived for so many years in cold climates the temperate weather of Rome was welcome, and Thomas and I spent many a day wandering around Rome looking at the art, which was beautifully varied. There were the old monuments, the Coliseum, Villa Borghese and Teatro Marcello, the Trevi fountain and the Quattro Fontaine, and of course the artworks in churches and palaces by Michelangelo, Da Vinci, Raphael and Botticelli.

It was Christmas Eve and I was determined to make this, our first Christmas in Rome, as memorable as possible. Busy preparing for Wigilia, the traditional Polish Christmas Eve supper, I had turned on the radio searching for something to fill the background when I heard the announcement that the famous American, Ely Culbertson, 'King of Bridge', was passing through Rome and would be staying at the Grand Hotel.

Amazed by this wonderful coincidence we straightaway contacted the hotel and were put in touch with him. His deep voice greeted me on the phone and immediately brought back so many memories; we arranged to meet for breakfast the following morning. As soon as we entered the hotel lobby we spotted Ely. The passing of the years had not changed him; he retained his characteristic elegance and wore a dark blue coat and a homburg, ever fashionable. Walking through the door I ran towards him and, after a hug I introduced him to my family. During breakfast we tried to recall our last meeting. Thirty years had passed I said, it was in Ekaterinodar. We talked about all the intervening events that had affected both out families. The revolution, the civil war, the world war and now, on the horizon, troubles with Germany. Surely, we thought, there cannot be yet another war, after all the disastrous consequences of the previous one.

Ely told me all his news, how, after the war of 1914, he found himself in America with his father. His younger brother, Sascha, had achieved success around the world but was in the throes of a nervous breakdown and was fighting his illness. Eugene, the older brother, after years at the front as a fighter, eventually went to France and had taken vows in the convent of the Franciscan Bernardines cloistered near Le Vesinet. With his family dispersed Ely began to give lessons in foreign languages and, in his free time fell in love with the game of bridge. As a member of a private club, he found a partner in the incomparable Miss Josephine Dillon and, aside from her beauty, he fell in love with her uncommon intelligence and singular elegance. Having studied the game of bridge and all its complexities, he felt there were flaws that could be improved upon, and set about changing the current standards of play and bidding.

Ely continued his story: "The result was a success and my partner, Miss Dillon, congratulated me and suggested I should write a book, assuring me it would be a great success and read by both good, medium and poor players alike. 'I would need your help,' I said, 'can you devote the time?' 'With pleasure' she had replied and since then my life has changed in every conceivable way. We married, became famous and are now invited all over the world, to talk about, teach and play bridge."

That was why he was in Rome, at the invitation of the Marquise Z, and to partner the former King Alfonso and King George of Greece.

"Do you believe that the world is threatened by another war?" I asked.

"My opinion," Ely said, "is that there are dangerous currents and each new influx of water may break the dams that protect the peace. I suggest you come to America where you will be safe!"

Gaby, ever the firebrand, leapt upon this invitation and suggested she accept and that she should take advantage of the situation to travel as a companion for his journey.

"Time is short, I'll leave you three days to decide," said Ely taking his leave.

Sometimes events follow one another so rapidly that they do not, nor should they, give us time to reflect on the correctness of our decisions. Gaby left with Ely, and from Paris they travelled to Cherbourg and then on the steamer *Bremen* to America.

Every day that passed increased the pleasure of living in the eternal city, but the official announcement of the visit of Hitler shook me deeply. Rome was preparing feverishly for the occasion and I had a phone call from a friend who lived in the Aventine quarter overlooking the Circus Maximus. She was enthusiastic about the preparations that had seen the removal of all the rubbish in the streets, the replacement of broken lamps and all the statues and fountains repaired. It was, she said, like the Arabian nights in its beauty and magnificence. Dusty squares had been restored and re-presented as velvety green meadows with fresh turves and flowering azaleas that had been artistically arranged so they looked like a painting.

On the day of Hitler's arrival we found ourselves in the midst of a huge crowd of onlookers. In a splendid carriage drawn by four horses, harnessed luxuriously and escorted by cuirassiers in dress uniform, the King of Italy sat next to our visitor with the 'Charlie Chaplin' moustache. The procession passed the Coliseum, the Forum, the Quirinal Palace, and the fleeting greatness of the visitors was lost completely in the grandeur of these ruins of an ancient civilisation. They made these people seem timid and fearful as if they had tumbled by mistake through history into an environment that surpassed the significance of the people themselves.

We followed the procession with a certain sadness, Goebbels lost in his big carriage, and Himmler with his prince-nez looking for all the world like a stiff spinster from the last century. Thankfully they were far enough away from us in the streets that they could not hear the comments from my family, and indeed from some of those around us. We took advantage of the refurbished city to take in these unusual sights: the triumphal arches under the floodlights, the ruins of the Palatine and the lush vegetation behind contrasting with the ghostly remains of the ancient walls, the impressive view of the Coliseum, with its many arches lit with torches, spitting tongues of flame, the ancient monument seemingly enveloped in a cloud of fire. In Piazza Venezia we remained long in admiration of the artistic choreography of the Capitol. We returned home late in the evening, enchanted by our night tour.

Over the next few months our circle of acquaintances widened. One afternoon, we headed off to Via Archimede to visit Mercedes Retti-Massani and her family. We were greeted with the warmth I remembered of my native country, and were led into a bright and airy garden where, sitting around a table, we took tea in the midst of flowers, chatting pleasantly. The scorching heat of the day brought the discussion round to the subject of resorts and where to go when Rome is too hot. Mrs Retti-Massani was adamant about what should be first choice, a charming mountain village that was also, by coincidence, the favourite place of our friend Tola de Rudroff. My preference, I explained, was Santa Margherita Ligure where palm fronds wave in the breeze along the esplanade, or the nearby Portofino. Thomas, meanwhile, preferred the thermal treatment of Montecatini Terme. We spent until sunset trying to persuade each other of the wisdom of our choices but finally, with minds still set and no resolutions changed or made we parted with the intention of meeting again after the holidays. Before leaving for our resort, Portofino, we contacted a transport company to bring our furniture from storage in Gdansk to Rome so that on our return we could look in earnest for a suitable apartment.

The tropical heat emptied the capital, scattering the inhabitants across the entire Italian peninsula. I left with Benita, and after a long train journey of almost nine hours went direct to our hotel, the aptly named Splendido situated in a beautiful location, set high on a hill, overlooking the bay and harbour of Portofino.

In the morning we ate breakfast, and lingered on the large terrace to admire the small bay below. It was surrounded by hills that were, in turn, covered in thick woods descending almost into the sea. The small square that served as a miniature port contained groups of animated fishermen, some with half naked bodies tanned by the sun, others with colourful straw hats with wide brims to protect their heads. Still others were crouched by their boats, checking nets, scraping barnacles, mending ropes. Beside this scene sat the houses at the foot of the mountain, in a semi-circle enclosing the basin of the bay, with umbrellas that sheltered the early morning coffee drinkers from the already harsh sun. And finally, out on the bay itself, was an array of boats, some with engines, some with sails, and some just anchored and rocking in the soft swell of the tide.

The scene was so reminiscent of the shores of the Black Sea back home that I was lost for some while in a dream of remembrance. But then the figure of a man distracted me from my thoughts. Equipped for fishing with a long line and a bucket in hand, he headed across the square and to the shore, followed by a procession of cats which covered every breed, every colour and every state of fitness available in the feline world. The fisherman perched on the low wall of the jetty and went to work watched eagerly by his companions. They circled him greedily, observing his gestures and watching the bucket fill up quickly with darting fish.

Every morning the same scene would take place. He would come down to the jetty, accompanied by his feline friends who would wait patiently until he had finished his tasks. He would then distribute the fish amongst the waiting audience and each would politely take his or her turn before standing back. The meal would end, the 'table' would be cleaned and the fisherman would walk back to his house, followed still by the retinue of cats. It was curious, but a little investigation revealed the fisherman was English, had lived in Portofino for many years and owned a property on the harbour front, and everyday would practice his hobby.

Each morning as soon as I awoke I would run to the terrace to embrace that wonderful view. The beautiful yachts moored in the harbour brought a diversion from the usual scene. One day I noticed a yacht of outstanding beauty, painted black and with a large red stripe; the brass of the lamps, railings and port-holes shone like beacons almost blinding observers. Its owners, the Duke and Duchess of Windsor, were in the square getting into an equally magnificent car that would take them to Rapallo for a round of golf. It was by coincidence that we were due to meet Paul Scott Maurer at the golf club for lunch, so we very much looked forward to rubbing shoulders with royalty. And Rapallo was where the Germans and Russians met in 1922 to sign their treaty.

The concierge arranged for a driver to take us to Rapallo and he duly arrived later that morning. Given our rustic venue it was appropriate that we were going to be visiting royalty in a horse drawn carriage, albeit one where the horse wore a large straw hat! The small grey mare took us slowly down the narrow lanes and winding roads that snaked along the coast, all the while we were accompanied by the soft tinkling of the bells that were attached to the harness, like listening to never-ending tree frogs! Throughout the journey the driver spoke softly to the horse.

"Don't tire yourself, it's alright to go slowly."

'There is plenty of time, we'll stop and drink shortly."

I asked the driver why, and he told me that he had recently lost his wife and that only the horse could understand his pain, and therefore he spoke to her with much tenderness as the horse must surely be missing her as well. We arrived at our destination and left the coachman talking to his friend, patting her and awaiting our return.

At the Golf Club Paul Maurer had reserved a table for us. Paul was a journalist for the *Chicago Daily News* who had piqued my interest when he had written some short stories and impressions of his travels in Russia. I sat and listened to his thoughts: "I have already written a lot about what I could see, especially on theatre and art. Every small provincial town, lost in the endless territory of Russia, has its own theatre, and its choreography will be based on highly original concepts driven by immediate surroundings and experiences. The ideas are cutting edge and can be used as an example and inspiration to all artists, in whatever discipline, around the world. In each of these small theatres the representations are crowded and the audience composed of simple people who are moved by the unparalleled enthusiasm and intelligence of the performing artistes."

"In these places, the theatre is a new and effective teaching method. It is impossible to describe the drama caused when it is exploited for propaganda. The characters of the works embody figures of the past and can constitute cruel caricatures, stripping bare and exposing the weaknesses of the time."

"I visited Russia in three different periods. During my last trip, in 1937, I was amazed to see how many restrictions and how much surveillance was imposed, and how limited the freedom of the tourist had become. All those who go to Russia, whether in the countryside or in the cities, hoping to catch a glimpse of the atmosphere prior to the advent of communism, will be disappointed."

"The civilization of old Russia is buried and no one cares,

or wants to revive it. The population has now reached the point of not wanting to feel the need for history and therefore cannot appreciate or possess it. Those that do have left; those that cannot leave have changed. You Russians have a priceless wealth of the soul, and are strong in suffering, but there is a dictatorship that is trying to stifle your feelings. But be aware, large volcanoes can be dormant for many, many years; they are not dead, they are sleeping, recharging, and one day with the power they have stored nothing will prevent them from showing their strength and anger."

"A few years ago," continued Mr Maurer, "I met a Russian I will never forget. He had been invited to our estate in France, as an expert adviser on agriculture. Mr Wolkoff was friendly and engaging, soon we became good close friends. At that time a terrible tragedy struck when I lost my son in a storm at sea, here in Portofino. He was thirteen. None of my friends had managed to give me the strength and the courage to bear the sadness that I carried and the feeling that I could have done more to save his life. It was only in long conversations with Mr Wolkoff, with his deep religious convictions, and perhaps a certain Russian mysticism, that I was able to recover some equilibrium in my life and to look upon my son's life as a blessing rather than his death as a curse."

I listened with particular emotion to this last story of Mr Maurer's and finally asked, driven by the desire to know, whether his friend Mr Wolkoff was at one time the Head of the Imperial Cabinet of Tsar Nicholas. Surprised, he said: "He was his son."

The Storm Strikes

My return to Rome coincided with the return of Gaby from America. She brought back with her a gift from Ely, a most delicate and delightful Tiffany pillbox. Enamelled as if by nature with boughs and stems and which, when opened, shone like the sun from the bronzed and burnished interior.

We had by now found an apartment, newly built, in the Parioli district of Rome on Viale Bruno Buozzi. Our furniture had arrived from Gdansk and we began to be in a position to return the hospitality that had been given to us by friends and acquaintances. Because of Thomas's position working within the Polish government, our circle of friends included a good many embassy staff from a variety of countries. During the long winter evenings they would often come and take tea or coffee with us. We would sink into the plush armchairs that were scattered around the library and converse animatedly on the subject of the recent visit of Hitler and of a possible change of Italian politics. We would discuss our concerns and points of view, and the geographical position of Poland and the impact this may have on its fate. On the one hand the spectre of Soviet Russia, and on the other the hostility of Germany, clouded the peaceful enjoyment of freedom regained at such great cost, but whose existence was once again threatened, in spite of the clear understanding of the alliances that should be there to protect us.

During those days, laden with political concerns, we were invited to a reception at the Polish Embassy on the occasion of the arrival of our Foreign Minister Jozef Beck, and his wife. The doors of the Palazzo Caetani were opened to welcome guests, and the magnificent rooms were decorated with a profusion of flowers. None of us were aware of an unfortunate incident that happened that night to our ambassador, Alfred Wysocki, who had a fractured foot and was reduced to receiving his guests sitting in an armchair with the limb in plaster. It was for this reason perhaps that the atmosphere was a little stilted and the evening ended prematurely. As it was still early we went out with Colonel Romejko, the military attaché at the embassy, and it became obvious from our discussions that storm clouds were gathering.

Worried as to where things were going I proposed to Thomas that perhaps we should take a holiday and, given the proximity of the Riviera, it would be good to revisit Menton and introduce our daughters to the places where I had spent my youth with my father.

In Nice we stayed at the Hotel Negresco whose windows overlooked the Ligurian Sea, the waters calm and still and soothing. On the first afternoon we visited the last house of my father in Menton. I explained to the children the layout of the rooms, and how the door of the dining room opened out onto the terrace from where the scent of the magnolias would pervade the whole of the ground floor. In my mind's eye, I saw again the table I would sit at whilst I wrote letters to Thomas in Lviv, while, not far away, my father would be lying on his bed, talking to Dr Vaqueret. My father had wanted to return to the Caucasus, saying he needed to change a clause in his will to provide an equal right for each heir to use the family home. I can still hear the cautionary voice of Dr Vaqueret who felt that such a long journey would not be good for his health. It is a strange twist of fate that, after all that had happened, it would have been irrelevant anyway.

We spent many hours in Nice, the favourite haunt of all Russian refugees. One day we went to the outskirts of the city invited by Mrs Bezak. Her husband had been a high Russian dignitary, an energetic official, the idol for a time of the Russian patriotic press and a former officer of the Death's Head Hussars, the 1st Life Hussar regiment. She was waiting at the narrow front door of a huge block which, in turn, led down a long, narrow, dark corridor where she introduced me into a room whose only furniture was a table set for tea, some chairs and three bunks on which were stretched out army blankets. We sat for a short while and exchanged memories of home. She told me a story of when some friends of theirs, the Ericksons, who had been to the theatre and then had decided to go to Strelna, an exclusive restaurant just outside St Petersburg. It was late when they began their drive home, dark and with no traffic and they were the only car on the road. Suddenly they realised that a military truck was approaching and, concerned about her jewellery, Mrs Erickson took off her bracelet, necklace and rings, and hid them under the seats of the car. The military truck stopped and troops leapt out into the road and halted the car. They ordered the occupants out and thinking they were about to be searched Mrs Erickson gave a small sigh of relief, until that is the troops drove off with the car leaving her and her husband stranded! It was only then that she realised that the car itself was a jewel. I have to admit to smiling at the thought that perhaps the jewels are still in the car today, dusty and undiscovered.

It was the 1st September 1939, our stay in Nice was nearing its end and we were taking care of the final preparations for the return trip to Rome when we heard terrible news: Warsaw had been bombed by the Germans! Within a few hours panic had begun to spread through the city. In our hotel there was extreme agitation and in the lobby there accumulated a veritable mountain of suitcases. The staff struggled to maintain some sense of order from the chaos but they were overwhelmed by the demands of the guests anxious to return as soon as possible to their own countries. Although I knew Thomas would be worried about his family in Lviv we agreed it was impossible to return to Poland. There would be a serious risk of falling into German hands and we did not know whom to contact for advice. Once again it would seem our world was about to collapse around us.

All the roads out of Nice were blocked to civilian transport. We passed endless rows of French and Algerian soldiers in full battle gear, battalions marching with heavy steps. The beat of big military boots on the hot asphalt created a continuous thunder of noise. A long grey-green snake of regiments, interspersed with groups of overloaded mules, marched past the front of the fashionable hotels in Nice. Our memories of previous revolutions and wars came full circle; once again I saw us needing to adapt to the life of a refugee. Already I could feel the tears inside.

Back in Rome, our concerns were increasing day by day. For quite some time Mussolini had, had ambitions. In early 1939 he had delivered a long speech on international affairs where he began by claiming that the freedom of a country was proportional to the strength of its navy, and that Corsica, Tunisia, Malta and Cyprus were the bars of Italy's prison. He wanted to break the British control on Cyprus, Gibraltar, Malta and Egypt. What would Italy do now? We followed every speech Mussolini made, considered his every word, and tried to interpret them in order to better understand his intentions. A speech from Foreign Minister Galeazzo Ciano seemed to show sympathy for Poland, and appeared to wish victory for the Poles. For a while it gave us some hope for the neutrality of Italy, or even perhaps that it would help Poland in its hour of need.

Meanwhile the first fugitives from Poland began to cross the border. It was comforting to see that, at this time, there was great tolerance from the government towards the refugees and we were touched by the warm welcome bestowed upon them by the Italian people. The flow of refugees changed from a slow trickle to a flood, and the door of our house in Rome was open to every request for those asking for hospitality and sanctuary, but we were somewhat surprised by the closure of the Polish Embassy and the Consulate. In an attempt maintain some degree of support we began to organise meetings between our compatriots so they could discuss their problems and to improve the lives of exiles.

In our Sunday meetings, Princess Radziwill Bichette would

be greeted with reverence, as much for her kindness and humanity as for her high lineage. Mothers and children, tortured and separated from their families in the chaos of war, asked for help from the Princess and she listened carefully to their painful stories, asking for the names and precise information of the missing, promising her support. I remember the Princess, after listening to a lady, the wife of a Polish consul held in Hungary, who was in despair because she did not know if he was dead or alive. She simply said: "I will write to Horthy", who was at that time Regent of Hungary. And she did. A few weeks later the consul was in Italy, reunited with his wife. With the help of the Princess many Poles were able to emmigrate to distant lands, where they could start a new life.

Every Saturday I went to the Academie Française, at the invitation of Jacques Ibert and his wife. The meetings were held in a beautiful room and we were joined by many of the ladies of the diplomatic community with the express intention of organising charitable works for the benefit of all refugees. We were still optimistic about the neutrality of Italy and this optimism gave comfort and impetus to our work. It was at one of these meetings that the wives reported that most diplomats were in agreement with the opinion that Germany would force Italy to declare war. Given the other news from the front this was a disheartening turn of events.

For the next few weeks this news dominated conversation. Each meeting would at some point lose focus and discussion would start around the latest news from the front and the German war machine, but more importantly the fluctuations of Italian politics and Mussolini's viewpoint. A few more weeks passed and it was noticeable that the numbers of diplomatic wives attending our meetings was falling sharply; the room was beginning to look sparse, almost deserted. One afternoon Madame Ibert was relaying correspondence from France. They were thanking us for our contributions and for the charitable work our association was conducting. At that moment the wife of the French Ambassador, Madame Francois-Poncet, entered the room. Having also been the former ambassador to Germany we took in every word she said in the hope of being able to learn the latest news on the attitude of the Italian Government against Germany.

However perhaps the most telling point came when she asked the wife of the Swiss Ambassador which kind of salami would be most suited for a long journey. We were suprised, but the advice given was that perhaps the best would be salami from Milan. Subsequent conversation with the Ambassador's wife did not last long and she left probably feeling less than impressed by her welcome and our response.

"Do you not find," said Monsieur Ibert once she had left the room, "that the request from the Ambassador's wife is quite significant? To me she was trying to make us understand that our days of staying here are numbered!"

We all nodded wisely, although most of us had missed the intimation completely. The meeting concluded with some heavy sighs and I went home that day with a heart full of worries. Storm clouds were gathering over our heads and were once again in the process of ruining our lives. The following day, June 10th 1940, after withholding formal allegiance to either side in the battle between Germany and the Allies, Benito Mussolini, dictator of Italy, declared war on France and Great Britain. Hitler was deprecating in his comments, saying

"First they were too cowardly to take part, now they are in a hurry so that they can share in the spoils."

How much perfidy, how many intrigues, how much cheating and confusion, how many disasters are contained within the word 'politics'. It is certainly an art or a science which holds the reins of the world, directing the fate of millions of men, that turns friends into hated enemies, and vice versa. It seems to be above any human law, common to every mortal; it is accomplished by force, with a violent force and passes over all the best principles created by God and men.

The sounds of war followed quickly, air raid warnings, sirens, bomber formations flying overhead, all served to remind us what lay ahead. At night the sirens would wail, and sleepily we would descend into the cellar and sit, pressed on wooden benches, feeling like trapped rats. Our situation became particularly unpleasant, as being Polish we had moved from warmly received refugees to being considered as intruders and, effectively, the enemy. A deep sadness settled over us and we no longer had the strength to protest, to make it clear to others that war was more painful than ever for us, and that for so many years we were in search of our home, and now it seemed we were about to lose another.

A few days later, while we were away from home, our staff were called to the police station. I believe the gesture was more of a threat to us than to the staff but it was merely the beginnings of the persecution. They were interrogated, not about themselves but about us, then released.

On the 13th August 1940, we too were called to attend the police station. I cannot, indeed I do not want to, describe the suffering effected by this action. The police, as always, reigned supreme, and nobody could appeal their verdict. The interrogation ended, and my husband, suffering from angina pectoris due to the anxiety created, was detained. His crime? One of the servants had reputedly said, during their interrogation, that he heard Thomas listening to the BBC on the radio.

I spent my days praying and asking God to help him endure this unfair and forced isolation, and I have to confess. He answered in an unexpected way. After two months of separation we were ordered to leave Rome, together, within two days. We left our home, were given train tickets at the police station, and began a journey into an unknown with a dark destiny. All this could not disturb us though; we were just so relieved at the thought of being together again. As instructed we took a train to Naples and, arriving there, we climbed aboard a ramshackle local train heading for Avellino.

It was a voyage of discovery; there were only third-class cars and all were filled with farmers and peasants and their numerous miscellaneous goods. We were accompanied on our journey by chickens, a pig that would grunt and in return received a response of some plaintive bleating from lambs. This whole farmyard orchestral cacophony stood out because the passengers were taciturn and silent. We sat by the window facing forward, two by two, with our minimal luggage vying for space with most of southern Italy's livestock, or stacked on our laps.

Our thoughts went hand in hand with the monotonous and slow rhythm of the train. On the upward slopes the train would slow its march to walking pace as it struggled to pull the coaches. Occasionally with a great cough it would stop in front of one of the crumbling shelters of the villages that were scattered along the length of the line. There would be a moment's respite in terms of space as passengers would disembark, taking their sundry bags, cases and livestock with them, only to be replaced moments later by a fresh consignment of people and farmyard animals. With another cough, a sharp hiss and a breathless wheeze the engine would rattle its chains and begin the next laborious climb to the next crumbling shelter.

The air in the wagon grew fetid and became almost unbreathable and Thomas, particularly, was feeling the effect. I felt as though an iron ring had been tightened around my head. In order to try to reduce the mephitic atmosphere Thomas managed to force open the small windows and immediately we were rewarded by a blast of cool, fresh mountain air. Around us we could hear the welcome by way of deep breaths and muttered gratitude from fellow passengers who, although still broodingly silent, rewarded us with a short sharp nod of acknowledgement.

At sunset we finally arrived at Avellino, and thankfully someone was waiting for us, for we had no idea of what we should be doing or where to go. A farm cart pulled by two horses stood outside the station house. The cart was good for firewood, the horses for anatomical studies, but there was no alternative, so needs must. The driver helped us load our few small cases and we set off for our final destination.

During the long journey we could see the obvious signs of poverty around us. People were sitting in the doorways of the shanty houses, their eyes dull, their skin dark, burnt by working in the sun, their hair dishevelled and unkempt. The women were clothed in long cotton dresses, with more darning than original material. They looked tired and watched as we trundled by on our cart, well dressed, groomed and with cases that were made of leather. We felt more than a little guilty. Ragged children ran alongside us or played in the street. Although we tried to ask our driver several times our destination we received little response, perhaps a grunt of acknowledgement, and that was all.

It was dark when we arrived in a small square and the coachman stopped in front of a hotel that was perhaps best described as modest and had seen better days. It was here where we would spend our first night before we reported to the police headquarters at eight in the morning.

Resigned, we lay down but the bedbugs seemed to have got there first and had now laid siege to us in order to protect their territory. We began a ruthless hunt but the results left a lot to be desired, so fully dressed with gloves on our hands and our trousers tucked into our socks we tried, in vain, to get some sleep.

The next morning the sun was high and flooded the road leading to the offices of the police headquarters, and the village took on a much more welcoming appearance. We introduced ourselves first to police headquarters where our details were checked and we were registered. We were then directed to a Dr Bianchi who informed us that the last leg of the journey, by car, would be about ten kilometres, and take us to our final destination, Ospedaletto.

The last kilometre into the town was steep and uphill. Another small square and we were suddenly presented with a small village in all its squalid primitiveness. An employee from the town hall ticked our name off a list and told us to go to our accommodation at the Hotel Zia Raffaella.

The owner, Raffaella, was a woman of uncertain age, small in stature and plump, vivacious in temperament and apparently wearing a sample of every piece of clothing in her wardrobe. She took us up to the first floor and down a long corridor and towards the end on the right and, with a natural showman's flourish, she opened a door and announced with pride, "For the parents I offer my bedroom!"

We entered and our eyes were immediately drawn to a picture above the bed and no matter how hard I tried I could not tear my eyes away. I was riveted by a picture of a body, in a coffin, surrounded by four lighted candles. Raffaella explained that was her dead husband and that he looked so beautiful in death, and was dressed so smartly, that she wanted him to be looking down on her and protecting her.

It was difficult to refuse such sincerity but I was able to persuade Raffaella that her husband should be looking down on her bed, not mine, and we came to an accommodation that she would exchange pictures and find something a little more appropriate for her lodgers. Benita and Gaby were allocated the room across the corridor, that overlooked the village square. It contained bunk beds and a wardrobe. The remaining three rooms on this floor were occupied by the hotel owners, Raffaella who had no children, and Raffaella's extended family which was her sister, Vincenza, her husband and six children, five girls and a boy, who helped in the tavern. In addition to the income generated from the hotel Raffaella also owned a bakery in the same row of buildings. Although prosperous it could not be compared to the income from the tavern that was frequented by pilgrims who had come to Montevergine to pay homage to the miraculous Virgin.

From early spring until late autumn, the streets of Ospedaletto were crowded with a multitude of colourful pilgrims. They arrived in the village using a variety of transport: horse with cart, horse without cart, on foot, by car, taxi, lorry or bus. Both the transport and the pilgrims were adorned with artificial flowers, some wearing crowns of foliage and the majority dressed in traditional costumes. The echo of hymns drifted on the cool air up to the tavern where it was customary to pause before attempting to climb the mountain. The pilgrims would leave their cars and horses in the large courtyard and, before setting off to purify themselves at the feet of the Madonna for their sins, they took advantage of the break for some revelry.

Between the various courses of food, and the toasts to the Virgin made in wine, they sang hymns. Their voices, clear at first became, with the passing of hours, raucous and increasingly weakened. Finally their heads heavy with too much food and good wine, sleep would overtake them and silence would reign. They slept sitting at the tables, lounging on benches and on the floor; they slept in the dining room and on the adjoining terraces, illuminated by the full moon. In the morning they got up with the first ray of sunshine and barefoot, and some on their knees, they would climb to the top of the mountain. The mountain rose fifteen hundred metres and, having overcome the steep and dizzying 4,500 steps, the humble devotees would kneel before the image of Our Lady, and invoke her grace. The pilgrimages were only interrupted in the winter, when the heavy snow arrived but given that a good season would encourage nearly a million visitors it was a welcome respite.

The last days of autumn, with their golden glow, moved inexorably into winter. The trees, from being lush and green had passed through russet and gold and then their leaves had been carried away by the first gusts of winter wind, they were now bare. The harvest had been and gone and the rain fell with greater regularity, and as the season moved on the rain turned to snow and the nights became longer and colder. Then we began to look for things to occupy us closer to home. With Raffaella's permission we explored the barn and found some old tables and chairs, which were elegantly refurbished with the help of a local carpenter. Some fruit crates were turned into a library, the skeleton of a bottomless chair revived with padded rags and a small coffee table were put in the place of honour next to the window.

December 1941, and with Christmas Eve fast approaching we began to prepare our rooms in anticipation of the celebration of the nativity. We found a small tree which we lit with candles and decorated with coloured paper chains. Raffaella was in a state of high anticipation and admiration, never having experienced Wigilia before. Both families gathered in the dining room, the tree was lit and small presents and greetings exchanged and Raffaella's family were invited to join us for the traditional Christmas Eve dinner.

In the hall of the inn a large rustic fireplace warmed our cold limbs. We sat around a long table set with a beautiful white tablecloth and lit by candles provided by my daughters. In that distinctly primitive environment there was a feeling of sincerity on the part of all those present. Peace and harmony reigned undisturbed around us, and the atmosphere was so pleasant that we spent the evening exchanging memories. We regaled our newfound friends with stories of the past, and strove to forget, at least for this night, the thoughts that plagued our hearts.

The fine dining was completed with a delicious cake, a specialty of Carmelina, and Raffaella's talented sister, Vincenza. Refreshed by the warmth of the dying flames of the fire we summoned up the courage to return to our rooms. They had no heating and the temperature outside had dropped to ten degrees below zero. It was no surprise, therefore, to find the pipes frozen and the water in the sink a solid block of ice. In addition the large amounts of snow that had fallen, while we had been busy celebrating Wigilia, had blocked all access to the village, and we were now prisoners of Mother Nature.

The following morning the true nature of the snowfall was revealed in all its majesty. The village was buried by a pristine soft white blanket, some of the houses, through drifting, were buried up to their mezzanine floors, for all the world looking as though they had no foundations. The post office, church, and bakery all looked like toys on a white blanket, and the wind would drive the snow through the cracks in the window frames and under the doors, leaving behind patches of ice. With opportunities to do anything else severely restricted, we began to read, and imitated the custom of Raffaella by wearing a collection of warm clothes.

The winter was hard to bear. With no heating my daughters often suffered from bronchitis, and it was difficult for us to reach the doctor, who lived in Avellino. As the weather deteriorated so did the utilities. Water pipes were frequently frozen and then burst, electricity was intermittent and heating was almost non-existent. The hotel was built for pilgrims and tourists not for year round occupation. As a result the fire-places were in the communal areas not in the rooms.

Food was an issue for everyone in the village. The bread was made with poor quality ingredients and the supply of fresh produce was limited due to the fierce winter. Allied to this lack of supply was a lack of money for the villagers; the poor peasants were starving, and the mothers surrounded by broods of children, pale and dull eyed, struggled to survive on the restricted rations. Even Raffaella was affected and could only offer us a modest lunch of beans and peas.

We tried to help by selling some precious objects to the occasional customer of the tavern, at the price they were willing to offer. Bracelets, brooches, earrings and watches were exchanged for very little money but they served to cover our budget for a certain period of time. The menu was not very substantial, but often my imagination, excited like a starving poet, managed to enrich them. Most of the meals were cooked in my room but every so often I would go down in the Raffaella's kitchen, next to the bakery, and prepare more complicated dishes. It was where the whole family gathered, commuting between the kitchen and the bakery in the execution of their various chores. Driven by curiosity they would frequently stop and watch my culinary manipulations and the dishes that were made. Their criticism was faint but motivated by curiosity:

"But signora, who will eat that 'stuff'?"

"Where is your country?" Raffaella asked me, not for the first time.

"We are from Poland," I would answer.

"I know it well," would be Raffaella's response. "Bologna, very nice."

After trying several times to explain to her the difference between Poland and Bologna, I realised it was a battle I would never win, and left her to her charming misconceptions.

In spring 1942 we were able to once again resume our walks and our life in Ospedaletto settled down to a routine, one that was about to be disrupted, but happily. For some time in Rome Gaby had been seeing a young man, Cesare Meneghini, and they had fallen in love. But as with all things fate took a hand and first Cesare was called up to join the Army and sent to serve in Africa, and Gaby was interned in Ospedaletto. Communication between them was non-existent until, out of the blue, a letter arrived addressed to Gaby and written in a familiar hand. Cesare was in Italy on leave and wished, while he was here, to marry Gaby before he returned to the front.

Thomas and I were delighted. Having met Cesare in Rome we found him engaging, intelligent and, as far as we were concerned, perfect for our daughter. We immediately sat with Raffaella to see if she could assist in arrangements. First were meetings with the priest followed by meetings with the police and then meetings with the local mayor and finally with the local councillors. The end result was permission being granted for the marriage and permission granted for Gaby to leave Ospedaletto with Cesare. The ceremony was modest and held in the small church of the Virgin Mary, and the wedding breakfast, meagre but happy, at Raffaella's tavern. Then suddenly it was time for them to leave. Gaby would stay with Cesare's parents in Rome but her going would leave a vacuum in our hearts and lives. From the balcony of our room I followed their departure out of Ospedaletto. I watched as Cesare's car retreated down the winding road to Naples and beyond, and for all my sadness I was happy that Gaby had found someone who would cherish and love her and who would, with his goodness, become an irreplaceable part of our family. As I watched I gently squeezed Thomas's hand and hoped they would be as happy as we had been. Her absence was like the lack of an instrument in a quartet for some time well knit.

Meanwhile 1942 ran into 1943 and the events of the war came closer and the news left us continually dismayed. Now we heard the hum of aeroplanes, continuously passing overhead; they woke us at night and the formations were becoming more frequent and larger. In the absence of any other information, rumours ran rife and were king. We heard that the Americans had attempted to land in Sicily; we didn't know if this was true or purely wishful thinking. Allied to this rumour was the fact that the Germans were approaching the area and would be seeking shelter. The uncertainty surrounding our fate terrified the internees. There was talk of reprisals, transfers to other locations, and of atrocities committed by the German troops in Italy and elsewhere. Stories of concentration camps circulated and people began to panic. They barricaded their rooms; they fled to the woods in search of refuge. An English lady came to us in a state of delusional terror having learned that the Germans had occupied Avellino and were next coming to Ospedaletto.

On a night with a full moon we heard the first cry of alarm: "Help! Help!"

Another voice answered: "Wir zeigen Wreden say!" (We'll show you help!)

As soon as we heard the guttural German language, we told Raffaella's grandchildren to run upstairs in the barn, pull up the ladder and hide under the straw. Once up and hidden we closed the hatch from underneath, hurried back into the inn and closed and bolted the doors behind us. Thomas and I ran to our room and again shut the door. There was no lock so we wedged a chair under the handle. We knew it would do little but might, perhaps, buy us a moment of time. We sat low on the balcony of our room with Benita in our arms, staying below the rail so that we would not be seen. At the same time we were ready, if necessary, to jump down.

From downstairs at the front of the inn we heard blows on the door and voices shouting: "Aufmachen!" (Open.) Even though it was expected the order still made us jump!

Vincenza and Raffaella hammered on our door and I ran and let them in. And at the same moment there was the shattering sound of breaking glass from the room across the corridor. A woman staggered out calling: "They are already here, they came over the balcony of our room!"

We reflected for a moment on the danger that threatened our daughter and then, telling Benita to stay exactly where she was we stepped out into the hallway and closed the door behind us. A group of German soldiers came from the room across the corridor; they blocked the passageway and asked arrogantly:

"Wo sind ihre fräulein?" (Where are your girls?)

"Wir haben ein gehört siehaben harem." (We've heard that you have a brothel.)

They began entering all the rooms in the corridor: "Her damit!" (Next)

Two of the younger soldiers took hold of Raffaella and, threatening her, repeated their request for women. They then grasped her hand and began trying to remove the rings from her plump fingers. I looked at Raffaella, "Lassen sie doch, es ist nicht echt gold" (Let them but it's not real gold) I said to her.

"Sieh mal! Sie spricht Deutch. Von wo sind sie?" (Look, she speaks German! Where are you from?)

"Aus Danzig" (Gdansk) I replied.

"Hans, hormal, from einige sind aus Danzig" (Hans, look, here's someone from Gdansk.)

"Kom hier."

Hans came over and asked what we knew about Gdansk, his hometown, where we lived and how we were in Italy. The conversation seemed to have calmed everyone down and we were now a little more peaceful, although still trembling inside. These soldiers were little more than eighteen, Hans told us; they hadn't heard from home for a long time and had had no news about their parents. All they heard is what we were told and rumours that abounded. One of the soldiers began to tell us about his mother, his eyes filled with tears, another remembered his sister and in moments the war was forgotten. With a certain shyness they asked us if we had anything to eat. I told them we had nothing but if they wished I was sure we could make them a cup of tea with honey. My proposal was greeted with an explosion of joy.

"Ah wunderbar! Seit jahren wir haben kein honig gegessen, und da zu te." (Ah wonderful! For years, we have not eaten honey, and as to tea.) "Fabenhaft." (Perfect).

I went down to the kitchen to heat water and the whole company, guests, Raffaella, Vincenza and the soldiers came with me to help. I called Benita to come down from our room and bring the honey. Now, with tea ready, we settled on the porch, with Raffaella and Vincenza now calm. Benita brought the honey and each guest received a teaspoonful to go in their tea. We drank sitting on the floor.

"Gott, dass ist gut." (God, how good!) exclaimed the young soldiers. Our conversation lasted until dawn. The youngsters showed us letters and photographs of their loved ones but eventually there came a time when, although reluctantly, they had to leave.

"Horen sie, diconom-wenn mal andere ... hier kommen und sie werden Belastigt, rufen sie uns! Wir sind hier in der nähe in wald. Wir werden Ihnen helfen." (Look, if others come and harass you and you need help, call us. We are near here, in the woods and we will help you.) And with that they left.

As soon as we were sure they had gone, Raffaella and Vincenza opened the loft hatch and the girls lowered the ladder and came back down. We felt secure now with our new protectors, but in the back of my mind was, for how long? The peaceful character of Ospedaletto had changed completely, there was now continuous troop movement on the road that connected us to Avellino that created indescribable chaos, blocking any private travel between the two villages.

The chestnut forests on the lower slopes of the mountain had turned into a bivouac for soldiers and the fountain in the square served for their morning ablutions. The country now appeared to be under the orders of the Germans and there was a continuous formation of allied planes flying low over Avellino and its surrounds. The planes were targeting the roads on which there were military vehicles, but served to make any travel even more unsafe and unwise. The Germans were frequently forced to take cover under the trees of the forests, and even in the barns of the farms, their vehicles loaded with explosive fuel. Even covered in camouflage, they were obvious to the low flying fighter planes of the allies.

On one of these forced stops, we saw German soldiers carry a wounded comrade off a truck, bring him into the tavern and lay him on the ground. He looked no more than a child, sixteen or seventeen, and the wound to his arm was severe, gangrenous. His cries were muffled by the sound of the persistent bombers overhead and I suggested that they move him off the floor and onto a bed. His companions agreed and he was transported to a spare room on the ground floor. I was troubled by the state of the wound and the suffering the boy was going through. I recommended we called the doctor who was resident nearby. My offer was rejected with the excuse that they were prohibited from seeking treatment from doctors who were not German.

While we were discussing the issue the boy called out, in English. "Mother, where are you? Mother I want to see you! I like New York, I don't want to be here ... my sister Lilibeth ... I love you so much ... take me to America."

Each phrase the wounded boy said was interrupted by the soldier sitting next to him, who warned: "Fredy, so darfst. Du nicht sprechen. Was wird unsere Fuhrer sagen?" (Freddy don't talk like that. What do you think the Fuhrer would say?)

Then turning to us, as if to excuse the behaviour of the boy, he told us that he lived in America with his parents and had been on a visit to Germany, invited by an uncle. Surprised by the outbreak of war, he had been unable to return to the USA and, despite his young age, he had been called to arms.

"In the last battle" he continued, "Fredy was injured and also witnessed the death of his best friend. He has been in shock and depression ever since and has not the will to recover."

Fredy, meanwhile, wept and continued to call his mother. Torn by grief, seeing the agony of the boy, I sent for Dr Greek, regardless of the protests of his companion. The doctor cleaned and dressed the wound as best he could in the circumstances, and gave young Fredy an injection of morphine, after which the boy calmed down.

The roar of the aircraft moved away and his colleagues picked up Fredy off the bed and tried to persuade him that he must continue his interrupted journey in order to get to a field hospital and have his wound treated properly. As they carried Fredy to the truck and laid him, at least on a mattress, but admittedly between cans of gasoline, I could hear his cries: "Please let me stay here, let me stay with these people!"

"Fredy, du weisst Dich doch Ich muss weg bringen" (Fredy, we can't, we need to get away.) They turned on the engine and departed in a cloud of exhaust and dust, and then were gone.

One morning at dawn we were awakened by a salvo of cannon fire that seemed very close to the village. We ventured onto the balcony and looked in the direction of the echo but could see nothing: there was no smoke and the air was once again silent.

"An explosion perhaps," said Thomas.

Later that day, and into the night, the cannonades returned, this time unabated. For several days the sky was alight at night with the sporadic flare of flame from gun barrels. The sky would, for a moment turn bright orange and back to black. A few minutes later it was repeated. It was difficult to judge how far away the fighting was, but it seemed to be getting ever closer. We received no news, not even rumours now, and we were unaware of either political or military events. Our imaginations ran riot; we wanted explanations. One night we watched a huge fire envelop part of the forest. Swirling flames and burning embers flew high into the dark sky and we spent the night trying to explain to ourselves what disaster had occurred. Certainly there was a fight, but where? Who was bombarding with such aggression, the Allies against the Germans, or were the Germans repelling the Allies?

Then we saw the German convoys passing through the country, lorry after lorry without interruption, transporting the injured on Red Cross trucks, other cargoes on lorries covered with tarpaulins, trucks full of soldiers, looking weary but still armed. The vehicles came up the hill from Avellino, passing in front of us, and continued their journey to a destination unknown to us, unloaded their contents and, at breakneck speed came down again, only to do the same an hour or so later. The urgency of the military was evident and we watched with growing interest. One night we heard the sound of a vehicle, but it was struggling under whatever load it was carrying, barely moving up the steep hill of the mountain road. The engine strained as it wound round the serpentine roads, and the buildings shook to their foundations as it went slowly past. Intrigued I leapt out of bed and ran to the window to see what was the cause of such great endeavour. At that moment I heard a voice shout: "Halt, Jemand beobachtet uns!" (Stop! Someone is spying on us!)

For a moment my heart stopped, and without the strength to move, terrified and not daring to breath in case they could see my breath against the cold night air, I waited. The voices subsided, there followed a moment of silence and then, as God wanted, I heard the escort for the heavy convoy get back on his bike. Slowly, with difficulty, the enormous load tried to take the curve next to the inn but it was too steep and too tight for the huge, heavy calibre cannon being towed on the back.

The next morning we received the order to evacuate all the houses that were located near the main road. This in itself posed a difficult problem; where would we go, indeed where could we go? There was also very little time to reflect. Even as the order was being given the Germans were placing the heavy calibre cannon, delivered the previous night, in the courtyard of the inn right under our windows.

Raffaella and her family had already fled!

Thomas, Benita and I left the house with a small suitcase and headed to the village square where we met and discussed with other internees the order given and the gravity of the situation that faced us. The farmers were of little help and, not surprisingly, were in a mood of self-preservation. We were, after all, undesirables, which is why we had been sent here in the first place. They did not want to have any of the repercussions or reprisals to befall them or their families. Instead they went to the shrine of the Madonna of Montevergine to pray. By now we had lost the will to move any further, tired and worn out, we had begun to feel indifferent to the danger.

In the end we accepted the invitation of a Polish lady who lived far enough away from the main road. She offered us a room that admittedly we would have to share with our friends the Howells, (with whom Thomas had played bridge) and their son Jimmy. I have to confess that the accommodation was cramped, seven of us in a room that contained a bed, a table and two chairs, but we were grateful to at least have a roof over our heads, although sleep did not seem to be a real option!

We waited until night fell and then crept out to monitor the progress of events in the heart of the village. The darkness helped hide our bodies while the full moon gave enough light to observe all the activity. Along the side of the road we watched as a group of soldiers were intent on digging long ditches and then laying cables inside. Without getting closer and endangering everyone we could only hazard guesses at what they were for. Mr Howell was of the opinion they were communication cables although just whom they were communicating with was lost on Thomas and I. Aided by copious cups of strong tea we managed to stay awake until morning.

The next day we managed to scavenge some mattresses from a house that had been left vacant, we hauled them up to the house and lay them on the ground outside. At the very least it gave everyone a chance to lie down and most of us fell asleep almost immediately in the warmth of the summer sunshine.

Out in the country it was rumoured that a typhus epidemic had broken out in Montevergine due to the lack of clean water, poor sanitary conditions and the great mass of people; too many people, too few facilities. This had resulted in all the farmers, who had fled there from Ospedaletto now fleeing in the opposite direction and trying to settle back in their village, The Howells were telling us this news when our conversation was suddenly interrupted by a terrible air raid on the military tents and the streets of Avellino in the valley below. The effect of that bombardment caused a terrifying panic, not just amongst the Germans but the animals as well. They had been in the process of collecting all the livestock, seemingly getting ready to ship them away, when the bombing started. Both villagers and Germans were momentarily distracted and the street was now filled with chickens, sheep, pigs, mules and many other farmyard animals who, taking advantage, were running down the streets chased by frantic soldiers trying desperately to direct them to their collection point.

The villagers meanwhile, having moments before been pleading to be left with something, were now snatching the farmyard animals and hiding it wherever they could. Eventually calm was restored and the Germans went about retrieving all the livestock. Their owners were in despair and turned to us for help, asking that they at least be left with something to eat.

Thomas and I took to the streets. Three German soldiers were approaching, tired, sweaty and dirty; they were armed with hand grenades and one had a revolver in his hand. They asked me if I had any matches to light the cigarette. I offered him a box, saying in German:

"Here – keep them"

"Where are you from?" he asked.

"I'm Polish" I said a little warily.

"Your soldiers are brave fighters," was his reply.

Encouraged by the compliment I asked, "Is it possible to release some of the animals, to leave the villagers at least a little something to eat?"

There was a short pause and then the response, "We have no orders."

For a long while we sat together in silence; Thomas joined them in a cigarette and I just watched quietly and listened to their soft conversation. Long minutes passed. I did not move and then, after a while, I heard one of them, their leader, say to his companion, "Leave them the hens that flutter." And then turning to me he said, "For your sake, lady."

I thanked him profusely, so happy.

The farmers went away, taking with them the liberated chickens, and the Germans took away the rest of the animals, including the mule of the tavern.

The story of the tavern mule is poignant and unforgettable. The poor beast did not want to be moved, and was being as stubborn as any animal of that breed can be. It was as if he knew what lay ahead and, if possible, was going to have nothing to do with it. The soldiers tried to cajole, to tempt and to pull, all to no avail. They then tried pulling with more men and all that happened is the rope halter snapped sending three German's tumbling into the dirt of the road, much to the amusement of the villagers.

A soldier then resorted to beating the animal, but even this violence did not persuade the mule to move. Reinforcements were called upon and the beatings continued with fresh ferocity allied with more rope and more pulling. Still the beast refused to move, still he kept his head turned towards the house and brayed and wept. Furious, the soldiers managed to drag him to the corner, where there was another entrance to the house, to the rustic part. The mule stopped again, complaining, always watching the house, and expressing his despair of having to leave what had been his world. All of us were deeply moved and outraged. Finally they were able to take him away, and the irony of it all? We found him murdered, along with other animals, that the retreating Germans had abandoned in the woods.

Meanwhile, yet another group of soldiers arrived and hastily began to dig at the crossroad, one road of which led further up the mountain, the other through the village. The work was completed in a morning and we watched, fascinated, and with some trepidation, wondering why the effort? They finished and one of the soldiers asked a farmer if anyone in the village spoke German. The farmer brought them to my husband.

"Look," he said pointing to the houses that surrounded the ditches they had dug at across the road and beyond. "Go and tell the inhabitants that within fifteen minutes their houses, those houses," he said pointing again to make sure Thomas understood, "will be blown up!"

The villagers who had been standing around the group of soldiers and Thomas didn't need any further explanation. There was panic and terror on all their faces as they realised they had only fifteen minutes, just a quarter of an hour, to salvage their lives. On the stroke of fifteen minutes what was left in the homes disappeared into a pile of rubble. And a few moments later there was another explosion; the bridge in Summonte had been destroyed. We were now completely isolated. There was no longer any doubt, the Germans were retreating and ensuring that Allied troops would find it difficult to follow them.

We sat in the street in silence as we came to terms with these new developments. Then we prepared to move back into the inn from which the Germans had initially evicted us. Benita went back to the house where we had stayed with the Howells to fetch our case. Thomas and I went to clean the inn and our rooms.

Suddenly we heard Benita call out, "Mom! Mom!"

I raced out to the balcony and saw, in the street below, a group of villagers, armed with clubs, among them Benita, who called out in Polish and cried: "Do not let Dad out of the house, please. I will be back in a moment with the Archpriest!"

We were paralysed by this scene and, awaiting the return of my daughter, spent anxious moments. Benita finally reappeared on the square accompanied by the Archpriest who was in discussion with the leader of the rebellious crowd who was none other than a priest!

Their argument seemed endless and Benita looked terrified as she watched the Archpriest and the villagers talking and gesticulating wildly, pointing towards Thomas. Finally Benita said something to the angry mob, which was what they had become, and moved away from them, coming towards us to explain what was happening.

Apparently one of the houses that had been blown up by the German soldiers had belonged to the priest of the village. Animated by his desire for revenge he had now become the leader of the mob. He had incited the villagers to join him in his quest for retribution, but, with the lack of any German soldier on which to vent his spleen he had told them that the fault was all that of my husband, Thomas, because he had given the order!

He had then moved from prosecutor to judge and had recommended to the jury, the villagers, that Thomas was obviously guilty and that the penalty was immediate death! We were terrified, aware that the only person that stood between us and the execution of the penalty was the Archpriest. It was a paradoxical and incredible situation.

Fortunately the insistence and the exhortations of the Archpriest managed to ensure that the group of troublemakers melted away, but not before a few surly looks were thrown at the house where we were still refugees.

We began to retreat back to the inn, but along the way were surprised to see a group of soldiers walking, single file, on the roadside. They looked tired, indifferent to our curious gaze and their feet moved heavily. All were heavily armed and, although looking tired they were alert. One of the soldiers carried on his back a bulky portable radio out of which sprouted antennae and wires. One set of the wires led to a headset he was wearing into which he was constantly whispering. They were the first Americans, on patrol, and our hearts soared. It was some time before we saw anything more. The damage to the road from the explosions meant that, for a while, the American trucks had to detour. But before very long the rubble was cleared away and the road repaired enough to allow the heavy traffic through. From having to ration water because the Germans had bombed the supplies, we were transported to heaven when the trucks and jeeps started flowing through. Cigarettes, coffee, chocolate and tea were welcomed with open arms and I will never forget the day that some American soldiers of Polish origin arrived and brought loaves which were white and fragrant with a flavour that had never, ever, tasted better.

With the arrival of our allies, a new era began for the majority of the interns. They rejoiced in the hope of repatriation; a desire that, for now, remained impossible for the Poles, still deprived of their homeland. Thomas continued to remain optimistic, as for him it was the long lack of freedom that had been worst and was, furthermore, the cause of the deterioration of his health. The stress and worry had significantly affected his angina, which, along with the lack of any treatment, was beginning to have a severe effect.

The discussions now were all about captivity, when would it really end, and the pros and cons of good uncle Joe Stalin! He had helped defeat the Germans, but at what price for the Russians. I was totally absorbed in my thoughts when Benita rushed into the room, breathless and said, "Momma, Mussolini has been arrested by the King!"

I flew out into the street to try to confirm and clarify what had happened. I ran straight into Thomas who told me, "Mussolini had a short meeting with the King, Victor Emanuel, where Mussolini, looking disorientated and unshaven, was told that the war was lost and that General Pietro Badoglio would assume the position of Prime Minister. Mussolini apparently offered no objection, and, upon leaving the meeting, he was arrested by the police who had been planning to remove the leader for quite some time."

I stared at Thomas, trying to comprehend what he was telling me. I can remember stroking his face with my hand and looking into his eyes, slowly realising that this was an historic event.

Within days there were rumours that an organisation, headed by an American Colonel, had been formed to assist and help the repatriation of those who had been interned in Ospedaletto. Whether these were true or not, they fed the growing feeling that perhaps, at last, the war was really over. Mussolini had been arrested, the Americans were here in Southern Italy, and the Germans had fled leaving behind them only mayhem, bodies and disaster. Although the whole project seemed daunting, hope really does spring eternal. For quite some time all private cars had disappeared from the roads, no-one had any petrol, not even for tractors on the farmsteads. You can imagine our great surprise when, first we heard the sound of engines, and then we saw a car, a real car, coming up the road. It grew closer and this very long, very luxurious automobile drew to a halt outside of the inn. The driver leapt out of the car and hurried round to open the rear door. Out stepped a civilian accompanied by an American officer. All three, including the driver, were olive skinned, dark haired and immaculately tailored, even in this environment.

They entered the tavern and ordered lunch. Raffaella, impressed by the long limousine outside, mobilised the whole family and began to hurriedly prepare as special a menu as possible. Secret larders had obviously been raided, cupboards emptied and caches of food and wine revealed. It wasn't just the distinguished guests who marvelled at the menu, so did we. Exquisite dishes we could only have dreamed of moments ago made their way to the table; ham, macaroni and white cheese; suddenly our memories became realities! Wine appeared in carafes, red and white, and all the while the guests asked about the conditions for the internees. Raffaella suggested that perhaps they should talk to Thomas, who was himself an internee, rather than herself who managed the tavern.

The two gentlemen introduced themselves as Colonel Pomeroy and the Marquis de Vega, and they explained they were on their way to Summonte to visit the de Cristofaro family. The knowledge of common friends allowed for a more frank explanation of conditions in Ospedaletto. Thomas told them of the hardships the internees had experienced, and the friendship they had also received from the villagers. He also explained about how many different nationalities were in Ospedaletto, from the Howells who were British, to Russians, Austrians, Poles and others, all of whom would face varying difficulties in trying to get back home. Thomas spoke of his own desire to leave for Naples.

Having listened patiently the Colonel told Thomas that when they returned, the following morning, they would ensure there was a place in their car for him, and would take him down to Naples. My husband's happiness at these words knew no bounds. From such a period of forced inactivity and confinement, during which his health had suffered so badly, he felt his unshakeable faith had been rewarded, and, furthermore, bolstered his belief that Benita and I would soon follow him when he had made the necessary arrangements.

The winter's days in the mountains were short and seemed painfully slow. Already, by four in the afternoon, the sky began to turn brown and the long oppressive evening pressed in. There was still no electricity so in darkness we sat, a perfect environment for the mind to run rampant, and, invariably in the most undesirable directions. Benita and I were beset by worries about Thomas in Naples, and also from the lack of news from Gaby in Rome where there were constant rumours circulating, of the Germans who occupied the city and the allies who were bombing. The state of our nerves was far from enviable, and certainly improved nobody's health.

It was during one of these sad dark days that a note was delivered from the Marquis de Cristofaro. It informed me that both Colonel Johnson and his friend, the Marquis de la Vega, had returned again, this time as representatives of the Committee for Internees. They were primarily interested in those of Ospedaletto and, because de Cristofaro was not fully aware of the situation nor the details of the internees, he had been informed that I would, perhaps, be the person to help, and would I be kind enough to talk to them both? I read the note and was readying myself to go and pay them a visit when the door of the tavern opened and the Colonel's driver informed me that the Marquis de Cristofaro's car was waiting outside to take Benita and myself to Summonte.

The house appeared to be in chaos, of a good kind. The Howell family were there and immediately Benita ran off to play with their boys. I left her dancing around a gramophone with a smile I had not seen for a very long time. De Cristofaro's wife led me to a small sitting room and inside introduced me, once again, to Colonel Johnson and Marquis de Vega. After we were all seated, de Cristofaro explained that the purpose of the discussion was to identify which of the refugees needed the most assistance, and how they would be able to serve them in both their immediate needs, and furthermore, in terms of trying to repatriate them to their home. He also pointed out the amount of money they had to hand to provide this assistance. Encouraged by this, I tried to inform them as precisely as possible which of the internees were the most needy, and required their urgent help, and what would be required afterwards.

When I had finished my rather passionate speech, the two guests were silent and I had the distinct feeling that they did not feel at ease with what I had just reported, and indeed seemed to lack any real involvement. This feeling was not helped when, halfway through my analysis, Colonel Johnson had left the room momentarily. The situation was more than strange, it was embarrassing for me having been invited and perhaps I had misunderstood what it was the 'committee' wanted from me. Without seeming to lose any further face, or revealing my discomfort, or revealing my suspicions, I apologized to the two gentlemen and took my leave of the Marquis de Cristofaro.

The next day, I learned that the Colonel and the Marquis de Vega had visited our friends, the Howells, and talked in detail of their mission. They had also asked Mr Howell if, by chance, he could lend them the amount of money needed to pay the subsidies for the most urgent of the internees' cases. The country was devoid of banks, they explained: they lacked the immediate possibility of being able to underwrite the sums required at short notice and would be able to do nothing until they returned to Naples. I now began to understand why there was an atmosphere in the room when I was speaking.

So it was that Colonel Johnson and Marquis de Vega left for Naples, and promised that they would be back very shortly with the sum necessary for the payments. The internees greeted this announcement warmly, but perhaps with a little apprehension.

The Beginning of the End – and the End of the Beginning

My fervent wish for our relocation to Naples and to join Thomas coincided with the nerve-wracking period for the villagers who were waiting for the return of their husbands, fathers and children from the front. The armistice in Italy had been announced in September 1943, but still families lacked any real news. It takes time to recall troops, to withdraw them from the field of battle and to coordinate their return to their home. The days of anguish should have reached their end with the declaration, but until they were physically in the heart of the family, there was still a pang of fear. 'No news is good news' is not always the best adage.

Another winter came, Christmas was celebrated, but half-heartedly, and January came and went. It was March when the warm but watery sun had chased away the cold damp winter, when I noticed a group of young farmers walking down the road towards Avellino. I knew that their intention was to be able to greet the first one of their fighters, who had returned to the village, and I stood at the window watching the group from afar, wondering whom the first would be. They were going down the slope of a hill when the figure of a man on a bicycle, labouring up the last kilometre of the climb, came into view. The group paused as they waited to see who was on the bike, what uniform he was wearing, his hair colour. A small boy detached himself from the group and ran towards the bike, a quick look with young eyes and his high pitched childish voice called back on the wind, "Dr Sirignano's son... it's Dr Sirignano's son."

And then we saw him, tall and blonde, with blue eyes and the uniform of an Air Force Officer. The news was accompanied by squeals of delight and old Dr Sirignano, and his three children, ran to greet him and envelop him in the warmest and longest of hugs. Heads were buried in shoulders for a long time and I am sure the tears must have flowed, with relief and with gratitude and with release.

After spending the first day in the privacy of his family, he joined the circle of young people, under the aegis of the Marquis de Cristofaro. They took advantage of the proffered hospitality and they sang and danced, laughed and flirted, they were so happy. But fate was preparing yet another twist. The young aviator decided to go to Naples in search of new melodies to play on the gramophone, assuring his friends and family that he would only be gone a couple of days. On his return he was walking down the unlit country road accompanied by some playful children. Engrossed, he did not hear the truck behind him, running with no lights because of the blackout, and walking down the middle of the road he was hit from behind and killed instantly. His companions escaped unscathed but ran away, and the truck never stopped. The young man was found the next morning, his broken records scattered around him.

Weeks went by slowly. Saddened by the death of the young aviator, who had survived all that war could throw at him, and by a lack of news from Thomas I spent more and more time in the company of Raffaella. Finally, one eventful day, Thomas arrived in Ospedaletto with a truck to transport us back to Naples!

I never believed it would be so difficult to leave our friends from the tavern. Four years of generosity, kindness, memories and their greatness of soul will remain locked in my heart. They demonstrated their nobility time and again, and I will never forget them. They took us into their house, their home, and they gave us shelter and food and unconditional love and affection. We laughed together, we cried together, we argued together but through it all our friendship endured and grew.

Our last visit, after loading the luggage in the truck, was to the Marquis de Cristofaro. He was in his study trying to find accommodation in Naples for the internees. It was an almost impossible task given the lack of communication between the two towns, and much would depend upon the influence of the American Army in Naples. Nevertheless he did give Thomas and I an address that might be suited to a small family, given that until now Thomas had been almost camping as a bachelor.

The trip to Naples took three long hard hours and we reached the outskirts of the city just as the sun set and bathed the city and the view of Mount Vesuvius in warm orange and golden glows, before falling into the darkness of the night. Thomas drove the truck to the address given by de Cristofaro, via Roma (now called via Toledo). He stopped in front of an old house, which, at first sight, looked encouraging, but the entrance was dismal, dirty and bore good comparison to that of Raffaella's tavern. In many respects the latter (Raffaella's tavern) came out victorious. We kept our thoughts to ourselves and went to the first floor where we pulled on an old bell that sent nothing more than a grating sound into the hallway behind. We waited for a good few moments and then we heard a shuffling of feet, locks were turned, bolts drawn and the door opened a fraction.

A rheumy eye peered at us and we introduced ourselves as friends of de Cristofaro. The door opened further and we were beckoned in and greeted by something that even the most unbridled imagination would have problems conceiving.

The scenario was plucked directly from the pages of an Edgar Allan Poe novel. Spiders hanging from the ceiling swung from their silver threads, the light fittings were swathed in webs that in turn were thick with the carcasses of flies, presumably the previous meals of the spiders! Crowds of mice were running races on a ceiling of cardboard, producing a rumbling noise and giving the impression that everything was going to collapse on our heads at any moment.

I believe we slept that night fully clothed, trousers tucked into socks, shirts and blouses buttoned to the chin but at least we woke without bites. The next day dawned bright and we set about a radical cleaning programme for the house. Bathrooms, bedrooms, living rooms, kitchens, no room escaped our attention, no floor remained unswept, no wall unwashed and every spider was now homeless, with the myriad of webs wrapped in paper and deposited in the bin. Even the mice showed respect and stayed away. With housework finished, Thomas arranged positions for himself and Benita in the offices of the American Red Cross.

In the meantime I spent many hours wandering the streets of Naples, retracing the routes and tours my father had taken me on all those years ago. My memories overlaid the broken buildings and the skeletons of ruined houses. I was engrossed with the rebuilding of my life, of starting a new architecture for Thomas and Benita that would take us back to where we belonged.

Life was beginning to burgeon on the street again. On the road military trucks sped past, filled with human cargo, and shop windows were roughly repaired and filled with an odd assortment of goods: a pair of socks, a bust of yellowed cloth with drawstrings to tighten the waist, almost a copy of fashion from the previous century. A lace shawl and a pair of cotton gloves would sit next to a pair of spats. I could smell coffee and hear music, and at times I wasn't sure if this was real or just my memory playing tricks with me. Today the sun shone and my cheeks glistened with a few tears. Tears for my father and the image of us sitting in the café before our trip to Alexandria, tears for my freedom after almost four years as a prisoner, tears for those innocent victims who died on the whims of megalomania.

My husband and daughter returned one evening accompanied by two Polish officers whom they had met on the street. We spent the evening listening to their dramatic tales of war with the Russians and the Germans. They had endured the ups and downs in Russia, where first they had been prisoners of the Bolsheviks and then, with the sudden reversal of Russian policy, freed to fight with the Allies against the Germans under General Anders. The news of our presence in Naples spread rapidly in the Polish military circle and in no time at all not a day went by that someone, either alone or in the company of other compatriots, did not arrive, unannounced at our house, to drink our health and exchange a few words. They were mostly young, full of enthusiasm and rarely managed to keep any secrets, particularly after a few more toasts to health and future. They all wanted to return to Poland but first there was a serious mission to be achieved. Rumours circulated the city that in order to liberate Rome it was necessary first to take Monte Cassino.

Without ever touching this sensitive topic the Polish Officers could not hide the unrest that troubled them, and paradoxically the excitement that awaited them. They were proud of the mission they had been given, they were aware of the risks they were going to have to take, and equally aware of the consequences of those risks. They were willing to accept them for freedom.

They came to me to find comfort and to reinforce their hope. They wanted me to reassure them that they would return home, they would return to their Poland. They would hold out their hands, palms upwards, and ask if I could guess their future. With some I could be honest but with others I had to divert the conversation and would talk about my daughter, Gaby, in Rome from whom I had been separated for over a year and had received no news in all that time. Among my guests was an official, named Joseph Tomankievicz, who asked me, before leaving, for the address of Gaby in Rome. I gave it to him more in hope, but nevertheless with good faith.

Our accommodation, in via Roma, had by now been cleaned from floor to ceiling along with all the furniture. Everything now had a new position and the metamorphosis was mentioned and admired frequently by our visitors. The Marquis de Cristofaro came to see us one day and he was equally ecstatic at the extent of the transformation. He told us, with much laughter, that his two visitors, Colonel Johnson and Marquis de Vega had been discovered to be no more than well-known thieves. There was no money for the internees and, thankfully, Mr Howell had refused to underwrite their endeavour. Luckily for him his money remained safe. I don't believe anyone ever heard from them again!

The war continued, and during the nights we were often awoken by the sound of the air raid warnings, sirens wailing continually while a thick artificial fog would fall. We would run to take refuge in the basement, safe from the bombs. One evening just as we reached the cellar we heard the roar of a violent bombardment, so close it seemed the bombs were falling on our roof. The next morning the scale and extent of the damage was clear for all to see. The incursion by German bombers had not only caused significant damage and destruction to the port of Naples, but the fragile construction of via Roma had been reduced in parts to shards of glass and all manner of scrap which made it an impossible and dangerous passageway.

The air raids were the main topic of conversation until a sudden and spectacular eruption of Vesuvius in March. Small explosions took place over a number of days until, on the 18th March, she began a full-blown two-week eruption. We went down to the port several times a day to observe the summit of Vesuvius. From her crater a plume of smoke like a huge black dome rose into the sky and at night the red glow of the lava running down her sides could be seen. Thankfully the flaming streams were predominantly on the other side of the volcano where they destroyed a number of communities. An American Air Force base a few kilometres from the base of the volcano still lost some eighty aircraft from the heat and from the ash. Military leaders were commissioned to assess the probability and consequences of further eruptions and every now and then a gloomy forecast would be made and the levels of general nervousness would increase significantly, only to gently subside over the next day or so.

After three or four days the activities of Vesuvius fell silent and instead we were faced with a violent outbreak of typhus. Sitting on our balcony shortly after, waiting for some guests, I saw American vehicles unloading big bags of white powder and placing them on the pavement. A small detachment of American soldiers then began, with the aid of a special container, to spray passers-by, especially women, with this white powder. The military, regardless of the shouts and screams of protest from the well-dressed women who were merely parading looking for admirers, argued that this disinfection with DDT was a necessary evil. I looked through the groups of soldiers, trying to find those wearing the distinctive black caps with the insignia of the white eagle, the headgear of the Polish soldiers but I saw none.

"Maybe they have already left for the assault on Monte Cassino" I thought. All their faces, so young, went through my mind, like a moving kaleidoscope. "God help them and lead them to victory; they are fighting to regain their land, their lost homeland."

On March 20th I was awakened, disturbed by a dream, that announced the birth of a grandson who was christened Alessandro. I confided in Thomas and Benita, and wrote down in my diary the date and revelation of the dream.

The air raids continued, although with less frequency, Vesuvius calmed down, typhus was managed, and we spent our days waiting for the liberation of Rome. One day hearing the doorbell ring, I went downstairs and there stood Joseph Tomankievicz, the officer who had asked for Gaby's address. He stood in the doorway with a broad smile and said, "Here's a surprise for you, I hope you will be very happy." He gave me a letter from Gabby and Cesare announcing the birth of their son, Alessandro, born on the 20th March 1944. I called Thomas and Benita and confided to Joseph the contents of my dream, and even went so far as to show him the note I had written. In return he told Thomas, Benita and me about the fighting around Monte Cassino.

Victory had been achieved but at a cost of five thousand deaths in the Polish army; five thousand soldiers who will sleep forever scattered on the mountain slopes, watched over by the red and white banner that was hoisted on top of the mountain. The ancient Abbey was perched on a mountain and the Germans had turned it into an impregnable fortress. The first battle had taken place in January 1944 and resulted in huge losses for the Allies. The second battle was fought in February and the result, even with different tactics, was the same – defeat! A third followed but it was the fourth battle, in May, where the Polish troops, on 17th May, launched their second attack on Monte Cassino that was decisive. Under constant artillery and mortar fire from the strongly fortified German positions and with little natural cover for protection, the fighting was fierce and at times hand-to-hand. With their line of supply threatened by the Allied advance in the Liri valley, the Germans decided to withdraw from the Monte Cassino heights to the new defensive positions on the Hitler Line. In the early hours of 18th May the 78th Division and Polish II Corps linked up in the Liri valley west of Cassino town. On the Cassino high ground the survivors of the second Polish offensive were so battered that it took some time to find men with enough strength to climb the few hundred yards to the summit. A patrol of the 12th Podolian Polish cavalry regiment finally made it to the heights and raised a Polish flag over the ruins. The only remnants of the defenders were a group of thirty German wounded who had been unable to move. The Poles, on their second try, and the allies fourth, had taken Monte Cassino, and the road to Rome was open. At the end of the war the Poles erected a Polish Cemetery at Monte Cassino on the slope of the mountain.

Joseph Tomankievicz was saved and had arrived in Rome with the first units, and he had remembered to go looking for Gaby to bring our news. My gratitude to him and to the others, who had helped us, is endless and I will never forget them, although these pages do not reveal all of them. Their generosity and their sacrifice remains forever in my heart.

A few months later, in August, with help from the Military Red Cross we finally arrived back in Rome. Gaby and Cesare were there to greet us and, as we were still waiting for our apartment to become free they had offered to look after us in their small house. Thankfully high-ranking fascists from the government had occupied our own apartment in Viale Bruno Buozzi and as such most of our furniture had remained intact and undamaged.

Gaby and I spent long hours talking about the disastrous period of German occupation, both in Rome and in Ospedaletto. In Rome it was only Gaby's perfect fluency in German that saved friends and strangers alike. Friends of Cesare's would come to their house for help and the young couple had built a false wall in one of the rooms behind which they had hidden those being sought by the German soldiers, especially during the last air raid when the retreating Germans had killed many young Romans.

Our financial resources, in particular, were limited to the help of the International Red Cross. Thomas's health was suffering badly and allied with his age he had been forced to accept that he would no longer be able to work in any significant capacity. As a result the weight of responsibility for our future, our house and our finances became mine, much to the chagrin of Thomas. I often thought with regret of all those friends we had made, and had lost, of family who we would never see again. All seemingly dead or scattered throughout a world that had been ravaged by war, had its dreams shattered, in which I believed not one country remained unaffected by the devastation left behind. We now entered a period where we are lured by the artifices of a new era, where we are promised happiness and the end of conflict.

With all this turmoil I walked through the streets lined with the wreckage of the last air raid. Thankfully Rome had managed to survive the worst, its history remained largely intact, the Vatican relatively unscathed. There are not too many ruins to add to those of the past, but had we really made progress? Was there not a better way to resolve conflict? At times I felt my life had been stolen by conflict, and I had to confess to feeling aggrieved. And then I was stunned, I heard of a new weapon that had been used to devastating effect: the atomic bomb.

Postscript

Going through the boxes of photographs, documents and papers I came across a wonderful American newspaper article published in the *Glendale News-Press*, now part of the *Los Angeles Times*, that summarised my grandmother's life perfectly:

Glendale California:
1944
By: Carroll W. Parcher

I have today added to my list of interesting characters that I have met, the name of Baroness Alessandra Perutz in whose home in Rome I have been rooming for the last eight days. Her life story would be the plot for a first class movie thriller. The daughter of a wealthy Russian Baron, governor of a large part of the Southern Russia, the White Russian section, she grew up with every luxury imaginable. Her father was unusually enterprising, which he illustrated by personally financing a number of oil wells in the Caucasus region and finally bringing in a gusher which was the beginning of what still is Russia's third largest, the Maikop Oil Field.

She married a wealthy young Pole who held an Austrian passport and automatically became an Austrian citizen, an act that saved her life when the Bolsheviks took over. The mob stormed her forty-eight-room palace fully expecting to kill her, her husband and her daughter for being part of the Russian aristocracy. They were dismayed when she displayed her Austrian passport that they took to be English due only to the coat of arms on the front. However they occupied her castle and confined them to their rooms for eight months during which time she suffered indignities and witnessed horrors.

The story continues through a wild escape from Russia to Vienna and the outbreak of the First World War following the assassination of the Archduke Ferdinand. Later to Rome by way of Danzig where she settled down expecting to have a happy life at last with their two daughters. Her husband held a position as Italian manager of a Polish coal company and, with their two daughters, they leased a brand new apartment, the one I am sitting in as I write this. It is still one of the most expensively furnished places I have ever seen, although Mme. Perutz bewails the fact that poverty has, in recent years, forced her to sell much of her finest furniture.

The next chapter was the coming of World War II. The fascists arrested the whole family and carried them off without a moment for preparation. The husband was initially imprisoned and the Baroness Perutz and her daughters were placed in an internment camp in Naples.

After the arrival of the Americans in Naples, she returned to Rome. The family fortune had been confiscated by the Germans and her husband's health broken. Mme Perutz began to take in paying guests in order to make ends meet and by the time the war had ended she said, they had all learned "not to eat", and that's why they have been able to continue to exist and keep their apartment since.

They were lucky that a Fascist family that damaged it very little occupied the apartment during the war. In every word and gesture Mme Perutz still brings to mind what one thinks an 'aristocrat' of the old school must have been. She is a lovely and gracious hostess and a darned fine cook too. Today her apartment in the Viale Bruno Buozzi is the refuge of Embassy personnel and other Americans who find a steady diet of Italian pasta tiresome and heavy and fall eagerly upon the endless variety of Russian, Swiss, French, Austrian, Polish, Rumanian, Italian and even American dishes she sets before them. Mme Perutz is not a gourmet, she cooks for the pleasure and enjoyment of others, and she cooks with love."

Although his health was poor Thomas lived to the age of 76 and died, in Rome, in 1960. Alessandra continued to live in Viale Bruno Buozzi until her death in 1975. My abiding memory of her is from around 1974 when I visited with my fiancée, Penny. We had arranged to have dinner at grandmother's apartment but were distracted first by the beauty of Rome which I was introducing to Penny, and then taking the opportunity to see the Pope who was giving his Sunday blessing at St Peter's basilica. Staying longer than perhaps we should we were late arriving at the apartment and, as we reached the front door, could hear grandmother playing the piano. We sat outside, on the floor, ears pressed against the warm wood and listened for perhaps five or ten minutes until she stopped. Then we knocked. It transpired the only reason she was playing was because we were late and she was worried about us. However without that delay we would never had heard her play, so regrets but no regrets!

Dinner that evening was beautiful. Silver service, damask napkins and tablecloths, surrounded by wonderfully classic furniture. Alessandra regaled us with many of the stories in this book which, at that time, I never realised existed.

Benita, my mother, rarely used her first name after her incident at the Ursuline Convent. Everyone knew her as Krysha or Czoka. She moved to England, studied law and finally achieved her ambition by qualifying as a solicitor; she spent almost her entire career working for Herbert Smith, her greatest asset, speaking five languages fluently. It was an education listening to her on the telephone. The conversation would begin in one language and then, in order to find the right word with the right nuance, my mother would switch seamlessly to Polish, or German, or Italian, or Spanish.

Andrew George-Perutz

Dramatis Personae

ROGOZNY FAMILY

General Ilya Rogozny: Alessandra's grandfather. Army General who fought in the Russian Turkish war and was rewarded with a large estate by the Tsar for participating in the conquest of the Caucasus. He was one of the Cossack Atamans and lived in Illskaya in the foothills of the Caucasian Mountains.

Rogozny children

Yegor Rogozny: born: 1861.

Glafira Rogozny: born: 1867. Married General Konstantin Dolinin, a Russian aristocrat and senior official who had the responsibility for the Government's monopoly of vodka in the district.

Alessandra Rogozny: born: 1857 (Sania). Married Henry Kozlowski

Xenia Rogozny: born: 1854. At 23 Xenia's first husband lost his life in the Turkish War of 1877 fighting with the Cossacks. Her second was a "marriage by stealth", in true Cossack style, to Almon Culbertson, an American Oil and hotel entrepreneur, much to the outward disgust, but inward admiration, of her father. They had three children: Ely, Eugene and Sascha.

KOZLOWSKI FAMILY

Baron Enrico (Henry) Kozlowski: Alessandra's father married Alessandra Rogozny. Henry was a 'Russianised' Polish nobleman who had come to the Caucasus to seek adventure. He made his early fortune supplying lumber to the oil companies and later established some of the major oil wells in Maikop.

Kozlowski children:

Alessandra Kozlowska (Shoura): (1892-1975). Married Thomas Perutz

Thais Kozlowska: Died in Berlin in 1928. She never fully recovered from the attack upon her by her supposed colleague. For many years Thais wandered across Europe, her spirit broken. In January 1928 she was living in Berlin and had sold her last ring. Not wishing to be a burden to her relatives, and living a life which relied upon morphine, one afternoon she took an overdose – and never awakened.

Valentina Kozlowska (Tina): (1919-1972). Modelled for Maggy Rouff and Vogue in Paris. Married twice, initially to a "fabulously rich" Persian nobleman and then to a Mr R. Avedoff. She had one daughter, Irena. Valentina died in New York in 1972.

Vladimir Kozlowski: Vladimir was killed in action fighting for the White Army during the Russian Revolution in 1917.

Valerian Kozlowski: Survived the Russian revolutions and the First World War. Joined the Russian Liberation Army during the Second World War and fought alongside the Germans against Russia. After the war Vladimir was captured by the Allies and was forcibly extradited to Russia along with more than a thousand other Russian Liberation Soldiers. He was accused by the Russians of fighting with the Nazis, tried for treason, and found guilty. Vladimir was sentenced to ten years imprisonment, five years loss of civil rights and also confiscation of all property. Valerian was released from Karaganda and exile in November 1955. Recent attempts in 2002 to have the judgement set aside and property returned were denied with the statement "because it was on file – it therefore cannot be omitted!"

CULBERTSON FAMILY

Almon Culbertson married Xenia Rogozny and had three children.

Eugene Culbertson: (1887-?) The eldest of the three brothers. Around 1910 he enrolled to study Law at Cornell University and after graduation moved to France where he enlisted with the French Foreign Legion whilst he waited to be transferred to a regular artillery regiment. Badly injured during the war he spent many years recuperating in France in the small village of Le Vesinet. He rescinded his Greek Orthodox faith and became a devout Roman Catholic and planned, when he had fully recovered, to enter a monastery.

Ely Culbertson (1891-1955) is probably best known for his impact in the world of Auction Bridge and the development of the bridge bidding system alongside his wife Josephine Murphy Dillon. In the late 1930s the threat of war led him to abandon bridge and resume his political activities. He founded the World Federation, Inc., and in 1946 the Citizens Committee for United Nations Reform, which advocated world peace by means of an international policing organization. He wrote *Total Peace* (1943) and *Must We Fight Russia?* (1946). His autobiography, *The Strange Lives of One Man,* was published in 1940. Ely died in New York in December 1955.

Sascha Culbertson (1895-1944) became a world-renowned concert violinist, eventually making New York his home. The impact of his upbringing near the Carpathian Mountains in Russia defined his playing style where he blended the beautiful strains of gypsy, Russian and Cossack music, as well as classical music. He owned what would become known as the "Culbertson Violin" which had been made in 1772 by Giovanni Battista Guadagnini. Sasha died at home in America in April 1944.

PERUTZ FAMILY

Thomas Perutz (1884-1960) married Alessandra Kozlowska. Thomas returned home after internment and, although his health had deteriorated significantly, still managed to remain the dapper gentleman and regularly played bridge. He is perhaps summed up by a comment from Enrico Lamet, author of *A Gift from the Enemy* who met him during internment in Ospedaletto: "He was outgoing with always a joke on his lips. I saw him daily at the bridge table but little else."

Perutz children:

Gabriella Perutz (1914-1976) married Cesare Meneghini. Two Children, Aleksander (1944) and Christian (1947). Died at home in Padua in 1976.

Benita Christina Perutz (1925-2005). Married twice. And has two children. Myself and my brother Thomas. Unfortunately circumstances were such that my brother was adopted. I believe his new family emigrated and are now living in Australia.